FROM ASHES TO GLORY

A DRAMATISED LIFE OF

CT STUDD,

CRICKETER AND MISSIONARY

BY
DAVID MALCOLM BENNETT

From Ashes to Glory
Published by Even Before Publishing,
a division of Wombat Books
PO Box 1519, Capalaba Qld 4157
www.evenbeforepublishing.com
www.wombatbooks.com.au

© David Malcolm Bennett 2014

National Library of Australia Cataloguing-in-Publication entry (pbk)
Author: Bennett, David (David Malcolm), 1942- author.
Title: From ashes to glory / David Bennett.
ISBN: 9781921632761 (paperback)
Subjects: Studd, C. T. (Charles Thomas), 1860-1931
                 Missionaries--Biography.
                 Christian biography--Great Britain.
                 Cricket players--Great Britain--Biography.
Dewey Number: 266.0234106751

All scriptural quotations are from the King James Version.

All rights reserved. No part of this publication may be reproduced, stored in, or introduced into a retrieval system, or transmitted, in any form, or by any means (electronic, mechanical, photocopying, recording or otherwise) without the prior written permission of the publisher.

ENDORSEMENT

'*From Ashes to Glory* is a retelling of an old and remarkable biography. David Malcolm Bennett has used a different style to bring the story of Charles Thomas Studd to life and put it in the words of the participants. We are glad that he has done this and wish the book real success. We hope that a new generation of readers will enjoy the fresh challenge of Studd's story and see what God can do through anybody who has fallen in love with Jesus and is available to serve him in the tough places of the world. Today thousands enjoy being part of God's family because of Studd's pioneer example.'

Dr Evan Davies, former International Director of WEC International and author of *Whatever happened to CT Studd's Mission?* (2012, WEC Publications, Gerrards Cross, Bucks, SL9 8SZ UK).

ACKNOWLEDGEMENTS

I first thank Graeme Stephen of WEC International for permission to quote from Eileen Vincent's *CT Studd and Priscilla* and Adrian Brink of Lutterworth Press for permission to quote from Norman Grubb's *CT Studd: Cricketer and Pioneer* and Edith Buxton's *Reluctant Missionary*. I am very grateful to them.

In addition, I wish to thank a number of other people, who have helped in a variety of ways in the production of this book. They are Evan Davies, Rhonda Sallaway and Christopher Scott of WEC International, and Colleen Campbell, Dianne Cash, David Dooley, Liz Guntrip, Paul Millican, Jenny Norman and Walter Osborn. Most especially I would like to thank my wife, Claire, who, with her patience, tolerance and advice, has always been a great help and encouragement.

NOTES

This book is a genuine biography of CT (Charlie) Studd, cricketer and missionary pioneer, but I have taken the liberty of dramatising it. That is, I have assumed some details that the existing records do not contain and added speech to make the story more dramatic and more readable. However, all the major events in this account of Studd's remarkable life actually occurred.

The three Studd brothers Kynaston, George and Charles are best known in cricket circles by their initials, JEK, GB and CT respectively. Therefore, in the parts of this book that deal with cricket, they will usually be identified by their initials. However, the identifications vary in the later parts of the book.

A gentleman by the name of Vincent appears in the first chapter. In other books about Studd he is usually just called 'Mr Vincent', with no Christian name. For convenience, I have christened him William (Bill for short).

In chapter 2 a man named Witherby appears. In other Studd literature he is usually called Weatherby, Mr Wetherby or Mr W. However, he was probably Harry Forbes Witherby, a member of the Plymouth Brethren and the editor of the Christian publication, *Faithful Words for Old and Young*, and the writer of a number of books.

Writing about the great men and women of the Christian Church is a humbling and challenging experience. Researching the selfless, dedicated life of CT Studd has left a distinct mark upon my own life. From Ashes to Glory comes with the prayer that it challenges all who read it to walk more closely with the Lord Jesus Christ.

David Malcolm Bennett (Brisbane, 2013)

ABBREVIATIONS

AIM: Africa Inland Mission
CIM: China Inland Mission
HAM: Heart of Africa Mission
LMS: London Missionary Society
WEC: Worldwide Evangelization Crusade (later WEC International)

CONTENTS

Acknowledgements		iv
Notes		v
Abbreviations		vi
Chapter 1	Through the Needle's Eye	2
Chapter 2	Mr Witherby	8
Chapter 3	Cambridge University	17
Chapter 4	The Ashes	20
Chapter 5	The Tour	34
Chapter 6	The Turning Point	39
Chapter 7	The Call	44
Chapter 8	Spiritual Millionaires	48
Chapter 9	The Voyage	59
Chapter 10	The Land of Mystery	65
Chapter 11	Shanghai	70
Chapter 12	Adventures on the Yangzte	76
Chapter 13	On Foot to Pingyang	84
Chapter 14	Pastor Hsi	91
Chapter 15	'Foreign Devils'	97
Chapter 16	Priscilla	105
Chapter 17	In Partnership	111
Chapter 18	In Lungan	122
Chapter 19	'In Labours More Abundant'	134
Chapter 20	'In Stripes Above Measure'	142
Chapter 21	'A Thorn in the Flesh'	152
Chapter 22	Interlude	157
Chapter 23	No 'Chocolate Soldier'	162
Chapter 24	Africa	169
Chapter 25	No Sacrifice too Great	171
Chapter 26	Guess Who's Coming to Dinner	175
Chapter 27	The Heart of Africa	182
Chapter 28	Mission Established	188
Chapter 29	New Life in the Jungle	195
Chapter 30	Deti	204

Chapter 31	Reinforcements	210
Chapter 32	Strife and Blessing	215
Chapter 33	The End is Nigh	221
Chapter 34	To Glory	225
Epilogue		230
Bibliography		232

PART ONE

ENGLAND

CHAPTER 1
Through the Needle's Eye

Edward Studd loved horses. They were his great passion. Whether it was hunting, racing or just riding, they were an endless source of delight for him. His stables housed many beautiful beasts. One, Salamander, had won Britain's premier steeplechase, the Grand National, in 1866. Another of his horses came second and third in successive years, while yet another had finished in third place in 1867.

Edward Studd's third son, CT (Charlie), achieved fame in quite a different arena. This is his story.

In April 1875 Edward Studd wrote to his friend, William Vincent, to tell him he had bought a new racehorse. He urged Vincent to back it. A week or so later they met at the Tattersall's Club in London.

'Good to see you, my dear Vincent,' Studd enthused, as they shook hands. 'How much did you win on my new horse, may I ask?'

'Well, to be honest, nothing. I didn't back it,' his friend said.

'Why ever not? You're a fool if you don't back a certainty,' the surprised Studd said, raking his fingers through his mutton-chop whiskers.

Vincent smiled but said nothing.

'Well, fool or not, why not join me for dinner tonight?' Studd laughed.

'I'd love to.'

'Seven o'clock, then?'

'Yes, that will be capital.'

Bill Vincent arrived at Studd's new London residence at 2 Hyde Park Gardens in good time, was received by the butler and the two friends sat down to dine.

'Seeing you're providing the meal, old chap,' Vincent said, 'I trust you will permit me to choose the source of our evening's entertainment?'

'Whatever you say. We'll go wherever you suggest.'

As the meal drew to its conclusion, Studd grew curious. 'What item do you have on the agenda for us tonight, then? The theatre? A concert, perhaps?'

'I thought we might go to Her Majesty's Opera House.'

'The Opera? Splendid. Why not?' He then hesitated as he recalled something he had read in the newspapers in the last week or so. 'Isn't that where those two American fellows are appearing? What are their names? Moody and Sankey, is that right?'

'Yes, that's correct. We'll go and hear Moody and Sankey,' Vincent replied with a smile.

'My dear chap, that's an odd choice,' the astonished Studd spluttered. 'I mean, it would be like going to church and it's not even Sunday. Anyway, I understand that Moody absolutely murders the Queen's English.'

'Be that as it may, you said the decision was mine and that is what I have decided.'

'Why don't we go and hear the new Gilbert and Sullivan comic opera, *Trial by Jury*? That surely would be better?'

'You said the decision was mine.'

Edward Studd knew that he was trapped. He was unaware that his friend had been converted at a Moody and Sankey meeting in Dublin the previous year, and the thought of spending a weekday evening at a Christian service filled him with gloom. However, Studd was a gentleman and would keep his side of any bargain. He called a cab and directed it to Haymarket.

The scenes upon arrival were much like any night for any other show. Hansoms and other carriages spilled their passengers on to the pavement outside the Opera House. Smartly dressed men with high hats and ladies with voluminous skirts and the latest bonnets jostled each other as they moved in the direction of the entrances. One tiny corner outside was occupied by a young flower-seller, busily selling her wares, while another was the workplace of a boy shoeblack. The size of the crowd milling around outside the Opera House surprised Studd.

Studd and Vincent climbed down from the hansom and Vincent led the way to one of the ushers, a little man with a limp.

'We would like seats for two, if you please,' Vincent said.

'I'm sorry, sir,' the man said, 'but all the unreserved seats have been taken. The house is full.'

The two friends instantly exchanged moods. A feeling of relief immediately lifted Studd's spirits, while Vincent seemed to experience a brief moment of despair. But then he pulled out a visiting card, wrote on it and gave it to the usher. 'Take this to John Danvers, if you would.'

The man hurried off with the card, which carried the plea, 'I have a wealthy sporting friend with me and I'll never get him here again if we don't get in tonight. Please find us seats. Bill Vincent.'

Within a few minutes the usher returned with the good news. 'Mr. Danvers said you can come in by a side door, sir. There are some empty seats near the front.' He then led them round to a side entrance and directed them to two vacant seats.

Edward Studd was no stranger to Her Majesty's Opera House (also known as Her Majesty's Theatre) but on this day it appeared somewhat different. Certainly there was little changed in the makeup of the audience. They all seemed to be what Studd thought was the better class of people and he recognised quite a few familiar faces. However, some of the boxes were empty, and that reminded him that he had read in the *Times* that some had ordered that their boxes be closed for the duration of these unorthodox performances.

In addition, the curtain was drawn back revealing an unusual sight for that venue. Instead of an elaborate set was a podium, a small organ with a chair, and three rows of seats, most of which were occupied by various dignitaries, some of them obviously clerics and even a cabinet minister, Lord Cairns. Centre stage was a large be-whiskered man in his thirties, organising everything. In addition, and here Studd could not put his finger on the difference, there seemed to be an atmosphere unlike that which he had come to expect in that grand building. It all seemed rather confusing.

The two men had arrived only just in time. Dwight Moody approached the front of the stage and addressed his audience. Edward Studd was taken aback by what unfolded before him. It took a while for him to get used to Moody's accent and strange way of speaking, but Studd was not a bigot. He found something in the man that was rather endearing. He seemed open and warm, transparently sincere, and even though his grammar was awful it was no worse than thousands of English men and women, so he could be forgiven for that.

Sankey's singing, too, was not unpleasant. True, it was not as grand as some of the singers who usually paraded their talents on that stage, but his voice was certainly good and seemed less hindered by an accent than his colleague.

When the time came for Moody to preach, Studd was feeling more cheerful, if still a little confused. However, the preacher's message threw the horse-owner's mind into turmoil.

'My friends,' Moody declared, ''twas the blood that did it. As God said to the people of Israel, "When I see the blood I will pass over you. The blood shall be a token for you." (Exodus 12:13) And I tell you, my friends, the greatest question that can be afore you tonight is this: have you got the token? Have you got the blood? Are you sheltered by the blood of the Lamb? That is the question. If you are so sheltered, and if you have the token, then you're perfectly secure and safe.'

Questions rushed through Edward Studd's mind. 'What is all this about a token? Why all this talk about blood? What does all this have to do with me?' His mind switched back to the preacher, who was now warming to his task.

'My friends,' Moody's voice boomed, 'if you go to a railway station and you buy a ticket and get into a carriage, and the guard comes round and shouts, "Tickets!" You put your hand in your pocket and pull out your ticket and give it 'im.' Moody acted out the scene.

'The guard don't look to see if you are a white man or a black, learned or unlearned, great or small. He probably don't know who you are. He is just lookin' for the token. Oh my friends, God says, "If you have got the token, I will pass over you." Have you got the token? Young lady, have you got the token?' Moody's finger stabbed out to the left.

'Young man, have you got the token?' This time the finger was thrust to the right. Each time Edward Studd thought that the finger pointed to him and he felt guilty.

Moody continued on his way. Each moment seemed to increase Studd's burden. 'There is a woman in our country who was hopin' to be saved because she thought she was a respectable sinner. When people talk to me in that strain, I know they are *great* sinners. She heard a sermon, which showed her clearly that Christ died for the ungodly. It dawned on her that she, too, was ungodly and therefore Christ had died for her, and the light of eternity flashed into her soul.'

The preacher concluded his address with a story about a woman who sacrificed herself to save her baby son in a sea disaster, and he likened it to Christ's sacrifice on Calvary's cross.

'He left a life of glory to endure a life of shame', the evangelist proclaimed. 'While we were without strength, He died for us. He did not die for His friends alone. He also died for His enemies. I want you all to come to Him tonight. Won't you believe on Him and be saved?' Moody opened his arms wide, as if to embrace the whole audience.

Studd had not noticed a sound during the sermon other than the preacher's voice but now he was vaguely aware of a woman behind him quietly crying. Another to the left in his row was doing the same. His own emotions were in tatters but he showed little sign of it outwardly.

Moody invited those wishing to come to Christ to walk to the front and, while Sankey sang, men and women left their seats and approached the stage. Bill Vincent was in prayer. Edward Studd was in a state of confusion.

After the meeting had closed the two friends walked silently towards the exit and left the building. Studd was the first to speak.

'I'll come to hear that man again,' he said hoarsely. 'In a strange way he has told me everything I have ever done.'

The next night Studd went back to the Opera House. He kept returning until he found Christ. The night after his conversion he returned again and asked to speak to Moody. He was shown around behind the stage and introduced to the preacher. In the previous 24 hours Studd had done a lot of thinking and he poured out his concerns to him.

'Mr Moody,' he blurted out, 'I want to be straight with you. Now I'm a Christian, shall I have to give up racing, shooting, hunting and balls?'

'Mr Studd, you've been straight with me, so I'll be straight with you', Moody said. 'Racin' means bettin', and bettin' means gamblin'. I don't see how a gambler can be a Christian. Do the other things as long as you like.'

Studd was not satisfied. 'But, what do you really think about the theatre and cards?'

'Mr Studd,' Moody said warmly, 'you have children and people you love. You are now a saved man and you want to get them saved. God will give you some souls and as soon as you win your first soul, you won't care about any of these other things.'

'Thank you, Mr Moody. Thank you.' With that, Studd shook Moody's hand, left and returned home.

****

Dwight Lyman Moody had been born into a poor family in a small town in the American state of Massachusetts. As a teenager he left home and went to Boston with the intention of becoming a millionaire. Instead, he became a Christian. He then moved to Chicago, where he proved to be a successful salesman. He did evangelistic work in the Chicago slums and went on to become a fulltime Christian worker, and established a church.

Ira D. Sankey, by contrast, was the son of a member of the Pennsylvania Legislature. After a short period of undistinguished service for the north in the American Civil War, he went to work for the internal revenue.

The two men met at a prayer meeting in 1870. After hearing Sankey sing, Moody persuaded him to join his church in Chicago, to serve as choir master and soloist.

Three years later, almost entirely unknown in Britain, they commenced a series of meetings in various towns in the British Isles. The start was quiet, but it was not long before God blessed their work in such an extraordinary way that they became household names.

It was in 1875 that Edward Studd became a Christian through their ministry. It would not be the last time that the names of Studd and Moody and Sankey were to be associated.

CHAPTER 2

Mr Witherby

The next day Studd hurried back to Tedworth House, his country home. The three oldest boys were away at boarding school, Eton College, but with his wife, the younger children, his servants and neighbours close at hand, he found himself with an extensive mission field.

Dora Studd had the shock of her life when the enthusiastic new convert told her of his life-changing experience. Indeed, he had probably no need to have told her for the change was evident in his manner. Next he told his younger sons and his daughter, who greeted the news with varying degrees of perplexity. Before the end of that day he had called his servants together and advised them of the good news, too. Several of the staff, being Christians themselves, welcomed the news, while others were puzzled by the extraordinary announcement.

The changes in Edward Studd were evident. One visitor to Tedworth House soon after Studd's conversion asked the coachman, 'Is it correct that Mr Studd has gone all religious?'

The coachman scratched his chin. 'I don't know about that, sir. All I know is that though there's the same skin, there's a new man inside.'

The atmosphere at Tedworth House changed, too. From the time of Studd's conversion it became both a battlefield and a mission station. He gave no one any peace. He was forever asking all and sundry, 'Are you saved?' and telling them that he had been born again. He possessed boundless enthusiasm for his new faith and a great love for his Saviour, but he had a complete absence of tact.

One cool sunny morning he went to the stables with his son, Herbert. On his way he noticed one of the gardeners tending the flower beds and shouted to him, 'Giles, are you saved?'

'Not that I know of, Mr Studd,' the embarrassed man muttered.

'Then you'd better do something about it, my man. Hell awaits the sinner who won't repent.'

Soon after that he visited his sister and her husband, George. The meeting did not go well. George told him in no uncertain terms never to return.

Edward Studd had certainly become a new man and, in spite of plenty of rough edges, his new found faith made him rethink his whole life. He sold a number of his race horses but made sure that a horse was retained for each member of the family. Although he had severed connection with the racing fraternity, he still appreciated equestrian pleasures. Also in the main room at Tedworth he had most of the furniture removed and replaced it with benches. Guest preachers were invited to proclaim the Gospel to assembled friends and neighbours in this new chapel.

One of the preachers invited was DL Moody. He quickly accepted the invitation. Dora Studd dreaded his visit, for she blamed him for turning their happy home upside down. She found her husband's behaviour, especially when he asked everybody about their spiritual condition, very embarrassing. If Moody's religion had turned her husband into such a fanatic, she thought, what must Moody himself be like? She was terrified that the American would walk through the door and pounce on her with a booming, 'Are you saved?'

When, eventually, the carriage bringing Moody was heard pulling up on the driveway, she hastily gathered her children around her as a shield. Edward entered and introduced Dwight Moody.

The American made a courtly bow. 'Mrs Studd,' he enthused, 'it is a pleasure to meet you.' Then, surveying the children, he added, 'What a wonderful family you have.'

Dora Studd immediately changed her mind about her visitor. He was nothing like she had expected.

In the middle of June, DL Moody found himself in the eye of a storm. There had been a request for him to conduct a service at Eton College, England's leading public school, the place where Studd's eldest sons and many of the nation's future leaders were educated. However, the idea of a non-Anglican layman conducting a religious service at a high Anglican school drew strong opposition and, eventually, the meeting was held in the nearby garden of a sympathiser.

About 150 boys attended the meeting, including Edward and Dora Studd's three eldest boys, Kynaston, George and Charles. Their father was on hand to make sure that they were there. At first the boys were taken aback to learn of their father's new found religion but they did not attach any great importance to it. They listened quietly to what Moody had to say but it meant little to them.

As that rather wet summer progressed, the time arrived for the three boys to return home for the holidays. The teenagers chatted excitedly on the train and in the carriage on the journey back to Tedworth House. For all three the summer holidays were the highlight of the year, with long days of unabated enjoyment, playing cricket, riding and generally getting into mischief. They had little idea of how their father's faith had changed him and what that might mean for them.

When the carriage pulled up in the courtyard, the boys clambered down and they were greeted enthusiastically by their younger brothers and sister. The three athletic figures stood tall amongst the whirling bodies of the younger children. Dora Studd greeted her sons and noticed that though Charlie was only fourteen, he was almost equal in height to his two older brothers.

Edward had decided to welcome them privately in the library. When the boys entered he was seated at his desk. He rose to greet them and warmly shook each by the hand. 'Welcome home, boys. It's great to have you back.'

He then stood back slightly from them and clasped his hands behind his back. His brow furrowed as he thought for a moment. 'Boys, I have asked you into the library because I have something very important to tell you.'

The brothers looked at each other with questioning glances but said nothing.

'Back in May I had dinner with an old friend, Bill Vincent, and he took me to hear Moody and Sankey. You remember them. You heard them last month. Moody and Sankey are two great men of God and, as I listened to what they had to say, it seemed that they knew my heart perfectly. Though really, it was the Lord who knew it, not them.'

The boys looked at each other again, confusion on each face. Was this their father? He had never spoken to them like this before. Perhaps the religion that he had spoken to them briefly about on his trip to Eton in June was more significant than they had first thought.

'The more I heard them,' their father continued, 'the more I realised my own unworthiness, my own sinfulness, before God.' His head bowed slightly as he made that confession.

'Anyway, boys, the short of it is that a little over two months ago, as you know, I became a Christian. I was born again. Since then my life has been totally different and my main desire now is to tell others about Jesus Christ.' He extended his arms out to them. 'Kynaston, George and Charles I want you to become Christians, too. Won't you believe in Him?'

There was an embarrassed silence. Once more the brothers looked at each other questioningly. The silence was broken by Kynaston, the mouthpiece of the trio.

'But, father, we don't understand. Surely we are Christians already.' He paused in frustration as he searched for the right words. 'I mean... Well, I mean, we are English and England is a Christian country, so we must be Christians. And, at school, we go to service every Sunday.'

'Don't you see, Kynaston, that these things do not make one a Christian. Each individual needs to have faith in Jesus Christ. It doesn't matter where you are born, or necessarily how often you go to church. What matters is your relationship to God.'

Again the three brothers looked at each other but remained silent.

'Anyway, you may go to your rooms now. I have placed a new copy of the Bible in each room and I want you to make sure that you read it.'

The boys quickly left the library and Charles went straight to his room. Sure enough, there on a little table was a brand new copy of the Bible. He picked it up, leafed through it for a few moments and put it down again. Then, with a little more enthusiasm, he picked up a cricket bat and walked towards his wardrobe, upon which was a full length mirror. On the floor was a carpet with a strategically placed seam running in the direction of the mirror. He faced the mirror and began to play a sequence of exquisite shots, silky smooth, using the seam to guide his stroke. He continued with his impromptu practice until the gong sounded for dinner.

Later, as Charlie prepared for bed, a knock sounded at his door. His father's head peered round the door. 'Have you thought about what I said earlier?' he asked, as he walked into the room.

'What about, Father?'

'About believing in Jesus Christ.'

Charlie scratched his beak-like nose tensely. 'Well, not really. No, I haven't.'

'But, Charles, you must. This is not a game. It is life itself. Your eternal destiny hangs upon what you do with Jesus Christ.'

The father's words were greeted by an embarrassed silence from his son. But though Charlie was silent he was thinking loudly. *My father has become a religious fanatic. I'd be better off at school than here.*

'Don't forget the Bible,' his father said, pointing in the direction of the table. 'Make sure you read it.' With that he turned and left the room.

The next night, the same thing happened, and again the following night. On the fourth night, when Charlie heard the anticipated knock, he dived into bed, closed his eyes and began to breathe heavily. His father opened the door and looked in, assumed his son was asleep and went away. From then on that was Charlie's practice. He listened for the footsteps approaching his door and when he heard them he hurried into bed and feigned sleep.

But, there was no escaping the fervent evangelist. In the day time his father would hunt him down and challenge him with the Gospel. Charlie would not listen. The boy began to try to avoid his father but it was not easy. He seemed to be everywhere. He appeared from behind doors in the house and emerged from behind trees in the garden. It almost seemed that in every room that Charlie entered, hoping to escape, he bumped into his father.

Charlie's main place of safety was on the cricket pitch, which was situated in their spacious grounds but within sight of the house. There he only had to fear a cricket ball propelled towards him at great pace or with devious spin, delivered by Kynaston and George and a stream of willing servants. He knew how to counter that for, though he was young, he was a cricketer of great ability and class. On Saturdays, when the miserable weather permitted, the three boys gathered together servants and friends and played against various local teams. They usually won. Indeed, such was the skill of all three boys that they had forged a reputation in the wider cricket community.

Summer ended with the status quo maintained. The boys returned to school. The winter and spring holidays came and went and still there was no change. Summer returned. The summer of 1876 was as different from its predecessor as chalk from cheese. Each day seemed to be sunnier and warmer than the one before, and there were many opportunities for the boys to ride and play cricket. The grass that had been so beautifully green the year before was now patched with brown.

One weekend, late in the holidays, two visitors came to Tedworth House. Edward Studd was still holding Christian services in his home on Sunday evenings and these men were to be the guest speakers. The two men were enlisted in the cricket team for Saturday morning, and one of them, Forbes Witherby, proved an abject failure. He was bowled first ball and in the field fumbled the ball every time it came his way. Kynaston, the captain of the side, decided it was wise not to let him bowl.

The game was followed by lunch and it was decided to go riding in the afternoon. The night before, Mr Witherby had gone riding with Edward Studd and the boys had noticed that the visitor was rather ill at ease in the saddle. So, they hatched a plot. They decided that they would let Witherby and their father go on ahead a little and then suddenly pass them at a gallop.

In due course the two men mounted their horses and began to slowly tour the grounds. The boys, as planned, held back. Then, at the prescribed moment, the three urged their steeds to a gallop and passed the two other riders at great speed, shouting as they went. Witherby's horse reared a little and the rider's hat fell to the ground. His discomfort was plain. The boys circled round and once more attacked from behind. This time, as they passed, Witherby's mount also took off at a gallop, with the rider desperately holding on. For a moment even Edward Studd had difficulty controlling his horse, but this was because he could not stop laughing. He had always had a mischievous sense of humour and this was one thing his new way of life had not changed. Witherby eventually brought his horse under control and they all returned to the house.

Later that afternoon Charlie had again donned his cricketing whites and, with cap pulled down firmly and bat under his arm, was walking out to join his brothers.

'Excuse me, Mr Charles. May I have a word with you?' It was Mr Witherby. His accent suggested north-country origins.

'Yes, Mr Witherby. What is it?' The boy's manner was polite but not friendly.

'Charles, are you a Christian?'

Oh no, Charlie thought, *this man's as bad as my father.*

He looked at the preacher and replied, 'No, Mr Witherby. I am not what you would call a Christian.' His voice sounded tense, not hiding the frustration within. 'I have believed about Jesus Christ since I was knee high, of course. I believe in the church, too.' Charlie hoped that would end the conversation.

Though Forbes Witherby was a poor rider and a worse cricketer, he was a determined man and not easily discouraged.

'Look here!' he said. 'Did you know that "God so loved the world that he gave his only begotten son, that whosoever believeth on him should not perish but have everlasting life"?' (John. 3:16)

Those words were familiar to Charles. He had heard his father recite them before, when he had talked to his sons about Christ. But the lad did not answer.

Witherby persisted. 'You believe Jesus Christ died?'

'Yes.'

'Do you believe He died for you?'

Charlie paused. 'Well, yes, I suppose so.'

'Do you believe in the other part of the verse: "shall have everlasting life"?'

'No, I don't believe that.' Charlie shuffled his feet uncomfortably as he spoke and then leant on his bat, with a nonchalant pose that did not reflect his mood. Perhaps he could bluff his way out of this situation.

Witherby was not deterred. 'Now, don't you see that your statement contradicts God? Either God or you are not speaking the truth, for you contradict one another. Which is it? Do you think God is a liar?'

Charlie was no heathen. There could be only one answer to that. 'No!'

'Well, then, aren't you inconsistent, believing one half of the verse and not the other?'

Charlie thought for a moment, and then replied, 'I suppose I am.'

'Well,' Witherby persisted, 'are you always going to be inconsistent?'

The boy was feeling hot and not only because of the sun. 'No,' he said, 'I suppose not always.'

'Will you be consistent now?' the evangelist challenged.

Charlie felt cornered. He did not like the idea of inconsistency in anybody, least of all himself. 'I do want to be consistent, Mr Witherby.'

'Don't you see that eternal life's a gift? When someone gives you a present at Christmas, what do you do?'

'I take it and say, "Thank you."'

'Then why don't say thank you to God for His gift?'

The teenager considered this for a moment and, in spite of Witherby's rather twisted logic, belief in Christ suddenly seemed very reasonable to him. This Saviour who died so long ago, died for him. He died that even he, Charlie Studd, might be saved. Charlie felt an impulse within him drawing him to God. It seemed to confirm these thoughts, and he believed, not just with his head but with his heart.

That evening when he returned to his room he picked up the Bible that his father had bought him the year earlier, read a few chapters from the Gospel of John and thrilled to it.

A week later the three brothers were back at Eton. Charlie had told no one about his new found faith, not even his own family. But, aware that he should share it with someone he wrote a letter to his father.

A few days later, the brothers received a letter from their father addressed to them all. Kynaston opened it and read it to himself. A smile lit up his face. The other two looked at each other and back at their elder brother.

'What does it say, then?' Charlie said, eagerly.

'You wait your turn, young fellow,' Kynaston responded, handing the letter to George. As George read it he too smiled and then passed it to Charlie. Finally, Charlie read it, looked up and they all burst into laughter.

The letter read, 'My Dear Sons, I find it difficult to contain my joy. It was so good to hear that you all became Christians during Mr. Witherby's visit to Tedworth House. May I encourage you to continue on with the Lord Jesus and seek to win more souls into His kingdom. Your affectionate Father, Edward Studd.'

Shortly after that the Studds began a Bible study group at Eton, which Kynaston led. Some of those who attended had been converted the previous year when DL Moody had preached for them.

****

One evening, the following year, Edward Studd left Tedworth House in his carriage to attend a Christian meeting. Suddenly he realised that he had left behind a servant that he had promised to take with him. He instructed the coachman to stop and he ran back the short distance to the house. As he ran, he burst a blood vessel in his leg and was forced to go to bed. A few days later he died. He had been a Christian for just two years.

The boys were called home from Eton, shocked by the sudden death of their remarkable father.

At the funeral, the local vicar paid tribute to him. 'Our friend Edward Studd did more for Christ in two years than most Christians do in twenty.'

It was almost as though he knew that he did not have long to live.

CHAPTER 3
CAMBRIDGE UNIVERSITY

In 1879 CT (Charlie) Studd, like his brothers before him, had become cricket captain at Eton College. That autumn he followed his brother GB to Cambridge University. The eldest brother, JEK did not join them until the following year, being previously engaged in business. Though none of the brothers were ashamed of their faith, it was Kynaston who did most to promote it.

It was at Cambridge that they met Stanley Peregrine Smith. His father was a prominent London surgeon and the family background was strongly Christian. The fair-haired Smith had become a Christian when he was thirteen. The year before entering Cambridge he had been seriously ill and this had left its mark on his health for a while. However, he had considerable physical strength and was a rower of great promise. In 1882 he was the stroke in the Cambridge boat in the famous series of races against Oxford, which was one of the highlights of the London sporting calendar.

Smith had taken an immediate liking to George and Charlie Studd. Later, when Kynaston joined his brothers at Cambridge, Smith discovered in him a like mind. The two of them often joined together to pray for other students. They also led the singing when the students in the university's Christian Union joined together to sing from Sankey's *Sacred Songs and Solos*, with Smith on piano and Charlie on the banjo. Charlie even, on occasions, attended the students' prayer meeting.

One of the students that Kynaston and Smith prayed for was Montagu Beauchamp, the fourth son of a deceased Baronet. Beauchamp, an imposing athletic figure, had been at Repton School with Smith and, like him, had a Christian background. His uncle, Lord Radstock, was in fact an evangelist who had turned his home into a hive of Christian activity. The popular Montagu was thought to have become a Christian as a teenager but his faith at this stage seemed rather half-hearted, and this had moved Smith and 'Kynnie' to show concern for him. During one holiday a dramatic change took place in Beauchamp's life. When he returned to Cambridge he entered vigorously into the Christian activities, and none were left in any doubt as to where he stood. While still at university, Stanley Smith and Montagu Beauchamp began to experience a desire to serve God overseas.

However, the most significant impact that the Studd trio made on University life was not spiritual, nor was it academic: it was sporting. All three were accomplished all round sportsmen, but their greatest endeavours were saved for the cricket field. All three represented their university in that sport, with George being captain of the university team in 1882, Charlie the next year and Kynaston in 1884. In nineteenth century England the captaincy of the Cambridge University cricket team was one of considerable prestige. Put simply, it meant fame. The remarkable exploits and striking persona of Dr WG Grace had made cricket a major sport in England, and sport was followed like a religion by many Englishmen.

In the early 1880s there was less international and county cricket than there is today. Many of the most important games were between such teams as the Gentlemen (amateurs) and the Players (professionals), or the All-England side and various local teams. In addition, any game that included Oxford or Cambridge University was highly regarded. In 1881 the three Studds represented their university against Oxford. That year they also played for Cambridge against 'the Gentlemen of England', with JEK scoring 154 and CT 113. The name Studd was, indeed, becoming famous.

In 1882 the Australians made their third official cricket tour of England. This Australian team was an especially strong one, particularly in bowling.

Mid-season it was the turn of Cambridge University to take on this powerful side. It proved to be a game of almost unmarred success for the Studd family. The Australians were all out in their first innings for a mere 139, with CT taking five wickets with his fast-medium bowling. When Cambridge batted JEK did not last long, but GB and CT joined in a productive partnership, with George scoring 42 and Charlie 118. Charlie's innings was one to be savoured. He had even got on top of Australia's most destructive bowler, Fred 'the Demon' Spofforth, and few did that.

Charlie's rather upright stance seemed to lend itself to graceful, elegant drives, particularly through the covers, and this innings was studded with them. He batted as though he was still playing down the line of the seam of his bedroom carpet, assuring that his wicket was securely defended. His powerful hitting to leg was also a treat. Australia did better in their second innings, scoring 290 and setting the university 168 to win. JEK and GB opened the final innings with a partnership of 108. Cambridge eventually won by six wickets, with CT hitting the winning runs.

In that season, which was a low-scoring one because of the bad weather, CT Studd scored three other centuries in first class cricket, including another against the Australians. The great WG Grace, by comparison, scored none that year in 37 innings. In addition, CT was the second highest wicket-taker nationwide. CT Studd had become a national hero.

CHAPTER 4
THE ASHES

The weather that summer had been terrible, even by English standards, but Charlie's cricket had blossomed wonderfully. With August approaching its conclusion he had become only the second man ever to achieve the double of 1,000 runs and 100 wickets in a season. As the only man to precede him to that feat was WG Grace, Charlie had every reason to believe that at the age of 21 he was one of the very finest cricketers in the world.

Though his cricket had flourished so brilliantly, his spiritual life had stagnated. He still held firmly to his Christian beliefs, but there had been little sign of real spiritual development.

The touring Australian team of that year had done much to impress. It had beaten all the major counties as well as other powerful teams. It clearly was high class.

From the middle of August the weather improved a little. Set to commence on the 28th of that month was the most important match of the season: Australia was due to play the All-England eleven in a Test Match. As is normal with international teams, certain players of proven ability were virtually automatic selections in that eleven. WG Grace was one of them, even though he had not been at his best that year. Dr Grace's medical calling seems to have been demanding more from him at this time. CT Studd, too, had very good reasons to believe that he was an automatic choice.

A few days before that game was due to commence, Charlie received the news he had been awaiting. He had been selected. If selection in the England cricket team was not quite as significant as it later became, this was still a moment to savour.

On the morning of the match he caught a hansom cab to London's Kennington Oval, a ground overshadowed by two enormous gasholders, which were later to enter cricketing folklore. It was believed by many that England's chances of winning depended on the level of gas in them; a superstition that is said to have governed the use of gas in that part of London during a Test Match. As the cab took Charlie closer to the ground he could feel his stomach knotting tightly with nervous expectation. He peered out the window at the cloudy skies.

'At least it's dry,' he said to himself. 'I thought last night's rain would go on forever.'

By the time he arrived the crowd was already beginning to form and there was a buzz of expectation. He made his way to the amateurs' dressing room. Already present were the two Lancastrians, Albert 'Monkey' Hornby, the team's captain, and Allan Steel, a good friend from Cambridge.

Steel stood up as Charlie entered and his piercing eyes lit up as he smiled. His abundant moustache did not hide the warmth of his expression. 'Hello, Charlie. It's good to see you,' he said, extending his hand in greeting. 'It'll be grand to be on the same side as you again.'

Charlie laughed as he shook the offered hand. 'I'm just as relieved as you.'

'You know Monkey Hornby, don't you, old chap?' Steel added, as he indicated the small man just rising to his feet.

'For the most part as an opponent, I'm afraid.'

Hornby shook hands. 'We're expecting a lot from you, young Stood,' he said. 'This colonial team has surprised us all with their ability. We'll need every man playing at his best to beat 'em.'

'I'll try not to let the team down,' Charlie assured his captain, though Hornby's comment had hardly boosted his confidence.

Hornby was already in his cricket whites, looking neat and smart, and the other two began to change. While they were doing so, two of the other three amateurs in the team arrived: the Right Honourable Alfred Lyttleton, the team's wicketkeeper, and Alfred 'Bunny' Lucas. Finally, the imposing, heavily-bearded figure of WG Grace burst through the dressing room door.

'Good morning, gentlemen,' W.G enthused. 'I hope we are all ready to do battle.' Several shouts of affirmation responded to the great cricketer's call to war.

Outside, the stands were filling quickly and by the start of play the ground had reached its capacity of around 20,000. Some of the crowd were even wandering on the field of play, but were being kept well away from the wicket, which was still a little damp after the previous night's rain. Eventually a bell sounded, warning players and spectators alike that play was soon to commence.

Hornby and Billy Murdoch, the Australian captain, made their way out on to the field to toss a coin to decide who would bat first. The good-natured Murdoch talked to his opponent animatedly as they made their way to the centre. He rubbed his hands together to try to bring some life into limbs that were more used to Australia's burning sun than this poor excuse for a summer's day.

Hornby tossed the sovereign. Murdoch called and won. 'We'll bat,' he said. They walked back to the pavilion and advised their teams of the decision.

At five minutes past noon the two umpires entered the arena, soon followed by the English amateurs through one gate and the professionals through another. The crowd greeted them with enthusiastic applause. The Australian openers, Charles Bannerman and Hugh Massie, were next. Their faces were tense. They knew that taking on the English bowling in such difficult conditions would not be easy.

Their fears proved justified. Ted Peate, the gruff Yorkshireman, opened the bowling with his accurate, slow left-armers, and continued to bowl for most of the innings. With his packed off-side field, he held the batsmen in a grip of steel. But the first wicket went to 'Happy Jack' Ulyett, the fast bowler. He bowled Massie for a single. Soon after that the quietly-spoken Dick Barlow, with his medium-paced deliveries, took over from Ulyett. By lunch he and Peate had reduced Australia to 41 for 6.

After lunch the innings continued its disastrous course and, in little more than another half-an-hour, Australia was all out for 63. Charlie Studd had not been asked to bowl. He had not been needed. The English players were over the moon. They had in their side ten men who had scored centuries in first class cricket, so even on this wicket a healthy first innings lead looked certain.

But Australia had Fred Spofforth: 'the Demon'.

Four years earlier, against a strong MCC side, the Australians had emerged triumphant in a game that lasted only five hours. They had dismissed their opponents twice in the one day. The bowling honours had gone to Spofforth and Harry Boyle. The next day an English newspaper called the tall Spofforth, 'the Demon', and Boyle, 'the Very Devil'. Those nicknames had stuck and these two demonic bowlers were again in partnership in this game.

England's first innings proved hardly more successful than Australia's. In a short space of time England was reduced to 59 for 4, at which point CT Studd walked down the pavilion steps and on to the field. Spofforth had been at his devastating best. He had taken three of the four wickets to fall.

Studd was nervous. The idea of saying a hasty prayer had not entered his head. At least he did not face the bowling immediately. The tall, strongly-built George Ulyett, who had been fighting heroically since the fall of the first wicket, scored a single before it was Charlie's turn to take strike. He took his guard, looked around the field and prepared to face 'the Demon'.

Spofforth was back on his mark, waiting. He wiped his well-trimmed moustache with the back of his hand and then began to approach the bowling crease with rapidly increasing momentum. He leapt into the air and his right arm swung over, propelling the ball with all his might towards Charlie. As Studd played at the ball he simultaneously, or so it seemed, heard the sound that all batsman dread: the sound of the ball smashing into the stumps. He was out first ball. England was now 60 for 5.

Later Maurice Read and the highly-talented Allan Steel gave the English score a little substance, before the innings concluded at 101, a lead of only 38. But, at least they had the lead and a gap of 38 in a low-scoring game could prove to be decisive. Spofforth had bowled throughout the innings and had taken 7 wickets for 46. The last man, Peate, was out only five minutes before the scheduled closed, so the play ended there for the day.

Charlie made his way home in a downcast frame of mind. He had failed and his team, though still in the stronger position, had thrown away a significant advantage. Thoughts of the momentous activities of the day – the superb bowling of Peate, Hornby and Spofforth; the courageous batting of Ulyett, and the dramatic fluctuations of fortune – filled his mind. He had little thought for God that night and contented himself with a quick prayer before retiring. But sleep would not come. Once more thoughts of the day's play coursed through his mind. The sound of the hard, leather ball shattering the stumps echoed in his brain. He had been dismissed for a duck before but this was the biggest disappointment of his short life. Briefly, thoughts of his two centuries against the Australians earlier in the year came to cheer him, only to be soon replaced by the sound of crashing timber and visions of flying bails. As he lay there, tormented, he heard rain pattering on the window panes.

Sleep came at last and so, finally, did the rays of the weak morning sun, peeping through his bedroom window. He awoke feeling as if he had never slept. Indeed, his body felt strangely tired and his head unusually warm. He put it down to the excitement and exertions of the previous day and his lack of sleep. He washed and shaved but did not bother to read the newspaper. Failing was bad enough and reading about it only made it worse. He had a light breakfast and then set off for the ground. As he sat in the hansom it began to rain again. He found himself shivering. *Strange, for August*, he thought. *Even one like this.*

This time Charles arrived first in the dressing room but it was not long before Allan Steel appeared.

His friend greeted him. 'Good morning, Charlie.' Steel then noticed Studd's pallid face. 'Are you alright? You look shocking.'

'I think I have a chill. I've been feeling unwell all morning.'

'Oh dear! That's not good. When the Doctor arrives we'll get him to have a look at you.'

Charlie sat down, feeling sorry for himself.

One by one the other players arrived. When WG appeared, Steel told him about Studd's condition. The Doctor gave the patient a quick examination then pulled a little bottle from his cricket bag.

'Try a sip or two of this tonic, Charlie. It always does me a power of good.'

The Doctor had more important things on his mind than what he assumed was a man suffering from the disappointment of the previous day. He knew that if England were to win this game, his side would probably need a substantial innings from him.

By the time play was due to start the rain had stopped and the ground was again full to capacity. The English team walked out on to the field for the beginning of the Australian second innings. Hornby beckoned to Ted Peate and the bowler wandered over to his captain.

'Yes, Mr 'ornby?'

'The wicket looks a bit too wet for you this morning. I'll give Dick Barlow and Happy Jack a bowl first. If that doesn't work, I'll try you.'

Peate was not happy with that piece of news. After all, he had played a major part in dismissing Australia for a small total in the first innings and he, with bold north-country confidence, believed that he could do it again. He just muttered, 'As you say, Mr 'ornby', and kept his thoughts to himself.

Hornby's decision was not a good one. While Bannerman defended patiently, the powerful Massie began to hit the ball to all parts of the compass. Three times he hit Barlow to the boundary and within 15 minutes the score was 20 for none. Hornby enacted plan B, with Peate from one end and, for the first time in the game, Studd from the other.

Just being out on the field made Charlie feel a little better, but to hold the ball in his hand with the opportunity of getting wickets for his country improved his health no end. Sadly he had a relapse when Massie on-drove him for four and then gave Peate similar punishment on the other side of the wicket. It was not long before the lead that England had worked so hard to obtain was washed away, and still no Australian wicket was down.

Another bowling change saw Billy Barnes brought into the attack. Once more Massie smote with power but this time the ball was not hit cleanly, and it flew high to long on. Bunny Lucas moved into position for the catch, and dropped it. The crowd groaned. The embarrassed Lucas quickly threw the ball back to the wicketkeeper and covered his face with his hands.

Massie continued on his merry way. The situation was beginning to look desperate. Charlie felt unwell again, his declining mood affecting his physical condition. He knew that if Massie proceeded in this vein, the Australians would soon have a stranglehold on the game. Hornby made another bowling change, bringing Steel into the attack. Steel soon settled into a good line and length, which had the aggressor thinking. But Massie was determined to see that his team did not lose the advantage gained by his positive approach, and hit another boundary off the new bowler.

Steel was well aware of his opponent's intentions and was determined not to panic. Once more he brought his arm over. Massie again flailed at the ball, but this time he missed and the missile smashed into the stumps. A vital blow, but Charlie and the other English players were relieved rather than excited by it.

Shortly after that Bannerman was also out. He lofted the ball in Charlie's direction and to the Englishman's immense relief, and with an immediate improvement in health, he caught it.

From then on only Murdoch, the Australian captain, withstood the varied attack. On 113 for 6, he hit a ball to the leg side and the batsmen crossed for a single. Sammy Jones, the other batsman who had been promoted in the batting order, unaware that the ball was not dead, wandered out of his crease patting the wicket down with his bat. WG Grace seized his opportunity and ran the astonished Australian out. Jones looked pleadingly at umpire Thoms.

'Sorry, Sammy,' the umpire said, 'you're out.' His finger pointed heavenward.

After lunch Charlie combined with Hornby and wicketkeeper Lyttleton to run Murdoch out. The Australian innings only lasted a few minutes longer, closing for 122; a lead of only 84. The players trooped off the field, the England team delighted at being in what seemed to be a winning position. However, while 85 to win would normally be achieved easily, this would be on a difficult wicket and against Spofforth and Boyle. The players and the crowd alike knew that it would not be easy.

Drama lay ahead, but not all the drama that day was to be on the playing field. As the English amateurs went through the gate to return to their dressing room, one of the nearby spectators suddenly leapt to his feet and then collapsed with a gurgling cry, blood spurting from his mouth. As he lay on the ground groaning, up went the call, 'A doctor! Quickly, we need a doctor.'

The nearest doctor, one appropriately dressed in white, was WG Grace. Grace's medical studies had taken years to complete, medicine having usually taken second place to cricket in his life. However, he had qualified just a couple of years previously and was recognised as a competent medic. He rushed in the direction of the call, barging his way through the excited crowd, and bent down over the writhing form of George Spendlove.

'Get this man into the pavilion and be quick about it,' Grace commanded, more like a general than a doctor. The order was obeyed immediately by the poor man's companions and by the time Grace had begun his examination he had been joined by another doctor.

Meanwhile, there was consternation in the English amateurs' dressing room over the whereabouts of their best player. Lyttleton had seen Grace disappear in a different direction from the rest of the team but, such was the confusion that surrounded Spendlove, he had no idea what was going on.

As they considered the problem a ground official suddenly entered the room, an anxious look on his face, and marched over to Monkey Hornby.

'I'm sorry, Mr Hornby, but Dr Grace is attending a patient. The man is very ill. The Doctor may be a while. It has been agreed to delay the game for as long as necessary.'

Hornby's well-worn face showed anxiety, too. His hand stroked his chin as he considered the problem. His face then lightened slightly.

'Go to the professionals' room and tell them about the delay. Tell them that we'll keep 'em informed,' he instructed the official. 'Oh, and tell Dick Barlow that I'll be opening the innings with him.' The man hurried off.

Then Grace appeared in the doorway. His clothes were covered with blood. His face was expressionless. His team mates asked no questions for they guessed the answer: the patient was dead.

Hornby went over to his star player. 'Are you alright, Gilbert? Can you still play?'

The big man stripped off his bloodied shirt and put on a clean one. 'Yes, I'm still playing. Just give me five minutes.'

'I thought I'd open the innings with Dick and you can come in when you feel ready.'

'I've lost patients before, Monkey. And, no doubt, I'll lose more. I'm still opening.' The determination in those final words left Hornby with the distinct impression that it was a waste of time arguing. In the end Grace did open the batting, but with Albert Hornby, not Dick Barlow.

Grace's condition was not England's only problem. Charlie Studd sat miserably in the corner shivering. The exertions of the day's play had left him feeling worse than ever.

'Charlie, you look shocking,' Allan Steel said, with concern.

'I don't feel at all well,' Studd muttered, as his body shuddered.

'I'll get you a blanket, old chap. I had better tell the skipper, too, though he has other problems at the moment.' Steel hastened over to Hornby, who was on the point of going out to bat with Grace, and advised him of the situation.

'Well, 'opefully, Steel, we won't need 'im. We'll slide 'im down the order if necessary. But there's only 85 to get. We should do it without 'im.'

****

In the Australian dressing room the mood was far from jubilant. They had their own problems. Bowling out a strong England team for under 84 would be very difficult and they knew it. But they were fired by what they thought an injustice, the dismissal of Sammy Jones, to what they considered a cheap trick by WG.

During the longer than usual delay between innings, the tall, lean figure of Spofforth sat slumped in his seat, muttering to himself.

'What was that, mate?' the giant George Bonner asked.

Spofforth stopped, looked up and fixed his penetrating eyes on his team mate. 'I said, "This thing can be done. This thing can be done."' Then, after a pause, he continued, 'We can still win.'

'That's as may be,' Bonner responded, 'but it won't be easy. Make sure you get that big fella out quickly for what he did to Sammy. That'll put 'em on the back foot.'

Eventually, the 'big fella', WG Grace, strode confidently through the pavilion doorway and on to the ground, followed by his captain. Cricket's most famous two hours was about to begin.

'The Demon' Spofforth opened the bowling from one end, with Tom Garrett from the other. The English score ticked over steadily but, in Spofforth's fifth over, Hornby's off stump was knocked back: 15 for 1. Dick Barlow replaced his county colleague at the wicket, took guard and prepared to face that wily Australian bowler. Once more Spofforth ran in, leapt and wheeled over his arm, sending the ball speeding towards the waiting batsman. The ball pitched, kept low, beat the bat and again the stumps were shattered: 15 for 2. Two wickets in two balls caused a concerned buzz to rise from the English crowd. What had appeared an easy target a few minutes before was beginning to appear difficult. But Grace was still there.

Back in the amateurs' dressing room Charlie Studd sat with his head in his hands and a blanket around his shoulders. The others peered out over the ground as George Ulyett walked onto the field.

Ulyett took guard and waited for the dreaded 'Demon'. Spofforth obliged with a snorter, which beat the professional's groping bat and missed the stumps by a whisker. From then on the English innings began to settle as the two batsmen, without ever seeming too confident, slowly added to the score.

Harry Boyle, 'the Devil himself', came on to bowl, to partner his hellish companion, Spofforth. Still the score mounted. The wicket was playing unpredictably. Some balls kept low and others rose chest high. But Grace was the master of all conditions and he stuck to the task like the champion he was. He and the gritty Yorkshireman at the other end brought the total up to 51; a mere 34 still to get, with eight wickets in hand. Once more the Englishmen seemed to have control of the game.

But 'the Demon' still had a stock of fiendish tricks up his hellish sleeve. Spofforth played a card. It was an ace: a quicker one. The ball took the edge of Ulyett's bat and went smack into the gloves of wicketkeeper Blackham.

'Howzat!' eleven Australian voices yelled in unison. The umpire raised his finger: 51 for 3.

By this time Studd was pacing the dressing room, the blanket still around his shoulders. But, Hornby decided not to risk a sick man at this stage and sent in Alfred Lucas instead. The crowd was hushed.

When Lucas arrived in the middle, Grace walked up to him. 'You just play your best defensive game, Bunny,' the doctor said. 'I'll make sure we get 'em.'

It was the end of the over, so Grace faced up to the next ball from Boyle and hit it for two. But, the following delivery was a little slower. Grace played a little early, the ball lobbed up and Bannerman caught it: 53 for 4. And Grace was gone. A gasp went through the crowd. Only 32 to get, but that target suddenly seemed a long way off.

The Right Honourable Albert Lyttelton was the next man in and the two ex-Cambridge University team mates batted slowly, slowly, ever so slowly. Yet the slowness of the play only increased the tension. Each run was greeted with a cheer from the crowd and each near miss by an agonised sigh of relief.

Lyttleton was the next to go, beaten by a vicious break-back that hit the middle stump: 66 for 5. They only needed nineteen to win and Studd was still to come. Indeed, by this time Studd had his pads on and was ready to bat, but Hornby decided to hold him back and sent in Allan Steel instead. He did not last long; caught and bowled by the tireless Spofforth, without scoring: 70 for 6.

If ever a situation demanded the presence of CT Studd, England's best batsman that year, sick or not, it was this one. But still Hornby left Studd in the dressing room and sent in Maurice Read. A gasp of surprise from the crowd greeted Read, followed by polite applause. If Hornby and the rest of England's team knew what was going on, the spectators did not.

'Why was Studd still in the pavilion?' they wondered. 'He should be out on the field.'

Two balls later Spofforth bowled Read for a duck: 70 for 7, 15 to get. Once more cricket's pendulum had swung, this time well in Australia's favour.

Still Studd remained in the dressing room, wrapped in his blanket, as Billy Barnes made his way to the wicket. The crowd's unease grew. Why was such an outstanding batsman as Studd being held back? Perhaps he was injured or ill. Perhaps he would not bat at all.

Barnes strode to the wicket. His walk looked a little unsteady. That came as no surprise to many, because it was known that Billy liked a drink. The tenseness of the situation had, indeed, made him succumb to temptation. However, he joined forces with the courageous Lucas, who was still obeying the doctor's orders and defending stoutly.

Drunk or not, Barnes scored a two. It was followed by three byes from a faster one from Spofforth, which Blackham, standing up to the stumps, hardly saw. The crowd cheered the byes as loudly as they had cheered anything that day. Only ten to get! The pendulum was swinging back to England.

Then Lucas defended once too often. He half hit one from the Demon and was unable to stop it rolling back on to his stumps: 75 for 8.

The sigh of disappointment was replaced by a hum of expectancy as the crowd looked towards the pavilion door to see whether Studd would come in. Surely now he would come to the crease, even if he had to bat on crutches. After what seemed an age, the tall figure of CT Studd emerged from the Pavilion. The blanket had gone and so, it seemed, had much of his vigour. He walked slowly to the wicket as the crowd applauded and cheered loudly. Surely Charlie Studd would see England to victory. After all, he had scored two centuries off the Australians already that year. He, however, just wondered why God had allowed him to get sick at a time like this.

Lucas had been out on the last ball of Spofforth's over, so Billy Barnes was due to face the bowling from Boyle. Studd spoke briefly to Barnes to urge him to do nothing rash.

Harry Boyle was the oldest player in the Australian team and he had bowled a lot of balls that day and was weary. But the Australians now had the scent of victory and that never fails to push tiredness away. Boyle ran in to bowl; the ball hit a bump in the pitch and rose unexpectedly. It took Barnes completely by surprise, struck his glove and lobbed to Billy Murdoch fielding close in on the off-side: 75 for 9. There were still ten runs needed to win, but only one wicket left. England was just one step away from disaster. Was it really possible that these colonial upstarts could beat the English Lion, full of cricketing power and pride?

Out of the pavilion strode the English slow bowler, Ted Peate. He, too, did not seem to walk quite straight that afternoon. The champagne ordered for the expected English victory was being used, instead, to calm the nerves of apprehensive batsmen.

When Peate reached the wicket, Studd went up to speak to him. 'Just keep your end up, Ted. Leave the runs to me. Do nothing rash.'

'Don't you worry, Mr Stood. You can rely on me,' the confident reply came back.

Charlie wandered back to the other end. Three balls to go in the over. *Can Peate survive those three balls and give me a chance to win the game*? Studd asked himself. A feeling of helplessness came over him as Peate took guard and prepared to face Boyle.

Boyle ran in and bowled. Peate took an almighty swing, connected, and the ball sped past the square leg fielder. The Yorkshireman clearly had no intentions of playing defensively. Charlie tore down the wicket, with Peate running in the opposite direction. When the run was completed, Charlie hesitated for a moment. There was an easy two in it, but a second run meant he would again be at the non-striker's end and Peate would have to face the final two balls of the over. However, Peate made the decision for him by charging down the wicket for the second run. Charlie had to respond. Eight runs to win. Two balls left in this over for Peate to face.

Boyle ran in again to bowl. Once more Peate took a swing at the ball and this time missed, but the ball also went past the stumps. At the other end Charlie shivered and felt a wave of nausea sweep over him. 'That was close,' he muttered.

Studd had another word with his partner, advising caution, and then retreated again to the non-striker's end. *If Peate can survive this one ball*, he thought, *I can win the game*. Then he would be the hero of the hour.

'The Very Devil' Boyle moved in for the 80th time that afternoon to bowl the last ball of the over. His arm wheeled round and the ball flew towards the bold Yorkshireman. Once more Peate swung. Once more he missed. This time the ball smashed into the stumps.

The crowd groaned. Australia had won!

Charlie stood there for a moment dumbfounded. The chance to be a hero had vanished. In this crucial situation CT Studd, the best batsman in England that year, had not faced a ball.

He walked disconsolately back to the pavilion, as the crowd stormed on to the field. The Australians carried Spofforth off the ground, for a remarkable effort that saw him take 7 wickets for a mere 44, off 28 four-ball overs. With the ball in his hand, Fred Spofforth was indeed a demon.

When Ted Peate arrived back in the dressing room and was asked why he had batted so recklessly, he thought for a moment and then replied, 'Well, lud! I couldn't troost Mr Stood.' Charlie wondered if he could trust himself.

****

A few days later Charlie felt much better physically, but was emotionally still exhausted and quite depressed. Spiritually, too, he was at a low ebb. As he sat picking unenthusiastically at his breakfast, Kynaston came in.

'Say, Charlie. Have you seen the *Sporting Times*? There's an obituary in it you ought to see.'

Charlie hesitantly accepted the offered paper. *Who on earth has died now*? he thought. *Can things get any worse*?

Kynaston pointed a finger at the spot, and Charlie read to himself:

In Affectionate Remembrance
of
ENGLISH CRICKET
which died at the Oval
on
29th August 1882.
Deeply lamented by a large circle of
sorrowing Friends and Acquaintances

RIP

NB The body will be cremated and
the Ashes taken to Australia

Cricket's greatest legend – the Ashes – was born, and CT Studd had played a memorable, if unfortunate, part in that birth.

CHAPTER 5
THE TOUR

In September that year Charlie and his brother George were included in the twelve-man England squad to tour Ceylon (now Sri Lanka) and Australia, under the captaincy of the Honourable Ivo Bligh. The *SS Peshawur* took them through the Suez Canal, which Britain had acquired a controlling interest in seven years before, and then on to Colombo in Ceylon.

The journey was a great experience for each member of the team, most of whom had not been to Asia before. The Studds, Bligh and Allan Steel spent their first night in Colombo in the home of a Christian friend. The remainder of the team lodged at a local sports club. The visitors found the heat and humidity very trying, the many statues of Buddha odd and the customs of the people strange, but they were delighted by the sandy beaches fringed by swaying palm trees. Charlie Studd subconsciously filed these experiences away in the back of his mind.

Ceylon had been a colony of different European nations since the sixteenth century. First it had been under Portuguese rule, then Dutch, and finally, from 1796, British. Within a few decades of the British arrival numerous coffee and coconut plantations were established. In addition, with the arrival of the English, cricket also emerged and by the early 1880s a keen cricket culture existed in the land.

During the English team's short stay a two-day game was scheduled between it and a team of eighteen local players. Protective equipment for cricketers in the Victorian era did not come close to what it is today, but some of the Sri Lankan players did not even bother with the then-available pads and gloves. Some even lacked shoes. On the second day England was just about to beat their opponents by an innings when the rain came down in torrents and forced an unscheduled close. At least that was something the English players were used to.

Their short stay in Ceylon over, they departed that afternoon in the *Peshawur* in a south-easterly direction. The Sunday after their departure, the Studds, Bligh, Steel and a few others were on deck having just attended an evening service led by the ship's Captain. Suddenly, a bulky sight loomed up in the darkened waters directly in front of them. The Captain urgently called for the engines to reverse and to go full speed astern, but it was too late. The fast approaching ship, the *Glenroy*, smashed into the *Peshawur*, with a fearful sequence of crashes. Ivo Bligh later recalled hearing 'the sickening sounds of great iron plates, bars and spars torn off in all directions like matchwood.'

Those up top went helter-skelter across the deck, falling over each other and everything else but suffered no serious injury. However, below decks it was different. Fred Morley, the powerfully-built English professional fast bowler, was catapulted with great force across the cabin, crashed into a cupboard and cried out in agony, collapsing on the floor. His roommate, Billy Barnes, no more sober than in the Test Match back in August, had fallen from his bunk but was uninjured. Barnes quickly crawled over to his friend, who was sprawled on the floor.

'Eh! You oright, Fred?' he asked urgently.

Nothing but a groan came from his semiconscious team mate.

Morley's condition was obviously serious and that realisation made Barnes quickly sober up. 'Don't worry, mate,' he said to his friend. 'I'll go and get Mr Bligh'.

He then clambered to his feet and rushed off to Bligh's cabin. Bligh was not there, so he went up to the deck, only to be confronted by a scene of chaos. Most of the fallen passengers were by this time back on their feet, though some were sitting, and were being attended for minor injuries by members of the crew or friends. Charlie and George Studd were looking after two young women, who were in an obvious state of distress. But the more chilling sight was the visible devastation to their ship, with debris liberally scattered all over the deck. The *Glenroy* was still nearby and clearly also in serious trouble.

Although no one knew the extent of the damage at this stage, the *Peshawur* had a gaping hole in its side – fortunately almost all of it was above sea level – and three of its lifeboats had been destroyed. There were only two serious injuries on the *Peshawur*. A steward had a leg badly broken in two places. The other was Fred Morley.

Charlie Studd looked up as Barnes arrived on deck. Seeing Barnes' panicky expression he asked, 'You alright, Billy?'

'Fred Morley's 'urt, Mr Studd. Where's Mr Bligh?'

'Hurt badly, you mean?'

'Yes, Mr Studd, I think so.'

'George and I are tending to these ladies, but I'll be down in a few minutes. I think Mr Bligh is on the port side.'

Barnes thought for a moment to work out which side that was and then hurried off. He eventually found Bligh and took him down to the cabin, with Charlie in pursuit. By the time they arrived Morley was sitting on his bunk, holding his side and obviously in a lot of pain.

Studd looked at the stricken man. 'It's a pity W.G's not with us.'

'Yes, but he isn't,' Bligh said. 'You had better get the ship's doctor down here as quickly as possible.'

Charlie rushed off, but it was a little while before he returned with the busy medic. The doctor diagnosed severe bruising, though in fact Morley had at least one broken rib. The medic confined the gruff northerner to bed, and he reluctantly became subject to more loving care than he was used to.

Both ships were in such bad condition that they had to return to Colombo for repairs, and the *Glenroy* was in no state to make it on its own. The *Peshawur*, therefore, towed it back on the long, laborious journey, fortunately without further mishap.

They eventually arrived in Adelaide ten days late, only just in time for the first scheduled game. By this time Morley was still incapacitated and Bligh, too, was injured. Their squad was supplemented by a couple of recently-arrived Englishmen with some cricketing ability, and they appeared in some of the less important games.

Prior to Christmas they played mainly minor games, the Test Matches being scheduled for the end of December and January. That Christmas was to be a very different experience for the Englishmen. It was hot instead of cold; very hot, in fact. But they, the amateurs at least, including Charlie and George Studd, were not denied the comforts of home. They were guests of William and Janet Clarke at Rupertswood, their family's stately home. William Clarke was the president of the Melbourne Cricket Club.

Janet Clarke had a companion, Florence Morphy, who also taught the Clarke children the piano. She was very attractive and the English cricketers, especially the handsome and moustachioed Ivo Bligh, inevitably paid her due attention.

On Christmas Eve, a Sunday, the Clarkes and their visitors attended the morning service at St Mary's Church of England in nearby Sunbury. The gentlemen in the party were dressed in black with top hats, and the ladies in voluminous skirts with eye-catching bonnets. They caused quite a stir.

Charlie felt it was good to be at church again. Because of all the travelling, opportunities for formal worship had not always been plentiful in the early part of the tour. Instead, the Christian members of the squad had met for more informal times of devotion.

Three Test Matches were scheduled and it was those games that would decide the destiny of the 'Ashes', though a fourth was later added. Morley was unavailable for the First Test, but, with great difficulty, courageously played in the last three.

The first game was played in Melbourne over the New Year period and Australia won by nine wickets. Charlie scored 0 and 21 and took two wickets, and would have had one more but for a dropped catch. The people of the rapidly-growing city of Melbourne, which had not even existed 50 years before, responded to the game in remarkable fashion. The total attendance for the three days' play was well over 50,000.

With, officially, just two Tests left, the Englishmen could not afford another failure. To win the Ashes they had to win the second and third games. Anything less would see the Ashes remain in Australia. The Second Test was also in Melbourne. This time England won a low-scoring game by an innings. Charlie scored 14, George just 1, but the latter had fielded brilliantly.

Travel in Australia was not by any means luxurious at this stage in its history. Although the major cities were linked by rail and sea, trips to games in up-country destinations were either by Cobb and Co coach or some other such vehicle on rough roads. It was not good preparation for playing cricket. Eventually the team sailed north to Sydney, Australia's other major city, for the Third Test. It was a must-win game. If they emerged victorious, the Ashes were theirs. If not, they remained in Australia. The mood between the two teams by this time was not friendly. Accusations came from both camps about bowlers deliberately cutting up the wicket with their boots to make it more difficult for opposition batsmen.

Once more the game was low-scoring. England batted first and gained a small lead in the first innings but collapsed dismally in the second. Charlie scored 21 and 25. George managed only 3 and 8. However, in their second innings Australia collapsed even more dramatically and England won by 69 runs. The still-suffering Fred Morley took a total of six wickets in the two innings. The following year Morley died from an illness brought on by his injury.

Ironically, Charlie did better in the unscheduled fourth Test, the game that did not count. It was won by Australia, but Charlie made the second highest score for his team in each innings: 48 and 31.

In spite of that game England had won back the Ashes for the first time and it was not long before there was an actual Ashes trophy to win. In Melbourne Ivo Bligh had met and fallen in love with Florence Morphy, Janet Clarke's companion. After the Third Test Florence Morphy and some of her friends presented Bligh with a little urn of ashes, inscribed 'The ashes of English cricket'. The urn's contents, still debated, were probably the ashes of a bail or bails. Since then English and Australian cricketers have risked life and limb for that tiny, but much-treasured, trophy.

CHAPTER 6
THE TURNING POINT

While Charlie and George were touring Australia, Kynaston had other things on his mind. In February 1882 he had written to Dwight Moody, then back in Britain, about conducting a mission at Cambridge University. Initially Moody had approached that request with less than his usual enthusiasm. He was painfully aware of his lack of education and the idea of preaching to England's young intelligentsia made him unusually nervous. However, Moody eventually replied encouragingly, and Kynaston sent an official invitation to Moody and Sankey, signed by a number of dons, students and local clergy. The mission was eventually held in November that year.

While his two younger brothers were enduring their eventful voyage to Australia, Kynaston was putting the finishing touches to the Moody and Sankey mission in Cambridge. The mission started badly, but blossomed into an exciting and fruitful time. Many students became Christians.

When Charlie returned to Cambridge after the tour he noticed a different atmosphere at the university. The students in the various colleges were organising regular meetings for prayer and Bible study and Christ was a common topic of conversation.

From the time of the conversion of the three brothers, it was Kynaston who seemed to take the Christian life most seriously. Charlie noticed on his return that his elder brother had matured considerably as a Christian. Charlie's development in the faith, by contrast, had almost come to a full stop. Kynaston had continued to meet with Stanley Smith for prayer, at which times the topic was usually the conversion or spiritual development of other students. One of the main people they prayed for was Charlie Studd. They could see that he was lukewarm about his faith, but they recognised that he was a young man with considerable charm and remarkable determination. They knew he had the potential to be a fine Christian leader.

Though Charlie was surprised about the changes in his brother and at the university, he was not reluctant to get involved in the Christian meetings on campus. He once again attended the occasional prayer meeting and, more often, joined with other students in the Sankey-inspired sing-alongs, accompanying them on his banjo.

But the long trip home from Australia ended at the start of the English cricket season. So out came the wand of willow, and once more CT Studd graced the cricket fields of his native land. The year 1883 was every bit as successful for Charlie as had been the previous one. He captained the Cambridge team and once more achieved the double of 1,000 runs and 100 wickets. Even the great Dr. WG Grace had to admit that Studd had a brilliant season both as a batsman and bowler. Was CT Studd, perhaps, the one who would take over the doctor's mantle as the world's greatest cricketer?

It often takes something startling to make people sit up and think. That winter George Studd fell dangerously ill with pneumonia. The three brothers had always been close, but Charlie was closer to George than he was to Kynaston. Charlie also knew that pneumonia could be a killer. In fact, one of WG's brothers, another fine cricketer, had died from that complaint four years earlier. Being a fit sportsman was not certain protection against death by such a disease.

The thought that his dear brother might die struck Charlie like a lightning bolt. It caused him to rethink his life. What was he doing? Where was he going? What should he do with his life? He could not play cricket forever. Indeed, should he even continue to play cricket? There surely were more important things in life.

George lay in his darkened bedroom in their Hyde Park Gardens home. Charlie sat by his bedside hour after hour. At times he wiped his brother's fevered brow. At other times he just kneeled at the bed and prayed. And suddenly prayer seemed real to Charlie. Before, it had been an occasional duty, now it was a vibrant necessity. He threw himself upon the mercy of God. Yet his faith was mixed with doubt. He read the Bible and felt assured that Christ the great healer would cure his brother. He looked at George's ashen face, listened to his coughing and desperate breathing and feared that he would not last much longer.

As he watched his brother's suffering, tears trickled down his face. Like Kynaston, George had shown a greater dedication to Christ than had Charlie. Now Charlie's mind pounded with regrets for his past half-heartedness.

What is all the popularity of the world worth to George, now? he thought. *What value is fame? He has popularity and fame, but now faces eternity. What worth is there in these earthly things? What about me?*

If I had to face God tonight, I would be deeply ashamed. My life has been a denial of my beliefs. I say that I believe in eternal judgment but what have I done to turn others away from it? Nothing! What value are runs and wickets when set against the backdrop of eternity? What can cricket do to get people right with God?

What value is wealth? We have so much but all our money cannot save George. It seems that nothing can. Fame; wealth; what good are they when one is faced with eternal matters? 'Vanity of vanities, all is vanity'. (Ecclesiastes 1:2)

'Oh, God,' he pleaded, 'heal my brother, George, and change me into the kind of person you would have me be.'

Early in 1884 it was clear that George was getting better. Charlie's prayers grew more optimistic. He was now more prepared to leave his brother for a while and took the opportunity to attend a Moody and Sankey meeting. He saw that service through new eyes and, as it drew to a conclusion, he whispered a prayer to God, 'Lord, everything, all I am and have, is yours. My life is only to be lived for you.'

From then on there was a dramatic change in Charlie Studd. Immediately, he began to tell others about Jesus Christ. He displayed the zeal of his father but not his tactlessness. When the cricket season commenced, once more out came the bat, out came the pads, but this time there was a different dimension to it all. During the day he played cricket. In the evenings he took his fellow players and associates to hear Moody.

One friend he took was Allan Steel, his companion in many a battle on the cricket field. At the end of one meeting Steel, deeply touched by Moody's message, walked slowly to the front of the hall, his normally blazing eyes glazed with tears. The Hon. Ivo Bligh, recently retired from cricket, was another who went to hear Moody. A few days after his visit Charlie received a letter from him which said, 'An address from that man goes right home, and makes one think more than any man I have yet heard.'

AJ Webbe was another All-England player who went to hear Moody and Sankey at Studd's invitation. Webbe was Charlie's senior by five years and had gone to Oxford rather than Cambridge, but a strong bond had formed between them when they both played for Middlesex in the County Championship. He too became a Christian.

CT Studd had come to learn of the excitement of influencing others for Christ. To him it was greater than all the pleasures he had so far experienced.

****

During one meeting in the London borough of Stepney, DL Moody noticed a young man walking out of the hall, while a clergyman prayed a prayer that never seemed to end. Moody quickly rose to his feet, and called out, 'Let's sing a hymn, while our brother finishes his prayer.' The unexpectedness of that interruption caused that young man, Wilfred Grenfell, to stop and, as the congregation burst into song, he returned to his place.

A few weeks later Charlie and Kynaston were participating in a meeting associated with the Moody and Sankey campaign. The hall was packed. Such notable sporting figures as the Studds attracted people who did not usually attend church services. Wilfred Grenfell was again in attendance.

Charlie gave his testimony but, in spite of his new boldness, he found it very difficult to address the large crowd. His words were sincere but halting. Kynaston followed him. He was more fluent. As the older brother brought his words to a conclusion, he said to the congregation, 'It is now over to you. What will you do with Christ? What I am going to ask is that if any of you wish to follow Jesus Christ that you stand up. That's right, just stand up where you are if you want to follow Christ.'

For a few moments the hall was still and silent. Nobody moved. No one even coughed. Grenfell experienced an intense spiritual struggle. He had been deeply moved by what the Studds had said, as he had by Moody's words on the earlier occasion. He did not dare stand, but his heart was being moved by the Holy Spirit. God was working in his life, he knew, but his mind was in turmoil and his legs were like jelly. As he hesitated a young man in naval uniform rose to his feet. That was the trigger he needed. Suddenly new strength coursed through his legs and he stood up. That night Wilfred Grenfell found Jesus Christ. He was to become a great missionary to Labrador.

In the middle of June the Moody and Sankey meetings in London ended. A few weeks later CT Studd graduated from Cambridge with a B.A. He then stopped playing cricket with more than a month of the season remaining. When another tour to Australia was announced for later that year, he declared himself to be unavailable. From that time on he was only to play a limited number of games in the sport that had made him famous. He was now intent on working specifically for his Lord and Saviour.

CHAPTER 7
THE CALL

Charlie wanted to dedicate himself to serving God, but how or where? Though he had withdrawn from the cricketing scene, the way ahead was far from clear. He had no awareness of any specific call; no particular Christian task before him. He was still winning his friends into the Kingdom, but his heart yearned for a special role, carved out for him by God.

His thoughts turned to his brother George. He had great respect for his brother's spirituality and wisdom, so he asked him for advice. By this time George had recovered almost entirely from his illness, though on occasions his breathing was still a little laboured. Charlie shared his dilemma with him. George thought for a moment before answering, his fingers gently stroking his moustache as he contemplated the problem.

'Well, it seems to me, old chap,' George began, 'that cricket may well have a bigger part to play in your future than you expect. After all, it has made you famous and God can use that fame to His glory. People will listen to you when they won't listen to their local parson, simply because of your cricketing skills.'

A look of frustration spread across Charlie's face. 'I know there's some sense in that, George, but somehow I seem to have lost all desire to play.'

'That may be so now, Charlie, but when the new season opens next year you may feel quite differently,' George said. 'Don't forget those players who have come to the Lord through your influence this year. I'm sure there are many more in the cricketing world who need Him, and you have an extraordinary influence over so many of them. Perhaps you can continue to be used in that way.'

It was Charlie's turn now to pause for thought. He shuffled his feet restlessly as he began to speak again. 'It's just that I believe I should be doing something else with my time. The Lord seems to be calling me to something new.' He shrugged his shoulders. 'I've no idea what. It's all so frustrating. I want to serve Him, but I've no idea where or how.'

'My dear Charlie, if you could see your face. You look so desperate.' George smiled encouragingly. His brother could only manage a weak smile in response. 'One thing for sure,' George continued, 'you don't have to decide your future tonight. Let's commit it to the Lord and see what transpires. Whatever you do, Charlie, don't act too hastily.'

The two brothers fell to their knees and placed the issue in God's hands.

But Charlie Studd was still not satisfied. He next spoke to Kynaston, whose advice was along the same lines as George's. It made Charlie feel no better.

In the next few days he approached various friends and explained his problem. The advice varied, but most of it followed the tack of his two brothers. None of it satisfied him. His mind remained as confused as ever. His health, normally so robust, was even beginning to suffer. He decided that it was best to get away from London so, mid-July, he went home to Tedworth. He stayed there throughout August and most of September praying and reading the Bible. By the end of that period his health had improved, but he was no nearer to knowing what his life's ministry should be.

In his confused state he decided to read for the bar and follow the legal profession until God directed him to a new sphere of service. But, on his return to London, even this seemed wrong. His heart was not in it. The thoughts of millions dying without Christ weighed heavily upon him. His one desire was to win men and women to his Lord but how was he to do that?

His call came from an unlikely source: a tract written by an atheist. Charlie read it out of curiosity rather than in a search for illumination, but it spoke to him.

'Did I firmly believe,' he read, 'as millions say they do, that the knowledge and practice of religion in this life influences destiny in another, then religion would mean everything to me.'

This man may be ungodly, Charlie thought, *but he certainly makes sense.*

He continued reading. 'I would cast away earthly enjoyments as dross, earthly cares as follies, and earthly thoughts and feelings as vanity. Religion would be my first waking thought and my last image before sleep sank me into unconsciousness. I would labour in its cause alone. I would take thought for the morrow of eternity alone. I would esteem one soul gained for Heaven worth a life of suffering. Earthly consequences should never stay my hand, nor seal my lips. Earth, its joys and its griefs, would occupy no moment of my thoughts. I would strive to look upon eternity alone, and on the immortal souls around me, soon to be everlastingly happy or everlastingly miserable. I would go forth to the world and preach to it in season and out of season, and my text would be, "What shall it profit a man if he gains the whole world and loses his own soul?"' (Mark. 8:36)

Charlie fell to his knees by his bed. 'Lord,' he prayed, 'this man's right. I have not been as zealous in saving souls as I ought to have been. Forgive me. Take all I have, and use me in the salvation of many people for you.'

He read through the tract once more. Tears filled his eyes making focusing difficult. He knelt by his bed for an hour or more, pouring his heart out to God. One particular phrase from the pamphlet kept pounding through his brain: 'I would go forth to the world and preach to it in season and out of season.'

The world! he thought. *I must go forth and preach to the world. But how can I do that*? He then prayed that God would show him how. In the days that followed, his determination to serve God with his whole being continued, though precise details of how he should do that did not appear.

****

On 1 November Kynaston Studd heard a knock on the door of their home in Hyde Park Gardens. Shown into the reception room was none other than his close friend from Cambridge, Stanley Smith. The two men shook hands warmly.

'It's great to see you, Stanley,' Kynaston enthused. 'To what do I owe the pleasure?'

'To Christian mission, Kynnie, old man. Christian Mission. There's a meeting being run by the China Inland Mission tonight at its headquarters at Mildmay. The main speaker's John McCarthy, who first went as a missionary to China nearly twenty years ago. He's just about to go back there. Why don't you come and hear him? I have a hansom waiting outside.'

Kynaston paused for a moment and then declined. 'I'm most sorry, Stanley. I can't make it tonight. I have another appointment, I'm afraid. But I'll tell you what, Charlie might like to go. I think he's in his room. I'll go and tell him. Take a seat, Stanley.'

He hurried up the stairs and spoke to CT Within a few moments both brothers descended the stairs.

Charlie greeted their friend. 'Hello, there, Stanley. Yes, I'd love to come. Just give me a few minutes to get ready, old chap.'

Smith nodded and Charlie bounded up the stairs. Surprisingly quickly, he reappeared looking his best. They said farewell to Kynaston and went on their way.

The hansom moved off and the two friends talked animatedly. Smith told Charlie that he had applied to join the China Inland Mission (CIM) and was anticipating leaving for that mysterious land in the near future.

Upon arriving at the hall the two men alighted from the cab and entered the building. It was already almost packed to capacity.

'Look, Charlie, I'm due to say a few words tonight, too, so I'll have to go and sit on the platform. But there's Monty Beauchamp over there. Why don't you go and sit with him?'

Sure enough there was that other ex-Cambridge student sitting in the body of the hall. In actual fact, Charlie knew Monty better now than when he was at Cambridge. Monty's sister had recently become engaged to Kynaston, which had drawn the two families together. Charlie went over and joined him.

Charlie sat through the meeting totally enthralled. He was entranced by John McCarthy's lilting Irish tones, but much more impressed by what he said. He spoke of the thousands of souls perishing every day and night without even an awareness of the Lord Jesus. Charlie knew what that meant for their eternal destiny.

After McCarthy had concluded, they sang,

> *He leadeth me, He leadeth me,*
> *By His own hand He leadeth me.*
> *His faithful follower I would be,*
> *For by His hand He leadeth me.*

In the hall that night, CT Studd, all-England cricketer, was aware of a leading he could not resist. By the end of the evening he was convinced that God wanted him to go to China.

He thought of offering himself there and then, but decided it was best to pray the matter through first of all and then advise the family. But, he was satisfied that he had now found his destiny.

CHAPTER 8
SPIRITUAL MILLIONAIRES

On his way home from the CIM meeting a difficulty came to mind. How would his mother respond to his decision? Travelling the country, even the world, playing cricket was one thing, but going to China as a missionary was another. He always came back soon enough from his cricket trips, with no more than a few bruises. Going to that mysterious, unknown land as a missionary seemed, even to him, both more permanent and more dangerous. Before arriving home he flicked through his pocket New Testament and came across Jesus' words, 'He that loveth father and mother more than me is not worthy of me.' (Matthew 10:37) That did not remove the difficulty but it did strengthen his resolve to overcome it.

However, unexpected opposition came from another quarter. The next morning, when he told Kynaston about his decision, his brother was horrified. Fine Christian though he was, Kynaston tried every way imaginable to make Charlie change his mind. He argued, he pleaded and he warned of the likely affect upon their mother. Charlie was shocked by the intensity of his brother's opposition. His eldest brother, after all, was one of the Christians for whom he had most respect. But Kynaston's stand did not waver, which was more than could be said for Charlie's. The would-be-missionary already found himself doubting that which before had seemed so certain. But the doubts soon disappeared.

The next stage was, as had been expected, harder. He broke the news to his mother. She, in the fashion of the time, fainted. When she recovered she berated her son for not loving her and for proposing to desert her, poor widow that she was. When fainting, anger and pleading did not change Charlie's mind she tried tears. Charlie could feel tears welling up in his own eyes, but he stuck to his guns. *I knew it would be hard*, he thought, *but does it have to be this hard?*

Later Kynaston re-entered the fray. 'Can't you see you are breaking mother's heart, Charlie? You really must reconsider.'

'Kynnie, I know I am hurting mother, and that hurts me too, but I believe the Lord wants me to go to China to tell others about Him. How can I say "No!" to Him? I believe that I must go.'

Silenced reigned. Neither of the two brothers seemed to know what to say next.

Charlie broke the silence. 'Look, Kynnie, I don't want to be pig-headed about this. Would you pray with me that we might seek the Lord's will?'

There was another pause, this time broken by Kynaston. 'Yes, Charlie, of course I will. I suppose that's what we both want when all's said and done.'

They knelt down together and prayed in great earnest.

The next day the opposition resurfaced. Mrs Studd enlisted various relatives, friends and Christian workers to try to dissuade Charlie from his proposed course. Once more he found himself wavering.

Later he went to his room and collapsed on the bed. Scoring a century had never wearied him as much as arguing with the family. That night he could not sleep. The arguments of the day filled his thoughts, but they were then replaced by a verse which just seemed to echo in his mind: 'Ask of me and I will give thee the heathen for thine inheritance, and the uttermost parts of the earth for thy possession.' (Psalm 2:8)

The next day, Tuesday 4 November, all opposition put behind him, Charlie went to meet James Hudson Taylor, the founder of CIM. Hudson Taylor went from England as a missionary to China at the age of twenty-one. Some years later, seeing the need to take the Gospel into the heart of that country, he established the China Inland Mission. He was now temporarily back in Britain to recruit suitable candidates for that mission.

At CIM headquarters Charlie was ushered into Hudson Taylor's office. It was the first time he had seen the man he had heard so much about. The stern but kindly face gazed through a grey, bushy beard. Charlie could feel Taylor's piercing eyes penetrating, seemingly, his whole being.

Hudson Taylor, for his part, knew much about Studd's background, but was well aware that a true missionary needed more than the courage displayed on the cricket field and a little Christian enthusiasm. What Taylor wanted to assess was whether Charlie Studd had a deep dedication to God, with a clear vision of the salvation of the lost, and a call to make that vision real.

'Sit down, Mr Studd.' Taylor directed Charlie to a chair. The voice had a distinct north-country accent, yet mixed with a lilt that Charlie had not heard before.

'Thank you, Mr Taylor. It is good of you to see me.'

'So you want to be a missionary!' Taylor was a busy man. He had no time to waste on small talk.

'Yes, that's right,' Charlie said. 'I believe the Lord is calling me to China.'

Taylor thought for a moment. 'Well, before we discuss it, we had better pray.' With that he dropped to his knees beside his chair. Charlie did likewise. Taylor then poured out a prayer to God, the like of which Charlie had never heard before. It was full of passion and intensity and demonstrated a strong belief in the reality of prayer. When he had finished they returned to their seats, and Taylor recommenced the interview.

'Perhaps you had better tell me about yourself, your family, your Christian experience, and that kind of thing.'

So Charlie told him 'that kind of thing.' Every now and then Taylor wrote a note on a sheet of paper, but for the most part the missionary statesman just studied the face before him and weighed the words he heard.

When Studd concluded, Taylor spoke again. 'And, your missionary call, Mr Studd? What makes you believe that you should be a missionary? And, why China?'

Charlie breathed in deeply. 'Well, Mr Taylor, I believe that while millions are going to hell I can't give God any less than everything I have.' Charlie leant forward in his chair as he earnestly presented his case. 'He must have my all. I desperately want to take the Gospel to those who haven't heard it, and have for some time, but I wasn't sure how I should go about it. Then when I heard Mr McCarthy the other night I knew God was calling me to China. Every time I open the Scriptures the Lord seems to confirm it.'

'What does your family think?'

Studd sat back in his chair and momentarily looked down at the floor, but then fastened his eyes back on the man interviewing him. 'I believe they think

I'm mad, Mr Taylor.' He paused for a moment. 'But, so did Festus think Paul was mad, didn't he? But he wasn't, and neither am I.'

Hudson Taylor smiled slightly. 'No, Mr Studd, I don't think you're mad either. I only wish there were a few more sane Christians like you. Thank you for your honesty. You realise, of course, that the way you are choosing is a very difficult one.'

Charlie nodded his agreement.

'Missionary work in China often involves isolation and privation, as well as the open hostility of the people you will be working amongst,' Taylor continued. 'I want to make it clear that going to China to serve is not a picnic. It is a venture that could cost you your life.'

'I realise that.'

A silence followed. It was broken by Charlie. 'When will I know if I'm accepted?'

Hudson Taylor rose from his chair and extended his hand. 'Now, Mr Studd! Now! From this moment you are an associate missionary of the China Inland Mission.' He paused to let Charlie take that in. 'At a later stage we may make you a fully-fledged missionary in the Mission, but we will discuss that on another occasion.'

Charlie leaped from his chair, took the proffered hand and shook it warmly.

Strangely, but perhaps not so strangely, on his way home the newly-accepted missionary was attacked by doubts, particularly with regard to his duty to his mother. As he waited at the station for a train home, he took out his pocket New Testament and opened it at random. His eyes fell on the words 'A man's foes shall be they of his own household.' (Matthew 10:36) Suddenly, once more, his mind was at peace.

The afternoon after Charlie had been accepted by CIM he sat alone in his room at Hyde Park Gardens. Suddenly the butler interrupted the quietness of his thoughts.

'Excuse me, Mr Charles, there are two gentlemen to see you. Mr Stanley Smith and a Mr Hoste.'

'Oh, indeed. Show them into the lounge, Ryall. I'll see them there.'

The servant disappeared and Charlie went down the oaken staircase and into the lounge. In a few moments the butler arrived, followed by the familiar, robust figure of the Cambridge stroke, Stanley Smith, and a thin-faced young man whom Charlie had not seen before. The two friends shook hands with feeling.

'Charlie, may I introduce you to Dixon Hoste? You'll remember his brother, William, who was with us at Cambridge.'

'Indeed, I do. It's a pleasure to meet you, my dear Hoste,' Charlie said, extending his hand in welcome.

'Call me Dick. Everybody does,' Hoste said shyly.

'Take a seat.' Charlie indicated the plush, leather armchairs.

The three of them sat down. 'And what do you do, Dick?' Charlie asked.

'Well, actually, I'm a soldier. I'm a Lieutenant in the Royal Artillery. Or, perhaps I should say, I was. Now I'm an associate missionary of the China Inland Mission,' the rather solemn soldier of Jesus Christ said.

Charlie's eyes lit up. 'Oh, I see.'

'That's why we're here, Charlie, old chap,' Smith interrupted. 'Mr Hudson Taylor wants the three of us to go to Oxford University tomorrow, and then to Cambridge, to tell them about the needs of China. A kind of recruiting campaign, I'd think you'd call it.'

Charlie laughed. 'He doesn't waste time that man, does he?'

'No, Charlie, he doesn't,' Smith said, 'and neither should we.'

Studd and Smith then joined in animated conversation, making plans for the visits. Dixon Hoste listened to them intently, but said little.

The next day they travelled to Oxford, where they held a series of poorly attended meetings, scattered over the next six days. On November 12 they returned to Cambridge, minus Hoste, who was not a Cambridge man. Montagu Beauchamp came in his place.

Since his Cambridge days Beauchamp, a Baronet's son, had become a Deacon in the Church of England. He had heard of Charlie's determination to go to China, in spite of family opposition, and had been deeply impressed by it. Montagu's situation was very different from Charlie's. It was his mother's dearest wish that her son would become a missionary. Beauchamp had first met Hudson Taylor many years ago, but had renewed his acquaintance with him in recent times. He also had made enquiries about going to China.

Though their trip to Oxford had met with little success, it proved very different in Cambridge. They were received like royalty. Led by Hudson Taylor, they spoke in various halls packed with enthusiastic men and women. On the second Sunday of their visit, after Hudson Taylor and Stanley Smith had spoken, Taylor asked any who wished to serve overseas to stand. Fifty did so. After the final meeting, forty five enquired about missionary service. Amongst them was Arthur Polhill-Turner, who had been converted through the earlier Moody meetings that Kynaston Studd had organised in Cambridge. The eloquence of Smith, the reputation and significance of Hudson Taylor, and the warm sincerity of Charlie Studd had been used by the Holy Spirit to move many to consider missionary service.

Suddenly the missionary enterprise became big news. The Press, secular as well as religious, took notice of these events and reported them widely. The ex-Cambridge men were dubbed 'the spiritual millionaires'. They were men of wealth and rank, but this they considered of little account compared with the riches found in Jesus Christ. Because of the considerable publicity, Hudson Taylor delayed his own return to China and used Studd, Smith and their companions to fill the many calls for speakers that Taylor was getting from churches and organisations.

One such request had come from Professor Henry Drummond of Edinburgh University. Studd and Smith were dispatched north to Scotland to stir up the interest there. So careless had Charlie now become about material things, he went with nothing but the clothes he was wearing, much to his mother's distress. She made sure that some additional clothes were sent on. When the two would-be missionaries arrived, preparations for the meetings were well underway. The organising body, a group of medical students, had hired the multi-towered Free Assembly Hall for some of the meetings, and arranged for men with sandwich-boards to walk around the university advertising them.

Charlie and Stanley spent their first afternoon in Edinburgh in prayer with their hosts, asking God to bless the gatherings. The two Cambridge men felt rather nervous as the time for the first meeting approached. Their minds alternated between optimism and doubt as they considered the task ahead. Of the two, Smith was the better speaker and Charlie felt rather in his shadow.

They arrived at the hall a half an hour before the scheduled start. Already there were many inside and hundreds were outside trying to get in. Charlie's mouth fell open as he gazed at the milling throng.

'Are these all here to listen to us, Charlie?' the equally astonished Stanley Smith asked.

'It's just like a Moody and Sankey meeting,' Charlie replied, hoarsely.

They were ushered into the building and directed to a small room behind the platform. As they sat there Charlie became aware of a noise he could not at first identify. He gradually realised that it was the sound of thousands of excited voices in the hall, muffled by the intervening walls.

The door of the room opened and in walked Professor Drummond, looking younger than any professor had the right to be. He smiled and shook hands with the two visitors. Then, in a voice that gently proclaimed his Scottish origins, he advised, 'Gentlemen, it's time we began. If you'll follow me…'

They followed the professor and mounted the platform stairs. A great cheer arose as they appeared. Once more Charlie and Stanley felt very nervous. The two friends were used to being cheered at sporting events, but not at religious gatherings. They found it all rather unsettling. What were these people expecting?

The meeting began with singing and prayer. Then Professor Drummond briefly addressed the audience. 'Ladies and Gentlemen, it is indeed a great pleasure to welcome you to this meeting tonight. The preaching of the Gospel of Jesus Christ overseas is very much our responsibility, and tonight we are going to hear from two young men who are dedicating their lives to that task. We need to hear them and we need to support them. First, let me introduce to you Mr Charles Thomas Studd.'

Charlie rose from his seat and once more a cheer went up from the crowd. He mounted the rostrum and gazed at the mass of faces in front of him. He was painfully aware of his problem: for one who had been commissioned to take the Gospel to others, he always found public speaking very difficult.

He opened his mouth but no sound came out. He tried again and in a hoarse whisper uttered a few words, which could not have been heard beyond the first two rows. He paused, silently said a brief prayer for strength, and started again. This time it was better. He told the story of his life, his conversion and his call to China. The hall was hushed as the people listened intently. When he finished, cheers broke out once more.

Next, Drummond introduced Stanley Smith. Smith proved more eloquent than Charlie. But the observable result was the same: silence followed by wild cheering.

Further meetings followed in subsequent days. There was opposition. But all the time more and more people were making enquiries about missionary service.

The two men eventually said their Scottish farewells at Waverley Station a week into December. Even the noisy engines were unable to drown out the din made by the large and enthusiastic crowd of students who had come to see them off. When Studd and Smith appeared, up went cries of 'Speech! Speech!' The two ex-Cambridge men obliged and were cheered once more.

The commotion attracted an even larger crowd. One man leant over to a porter and asked, 'What's all the noise aboot?'

The porter responded, 'They're all medical students, but they're all arf their heeds.'

They finally departed and returned to London. They arrived just in time for Kynaston Studd's wedding to Hilda Beauchamp, Montagu's sister.

****

Charlie, and his fellow missionaries-in-waiting, received invitations to speak, from far and wide. After Christmas it was decided to conduct a whistle-stop tour of Britain in the second half of January, with the dual purpose of proclaiming the Gospel and encouraging others to enlist for missionary service. Hudson Taylor, recognising the opportunity, agreed to postpone their departure for a few weeks, until early February. He, however, left to return to China in mid-January.

On 7 January two more candidates joined the ranks of CIM missionaries: Arthur Polhill-Turner and his brother, Cecil. The following day Hudson Taylor's farewell meeting was held in London's Exeter Hall. With the missionary-statesman on the platform were Charlie Studd, Stanley Smith, Montagu Beauchamp, William Cassels, Dixon Hoste and the Polhill-Turner brothers. It was the first time that they had all been assembled together. The next day they were dubbed 'The Cambridge Party', which was soon changed to 'The Cambridge Band', and then, to the name that stuck: 'The Cambridge Seven.' However, that title was not strictly accurate. Six of those young men had been to Cambridge University but the seventh, Dixon Hoste, had not, though his brother had.

Once more they found themselves big news with 'The Cambridge Seven' being prominently referred to in both the religious and the secular press. Their story jostled for newspaper space with the tale of 'Chinese' Gordon, another Christian, and his heroic stand at Khartoum. It captured the public's imagination that seven young men with wealth, learning and great potential would lay aside material prosperity to serve Christ in China. The oldest of them, William Cassels, was 25 and the youngest, Arthur Polhill-Turner, was a mere 21.

After Hudson Taylor had departed, Studd and Smith went on a preaching tour visiting Liverpool, Edinburgh again, Newcastle, Manchester, Rochdale and Leeds. They spoke in halls and churches to packed and enthusiastic crowds, with some coming to faith in Christ and others offering to serve Christ overseas.

Amidst all the excitement Charlie found time to write a letter to his mother. 'I cannot tell you how very much the Lord has blessed us,' he told her, 'and we grow daily in the knowledge of Jesus and His wonderful love. What a different life from the former one! Why, cricket and racquets and shooting are nothing compared to this overwhelming joy.'

Yet the joy was not unalloyed. He continued, 'Finding out so much about the poor in the great towns has increased my horror at the luxurious way I have been living; so many suits and clothes of all sorts, whilst thousands are starving and perishing of cold. So, all must be sold when I come home.'

They visited Liverpool again on 29 January and then returned to London. The official farewell to the Cambridge Seven was to be held the next day at the Eccleston Hall. Yet even after this there were further invitations to speak in different cities – Bristol, Oxford and Cambridge – causing their departure to be further delayed.

A final meeting at the Exeter Hall was scheduled for 4 February 1885. It was wet and cold, the kind of winter's day one would like to forget. Yet it was to prove memorable for the seven young men and the thousands who gathered to hear them. Amongst the crowd was Dora Studd, now accepting the inevitability of her son's departure, and other close relatives of the seven. William Cassels's mother, however, had stayed away, unable to face the trauma of the occasion.

Upon the platform sat no less than forty Cambridge graduates who had volunteered for missionary service. Behind them was a massive map of

China, which left no doubt as to the purpose of the gathering. At the proposed commencement time the seven filed on to the platform, led by Smith, and were greeted with the now customary cheers and applause. Each of the seven spoke briefly.

Though Charlie had spoken publicly numerous times in the last few weeks, he was still not comfortable with it. He had scribbled a few notes on a sheet of paper to assist him. As he looked out at the vast assembly his knees shook and his mouth felt dry. Facing 'the Demon' Spofforth on the cricket field was not as nerve-wracking as this. Yet, at the same time he found it exhilarating to speak for Christ.

He took a quick look at his notes, held in his shaking hand. 'I want to recommend to you tonight my Master, the Lord Jesus Christ,' he began. 'I have tried many ways of pleasure in my life, but in recent times I have been seeking after the best Master, and thank God I have found Him. But what are you really living for?' he challenged his listeners. 'Are you living for the day or are you living for life eternal? Are you going to care for the opinion of men here, or for the opinion of God? The opinion of men won't avail us much when we get before the judgment throne, but the opinion of God will. Had we not, then, to take His word and implicitly obey it?' He folded over the sheet of paper, placed it in his pocket and returned to his seat, while the crowd roared its approval.

The next day the seven assembled at Victoria Station to catch the boat train. Milling in the station concourse were many family members and friends, including the cricketers, Allan Steel and Ivo Bligh. Also present were Kynaston Studd, now accepting Charlie's missionary purpose, and his wife Hilda. Just before 10 am the seven boarded the train and on the hour it departed for Dover to begin their journey.

That day *The Times* gave generous coverage to the previous night's meeting. However, a day later the seven's departure was lost in the news of the death of General Gordon and the fall of Khartoum.

PART TWO

CHINA

CHAPTER 9
THE VOYAGE

The ship carrying the seven left Dover that afternoon. Travelling with them as far as Calais were Kynaston and Hilda Studd and Lady Beauchamp, Montagu's mother.

The Channel crossing went without incident and, after the brief stop in France, they journeyed south through a quieter than normal Bay of Biscay, round Spain and Portugal and through the straits of Gibraltar into the deep blue waters of the Mediterranean. The vessel then steamed round the foot of Italy and docked at Brindisi. On Friday 13 they arrived at Alexandria in Egypt. From there they travelled by rail via Cairo to Suez.

They then embarked on a smaller vessel, the *Kaiser-i-hind* ('The Emperor of India') for the remainder of the journey, as second class passengers. They shared the cramped quarters with three married couples and a bad-tempered sea captain named Bart Anderson.

Realising that their next port of call, Colombo, was a week away the seven sought to make good use of their time. They occupied it in two ways. The first was to try to win their fellow passengers to Christ. The second was to attempt to learn the Chinese language from books furnished by CIM. Without exception, they found the first task more to their liking than the second. Yet they each recognised that if they were to minister effectively in China, they had to master the language, so they studied hard.

On the first afternoon Dixon Hoste encountered Bart Anderson. 'Good afternoon. My name's Hoste, Dixon Hoste,' he said, extending his hand in greeting.

'And wet b'hind the ears you are, I can see,' Anderson slurred with a scowl.

Hoste ignored the comment and the strong smell of alcohol on the

Captain's breath. 'Everyone calls me Dick,' he continued. 'May I ask your name?'

'What's that to you? People should mind their own business, I reckon.'

Hoste was temporarily halted by the further rebuff but, like a good soldier, thought that attack might be better than defence. 'I'm on my way to China with some friends to tell the Chinese about Jesus Christ.'

'Jesus Christ?' There was something about the way Anderson said the name that made Hoste flinch. 'I've no time for religion, young man. The church is full of hypocrites.'

'You're not a Christian, then, Mr ...? I'm sorry. I still don't know your name.'

'Anderson, if you must know. Bart Anderson. And no, I'm not a Christian. Christians are all hypocrites, I tell you.'

'What do you think of Jesus Christ, Himself, then?'

'Huh! No one has ever been able to convince me he's ever really existed.'

'I'll tell you what, Mr Anderson. Why don't you and I read a few stories about Him from the Bible?'

'You must be mad, man. What interest would I have in readin' about someone who never lived? D'you want to make me as mad as you?'

Dixon's mind went back to a similar rebuff suffered by the Apostle Paul. 'But why not give it a try?'

'Not on your life. You can go to Hell.' With that, Anderson stormed off.

The next day Hoste was on the deck when he heard steps behind him. It was Captain Anderson. 'I'm gonna do what you said, Hoste.'

'What's that, Mr Anderson?'

'I'll read the Bible with you, like you said. I'll show you what rubbish it is.'

Hoste was delighted. They arranged a time and later that morning they met to read the Bible. Beginning with the Gospels, Hoste read a few passages and invited Anderson to do likewise. He did, but with a voice full of cynicism and contempt. The evangelist guided his reading but made few comments, preferring to allow the Scriptures to speak for themselves.

They met again that afternoon, and the next day, and the next day. They read and read. Occasionally Hoste would make an explanatory observation. Frequently Anderson mocked what they were reading. At the end of the third day he seemed no closer to accepting the Bible's message than when they began.

The *Kaiser-i-hind* had by this time sailed through the length of the Red Sea, into the Gulf of Aden, and was about to launch out into the Indian Ocean. Over their meal that night the seven missionaries talked about Bart Anderson.

'Just occasionally something seems to strike home, and I'm thinking I'm getting somewhere,' Hoste said. 'Then up goes the wall of prejudice again and we seem to be back where we started.'

'Satan's certainly having a field day in that man's life, Dick,' Stanley Smith responded.

'Is he beyond the Gospel, do you think? Too hardened by sin?' Montagu Beauchamp wondered.

'I don't believe anyone's that far gone,' Charlie countered. 'We just have to be persistent that's all, and consistent. He's still prepared to keep talking, so let's accommodate him.'

There was a brief silence while they considered the problem. 'Do you think it's time someone else took over? A new voice and a different approach might do the trick,' Hoste suggested.

'Why not let Charlie have a try?' Arthur Polhill-Turner said. 'It seems to me he's gifted with a way of reaching the unreachable. How about it, Charlie? What d'you think?'

'I'm game. I'll give anything a try. What do the rest of you say?'

'It sounds good to me.' It was Stanley Smith. 'Why don't we pray about it this evening and make a decision in the morning.'

'That makes sense,' William Cassels said. He had been silent up until that point. 'This sort of thing can only be done by prayer and fasting.'

Arthur laughed. 'Well, it's a bit late for the fasting, old chap, but there's plenty of time for the prayer.'

The rest of that evening they spent in prayer, and into the night. The next day they agreed that Hoste would introduce Charlie to Anderson to see what would happen.

Late in the morning they tracked the sea captain down. 'Good morning, Bart,' Hoste said pleasantly. 'I don't think you've properly met my friend, Charlie Studd.' Charlie held out his hand in greeting.

'You think y'need reinforcements, then?' Anderson responded gruffly. He ignored the extended hand.

Hoste smiled. 'Just thought you might appreciate talking to someone else.'

'Well, I don't appreciate it. I've had enough of this religion nonsense.' With that he turned round and quickly disappeared.

The two Christians looked at each other sadly. They then went back to report to their still praying friends.

That afternoon Charlie was walking on the deck when Anderson came up behind him. 'If it's talk you want Studd, I'll be in it.'

Charlie recognised the voice and offered up a quick prayer of thanks. He turned and replied, 'Most certainly, Mr Anderson. Why don't we sit down in these chairs?' He gestured towards two deckchairs.

Anderson said nothing but lowered his large frame into one of the chairs, which creaked as it took his weight. As Studd sat down next to him, he caught the whiff of alcohol on Anderson's breath. Charlie had no time for small talk. 'Where do you think your soul will go if you died tonight, Mr Anderson?'

The captain was shocked by the directness of the question. He hesitated for a moment and then replied, 'I don't think it would go anywhere, Studd. I don't believe there's anywhere else for it to go. Except six feet under, or in our case,' he extended his hand towards the sea, 'in the drink. I don't go for this Heaven and Hell nonsense that you Christians go on about.'

Charlie thought for a moment and then proceeded to talk about the Christ he loved. The two men spoke for an hour-and-a-half, but Anderson showed no sign of softening. Charlie was feeling unusually weary. This man was indeed difficult to deal with. He began to wonder if there was any point in continuing but a voice seem to sound in his head, saying, 'If not now, when?' so he continued.

'From my experience, Mr Anderson, I can tell you that there is no happiness to be compared with that found in Jesus Christ. I have had many blessings in my life. A happy family, good friends, sporting fame and wealth beyond what you could imagine. But I tell you, none of these things can be compared with the joy of knowing Christ and the power of his resurrection. True happiness is to be found in Christ.'

For the first time in the conversation Bart Anderson looked downwards. His eyes seemed fixed on the deck beneath his feet. He said nothing for a while. They could both feel the brisk sea breeze blowing their hair about and the ship rolling slightly in the gently moving ocean. Studd sensed there was a slight change in the hardened man.

Anderson looked up and spoke once more, but this time his voice was more subdued, less aggressive. 'You ought to be thankful for that. Many have been seeking happiness for years 'n years with all their might and ain't got it.'

He paused for a moment. 'Life has been hard for me, Mr Studd. I've been at sea since I was a lad and a drunk for almost as long. There's not been much happiness for me. I've never got on with family. When I left England I didn't say goodbye to any of 'em, not even me mother. Over the last twenty-five years I've nearly died many times, too. Once I was shipwrecked and only three of us survived. Another time I was attacked by a mob in Portsmouth. They nearly killed me, Mr Studd, they nearly killed me.'

Charlie wondered why a mob would have attacked Bart Anderson, but he did not ask. The man was clearly thinking and opening up and he did not want to stop the flow.

'Another time I had cholera but I lived. It's almost as if someone has been looking after me all this time.' He paused to reflect. 'Do you think it could be God?'

'I'm sure it is, Mr Anderson. Certain of it!' Studd eagerly replied. 'Don't you see that He cares for you? He sent His Son to die for you. Won't you accept Jesus Christ as your Saviour? Won't you believe in Him? He can lift you out of this sin you have been living in. He can change you.'

Anderson looked down at the deck once more, lost in thought. Then, he lifted his head slowly. 'If I did that now, Mr Studd, it would be words, just words. I don't think I would really mean them. I must think about it some more.'

Charlie placed his hand gently on the captain's shoulder. 'Yes, I understand. Think about it more and I will see you again tomorrow. I'll say goodbye for now, old chap.' Studd rose from his deckchair and returned to his cabin. Anderson remained in his chair, deep in thought.

The next day Dick Hoste was back on deck when he encountered Anderson. At least it looked like the sea-farer, but this was the first time Hoste had seen the man with a smile on his face. Hoste had to look twice to make sure.

'Mr Hoste!' The sailor hurried up to him. 'Mr Hoste, I've something to tell you.'

Dick thought he knew what that might be but he asked anyway. 'What's that, Bart?'

'I've become a Christian, Mr Hoste. I've become a Christian. I was very distressed after speaking with Mr Studd yesterday. All my sins seemed to be piled up before me in a great mountain and I couldn't bear to look at 'em. I just had to ask Jesus to forgive 'em all and take 'em away and He did, like Mr Studd said He would. He did!'

The usually solemn face of Dixon Hoste also broke into a smile. 'That's wonderful news, Bart. I am delighted.'

'There's more, too, Mr Hoste, I've written to my mother and asked her to forgive me. I haven't posted it yet, of course. I'll have to wait till we arrive in Colombo for that. I've told her too about me becoming a Christian. I'm not sure what she'll make of that.'

Hoste permitted himself a rare laugh. 'I'm sure she'll be delighted, though surprised no doubt.'

'She'll certainly be surprised. It's the last thing she'd have expected.'

The missionary could not help being swept along by the new convert's enthusiasm and he laughed again. He then extended his hand and shook the sailor's giant paw. 'Bart Anderson,' he said, 'welcome to the family of God.'

The following day, Sunday, the Cambridge Seven were given the privilege of leading worship on the quarter-deck. Arthur Polhill-Turner led the service, his brother and Charlie gave brief testimonies and Stanley Smith preached. Charlie also accompanied the singing on his banjo. Gathered for the service were several members of the crew, Bart Anderson, all of the second-class passengers and most of the first-class. Some of these, too, later became Christians.

Later that week they arrived in Colombo. Charlie found himself reflecting on the past. Two-and-a-half years ago he had visited this city to play cricket, but now he was on a very different mission.

What a great deal has happened in those thirty months, he thought. There had been a trip to Australia; a full season of cricket in England; George's illness; his own deepening Christian experience; Moody and Sankey meetings; his call to the mission field and the whistle-stop tour of Britain. He had experienced so much in such a short time. God had, indeed, been good.

From Colombo they travelled to Penang, Singapore and Hong Kong. On March 18 they arrived in the Yangtze estuary and before them they saw, for the first time, the mighty city of Shanghai. Their dreams were about to be fulfilled.

CHAPTER 10
THE LAND OF MYSTERY

To most in the west, China had long been a place of mystery. It had been a massive empire, largely on its own, for centuries. In the thirteenth century, in the reign of Kublai Khan, the young Marco Polo had been the first European to penetrate its life with any success and return to tell the story. The tales he told on his return were so strange few believed him.

Civilization had existed there for 2,000 years before the birth of Christ. Over the centuries the various dynasties had come and gone, each making its artistic and social imprint on the nation's heritage. The Shang dynasty, of the sixteenth to the eleventh centuries BC, was noted for its bronze vases and silk weaving. It was followed by the Zhou (or Chou) dynasty, which lasted about eight centuries, and for some of that time operated two separate and, at times, warring empires: the Eastern and the Western. During that era bamboo books were developed, bronze work furthered and in 776 BC Chinese astronomers recorded an eclipse. It was also an era of social growth and agricultural development.

In 221 BC Qin Shi Huang overthrew the Zhou dynasty and for the first time united the whole of China. It was during the reign of the short-lived Qin dynasty, of which Shi Huang was the founder, that the Great Wall of China was built. Its purpose was to keep out the barbarians from the north. When Qin Shi Huang died, thousands of life-like, terra-cotta warriors, some with horses, were interred in his tomb with him. These were only re-discovered as recently as 1974.

Under the following dynasties China did not always exist as one empire. Sometimes it was split into two, three or even more divisions. At times they peacefully coexisted and at others they fought fiercely.

The Chinese people were advanced and innovative. They invented the magnetic compass in the third century BC; produced paper around 100 AD; invented gunpowder in the tenth century and movable type in the twelfth.

The nation's religion and philosophy appeared in a number of forms. The first was Taoism, developed by Lao Tzu, in the sixth century BC. It was both a religious and a philosophical system. Its adherents worshipped a number of gods, and rejected excessive organisation and legal restraints. Taoism taught a belief in inaction: specifically that one should not react against aggressive behaviour, for such a reaction only furthered the aggression. It became the state religion during the Han dynasty, which from about 200 BC ruled China for four hundred years.

Confucius was born in 551 BC, and his teachings were more philosophical than religious. In contrast with Taoism, he introduced various codes of conduct for the different strata of society, which emphasised justice, loyalty, propriety and respect for the Jun Tze (the Confucian ideal man). His aim was to promote a peaceful and orderly society. As the ages succeeded one another his teachings acquired religious trappings, influenced by the animist beliefs of many of his followers.

Around the middle of the first century AD, Buddhism came to China. Buddhism was founded in India by Siddhartha Gautama, at about the same time that Confucius was developing his ideas in China. Gautama taught the four noble truths: that suffering is universal; that suffering is caused by desire; that desire should be eliminated; and that to do so required the following of the eight-fold path. This included such practices as right views, right intentions, right speech, right conduct, right awareness and right concentration. It was believed that the devotee, through a process of reincarnation, would eventually reach Nirvana, which is virtual non-existence. The branch of Buddhism that entered China was the more liberal Mahayana form, which the Chinese further adapted.

By the time of the arrival of Protestant Christianity in China in the early nineteenth century, the influence of both Taoism and Buddhism had declined, but Confucianism was still strong.

The first Christians to enter China were the Nestorians, probably early in the sixth century. There is a reference to them in an Imperial edict a little over a hundred years later, in 638. They translated the New Testament into Chinese in about the ninth century and experienced considerable persecution in the following period. While their numbers declined significantly, there were still Nestorian services being held in China when Roman Catholic missionaries arrived in the thirteenth century.

From the sixteenth century on, mainly through the zeal of Jesuit missionaries, the Catholics gained numerous converts. Though, periodically, imperial edicts forbade Catholic teaching, and at times persecution was fierce, it was estimated that there were about 300,000 Catholics in China by 1726.

The first Protestant missionary to go to China was Robert Morrison, a Scot, who arrived in 1807. He had heard of the daring of William Carey in taking the Gospel to India, and vowed that he would do the same for China. In 1804, at the age of 22, he approached the London Missionary Society (LMS) with his vision. He had a gift for languages and had already taught himself Hebrew, Greek and Latin. He had begun to learn Mandarin from manuscripts in the British Museum and from a Chinese acquaintance then living in London, who was trying to learn English.

The LMS eventually dispatched him to China on 31 January 1807 and he arrived in Canton, a port just north-west of Hong Kong, seven months later. His efforts saw very few converts but, working in secret for fear of the authorities, he translated the Scriptures and compiled a Chinese dictionary and grammar.

Very few brave souls followed his example. In fact, the Chinese authorities frowned upon and discouraged the presence of foreigners in China, which made entry into the country very difficult. By the early 1830s there were only eight Protestant missionaries and missionary families in the whole of China. However, by this time the handful of Chinese converts had begun to have greater success in presenting the Gospel to their fellow nationals. The population of China at that time was approaching four hundred million and the task ahead, with so little support from the Christianised nations, seemed impossible.

The great scandal of that time in British-Chinese relationships was the traffic of the drug opium. It had been used medicinally both in China and Europe for many years. In the mid-eighteenth century Robert Clive, who established the British Empire in India, recognised the commercial possibilities of the drug. It was being produced in the territory he governed, so he authorised the East India Company to commence exporting it to China.

It is probably true to say that the full social consequences of such traffic were not realised by anyone at the time. But as more and more Chinese began to use the drug the problems became very evident. In addition, with little other transportation available to get from place to place, some missionaries had used the ships that had also transported opium. In the minds of many Chinese this put the missionaries in the same camp as those in this despised drug trade.

The Chinese had always been cautious about trading with the European powers and they, quite naturally, were only willing to conduct such business when they believed it served their best interests. The drug trade obviously did not do that. The resulting disagreement between China and Britain grew to such intensity that war broke out. British warships sailed into Chinese waters and shelled Chinese ports. Hong Kong was occupied early in 1841. On 28 August 1842 the Treaty of Nanking was signed, guaranteeing the opening of various major Chinese ports to foreign trade.

The war was strongly criticised by many in Britain. Dr Thomas Arnold, famous Headmaster of Rugby School, described it as being 'so wicked as to be a national sin of the greatest possible magnitude.' The Christian humanitarian Lord Ashley (later Lord Shaftesbury) called it 'one of the most lawless, unnecessary, and unfair struggles in the record of history.'

But, whatever the wrongs of the Opium War, China was now open not only to commercial trade but also to missionary enterprise. Official persecution of the Christian Church had also ended, for the time being.

From this time Protestant missionaries began to enter China in significantly greater numbers. One of them was James Hudson Taylor, who had been sent to China by the Chinese Evangelisation Society on 19 September 1853. He was 21 years old. That same day the British and Foreign Bible Society decided to print and distribute a million Chinese New Testaments.

Taylor based himself in Shanghai but travelled extensively inland, spreading the word. He went back to England at the end of 1860 to qualify as a doctor, and in 1865 was appointed the leader of the China Inland Mission. In 1866 he returned to China to continue his mission, but made other return visits to Britain to increase interest in this missionary cause and to recruit new workers. On his visit back in 1883-85 he recruited the Cambridge Seven and other Christians to help forward the work amongst the Chinese.

During the 1870s some parts of China had been devastated by severe famine. A number of mission agencies conducted famine relief at this time, which improved the image of Christianity in the minds of some Chinese, but there was still much opposition.

CHAPTER 11

SHANGHAI

As the Cambridge Seven left Singapore and sailed to the Chinese mainland they noticed the increase in the number of Chinese junks on the waters. Upon arrival in the mouth of the River Huangpu, a tributary of the Yangtze ('the Long River') the number increased dramatically. They saw literally hundreds of junks of varying sizes, with their brown pleated sails. But even the largest of them seemed small compared with the *Kaiser-i-Hind*. Charlie thought it was like entering a new world and, in many respects, it was.

Their ship made its way through the junk-cluttered waters and docked. The Seven were up on the decks looking at the sights before them, pointing excitedly at the various buildings and vessels that caught their attention. Signs of European influence were surprisingly plentiful, such as the many new buildings used to house the various commodities being imported or exported by the different trading companies. But, inevitably more prominent and more interesting to the visitors were the traditional Chinese buildings with their curving roofs and ornately decorated facades. More interesting, too, were the people, hurrying and scurrying on the dockside. Some were European – that was clear from their clothing – but the vast majority were Chinese, the people to whom they had come to minister, wearing garments of quite a different style. Their hopes and dreams of the previous months were about to be fulfilled.

Before they disembarked they assembled for prayer to thank God for bringing them safely to China and to ask His blessing on their future work. They then walked down the gangplanks and waited on the quayside for their luggage to be unloaded.

As they waited Charlie noticed a Chinese man walking towards them very purposefully. *Who's this*? Charlie wondered to himself. He tapped Stanley Smith on the shoulder and then pointed towards the man. 'Perhaps he's the welcoming committee, Stanley,' he said with a smile.

The man came right up to them, extended his hand in welcome and in gruff north-country English said, 'Welcome to China, gentlemen.' It was Hudson Taylor.

The surprise was greeted with laughter all around as they each shook hands with him. Taylor was decked out in traditional Chinese costume: a skirt topped by a long-sleeved gown and on his head a close-fitting, peakless cap. As he was shaking hands with the Polhill-Turner brothers, Charlie noticed the queue or pigtail extending down the back of his neck.

Charlie flicked it playfully. 'When do we get one of those, Mr Taylor?' he asked with a grin.

'Soon enough, young man! Soon enough!' Hudson Taylor said, turning around. 'But first I had better take you to what will be your home for at least the next few days. There I can brief you on what is expected. Don't worry about your luggage. I've already arranged for that to be collected.'

As they left the harbour, and Hudson Taylor led them through the crowded streets, they gazed in wonder at the buildings and the people. Though their guide left them little time for sightseeing as they marched to their destination, they could not help but sneak closer looks at the intricacies of the marvellous decorative work on the buildings they passed. They witnessed dozens of rickshaws dashing past with surprising speed, weaving in and out of the other, mainly horse-drawn, traffic.

Charlie thought, *They don't look half as comfortable as a hansom. And what chaos they cause.*

Some of the narrower stone-lined streets had banners crossing their entire width, proclaiming messages unknown to the new missionaries. Everywhere there was haste and activity as people went about their business. Many stared at the newcomers, dressed in their strange western clothes.

Eventually they arrived at their new home; one of two adjoining houses that the mission used for workers in transit. Hudson Taylor explained to them the everyday practicalities of living in China and then outlined his proposed strategy.

'Gentlemen,' he said, 'I know you are eager to take the Gospel to the dear Chinese people, but there are a couple of other matters that need to be attended to. First, how is your Mandarin going?'

The Seven answered almost simultaneously. Hudson Taylor laughed. 'Was that English or Chinese? I didn't understand a word. Mr Smith, perhaps you'd better answer for everyone.'

'We've all found it difficult, Mr Taylor. Very difficult! It's so different from English. But now we're here and can hear it spoken all the time we hope we can become fluent.'

'Yes, I hope that's so. Tomorrow I'll introduce you to some of our Chinese brothers. They'll teach you some phrases for everyday living. Also some short Gospel presentations, so you can begin work almost immediately. They'll also advise you about Chinese customs. I don't want you to end up in prison or worse, just because you don't do things the right way. Etiquette is very important to the Chinese, you know. Make sure you learn their ways and treat them with respect.'

Smith acted as spokesman again. 'Don't worry. We haven't travelled this far to impede the work, rather to aid it. We will try our utmost to get it right.'

'That's good. Now, the second matter. We have also arranged some meetings for you to conduct amongst the European population.'

The Seven looked at each other. Taylor sensed that news had not pleased them. 'I know the reason for your coming here is to take the good news of Christ to the Chinese, but at the moment your English is much better than your Mandarin. So for the next few days,' he said with a smile, 'you can evangelise the British. They need it too, you know. Anyway, let's leave it there for the moment. I'll let you settle in. Before I go, let's ask God's blessing on us all.'

Hudson Taylor knelt on the floor and the Cambridge men followed suit. They beseeched their God not for an easy time but for successful ministry.

The next morning Hudson Taylor arrived with the promised helpers: four Chinese men. 'Gentlemen, may I introduce Xianseng (Mr) Ho.'

The Chinaman bowed respectfully to the visitors, his hands clasped tightly in front of him. He smiled broadly. 'May I welcome you to China in the name of the Lord Jesus,' he said in Mandarin. The Englishmen sensed the meaning of the words, rather than understood them.

'Xianseng Ho is a schoolteacher, so he should be of great help to you.

Although, I suspect he's never had a class quite like you before. I'll leave him to introduce you to the other members of the team. I'll look back later and see how you're going. Oh, by the way, he'll also be accompanying some of you to Hanchung in the north-west next month.'

Under the tutorship of Ho and his colleagues, the seven Englishmen did their best to think and speak Chinese. For the next three days almost the whole of their time was engaged in those pursuits. The Chinese found their students' struggle with their language, amusing. The Seven, for all their frustrations, joined in their hosts' laughter when their mistakes were pointed out.

On their first Sunday in their new home they worshipped in the newly-built Anglican Cathedral. The majority of the congregation was European. None of the Seven were invited to participate.

The next evening a gathering was held in the Temperance Hall, led by Hudson Taylor. For the most part it followed the pattern of the meetings held prior to their departure from England. Several of the Seven spoke, including Charlie, who once more gave his testimony. The audience had previously been given the news of the arrival of the Cambridge Band and some were well acquainted with the sporting endeavours of Studd and Smith. If the meeting lacked the fervour of those held previously in Britain, they felt that it had gone well enough.

Another meeting had been arranged for the following night. One of the speakers for that was the Rev. Fred Smith, the chaplain of the Cathedral. When his turn came to speak he shocked his listeners.

'Good people, I have a confession to make,' he began. 'Before last night, if the Lord had come I should have been a lost soul.' He hesitated as he tried to continue. His voice seemed to catch as he spoke. 'I did not know the Lord Jesus Christ. Outwardly I was His servant, but inwardly I was not His son. But if the Lord comes tonight, I shall be a saved soul. I wonder how many there are here tonight who, like me, have oft frequented the house of God, who many times have taken the blessed sacrament, yet do not know Him. If you are in that position tonight, I beseech you to believe in the Lord Jesus Christ. I thank God that I can say tonight, "I am the Lord's and He is mine." Can you say that?'

As the Chaplain returned to his seat the hall was in utter silence. Hudson Taylor, who was as surprised as anyone by the clergyman's words, decided to let the impact of Frank Smith's confession sink in before he continued. He then rose from his seat and addressed the congregation.

A few days later Xianseng Ho arranged to have the Seven fitted with Chinese clothes. 'We have had some difficulty,' he explained, 'because some of you are so big. Most of us Chinamen are smaller. But, with our loose-fitting clothing you will find that an exact fit is not necessary. First, let me do your pigtails.'

For the next hour or so Ho and his companions did their best to transform the seven Englishmen into Chinamen. The procedure was hilarious and, in some cases, so were the results. Charlie, Smith, Beauchamp and Arthur Polhill-Turner elected to have their moustaches shaved off. The other three decided to keep theirs. Though all had now grown their hair longer than they were accustomed to in England, it still proved difficult to plait the hair of Hoste and Arthur into authentic pigtails. The results for those two looked more like stalks sticking out horizontally, than pigtails hanging down. Charlie, Smith and Beauchamp were the tallest of the party and, when dressed in their Chinese garb, looked like a trio of ugly sisters from a pantomime.

'It's a bit different from your other uniform, Cec,' Arthur Polhill-Turner said to his brother, with a laugh.

'Yes,' his brother said, 'I don't think I'll be accepted in the Dragoons in this outfit.'

'Nor the Royal Artillery,' Dick Hoste added.

'I'm not sure what they'd make of it if I arrived at my old church in Lambeth looking like this,' William Cassels said.

After they were all suitably attired they assembled outside for a photograph to be taken.

'If your mother ever sees this, Monty,' Charlie whispered, as the photographer was getting ready, 'I guarantee she won't recognise you.'

They knew though that they could not treat their new clothes as a novelty for long. If they were to mix with the Chinese people and challenge them with the Gospel, this is how they would have to dress.

During the next few days their tutors continued to train them in the Mandarin tongue and sent them out on shopping and evangelistic expeditions to test their skills. Stanley Smith proved the most able student. He took to it very quickly, though he inevitably struggled with the subtleties of the language. The rest had great difficulty, particularly with its grammar and tonal nature.

One day Hudson Taylor took them to visit the local temple. 'It is Qinming, which means pure brightness. It is a very special time for those who wish to pray for the spirits of their ancestors,' he explained as they made their way through the busy streets.

'Is that a common practice?' William Cassels asked.

'Very common in the country districts, though less so in major cities, like Shanghai, but still common enough.'

'Blatant superstition!' Monty Beauchamp said.

'True enough,' Taylor responded, 'but to witness such practices will help you understand these people. If you understand them, it will help you reach them.'

They continued on their way and eventually arrived at the temple. They did not enter but just observed from outside. Within the building were dozens of red candles burning, brightening the dull interior. Not that the purpose of those candles was for light. The smoke they gave off represented the spirits for whom the assembled people prayed. Each devotee burned a piece of paper in a brazier, which had been placed there for the purpose, clasped his or her hands together and prayed. They then collected the ashes of the paper and left the temple.

After they had stayed there for about half-an-hour the missionaries departed in silence. As they walked home in reflective mood Charlie suddenly blurted out, 'For there is one God, and one mediator between God and men, the man Christ Jesus.' (1 Timothy 2:5)

'Indeed, Mr Studd,' Hudson Taylor said. 'They are without Christ and without hope. That's why we're here.'

On their way home Taylor explained his plans to them. Charlie and the Polhill brothers (they had by then decided to drop the Turner part of their names) would go inland with John McCarthy, who had made such an impression upon Charlie the previous year. They would travel west along the Yangtze and then north to Hanchung. Beauchamp would go part of the way with them, while the other three would venture north to Shansi with another experienced missionary, David Thompson, as their escort.

CHAPTER 12
ADVENTURES ON THE YANGZTE

Partings had become a common place in their lives during the past few months. On their travels around Britain they had farewelled many good friends. When they left England just two months before, they said goodbye to many more, including those especially close to them. On the *Kaiser-i-Hind* they had also made friends, like Bart Anderson. When they disembarked from that ship it was once more time for goodbyes.

In all this the Cambridge Seven had become a team, in the popular mind in England at least, who were going to 'play the game' of missionary life together, taking the Gospel to the Chinese. Each one of them, though, when he had accepted this call was prepared to go where he was led. In this case it was Hudson Taylor who was doing the leading, in human terms at least, and he had decided that the best plan was to divide the team and send its members to three different destinations.

It was not easy to say goodbye to friends, with whom one had formed a close bond, yet they did not question the wisdom of the separation. Charlie related well enough to the Polhill brothers, who were to be his partners in the attack upon Hanchung, over 1,500 kilometres away to the north-west. But over the years he had formed especially strong friendships with Smith and Beauchamp, and saying goodbye to them in this strange land would not be easy.

Smith was due to go with Cassels and Hoste north to Shansi, while it was Hudson Taylor's plan to take Beauchamp with him on his own travels. However, as his departure was not to be immediate, he decided to let Monty go part of the way with Charlie and his companions, so that he would gain some experience of inland China, and then to return to Shanghai.

On Saturday April 4 they all went back to the Shanghai dockside, where Charlie and the other three were due to catch a steamer for the first part of their journey. CT found himself close to tears as he shook hands with Stanley Smith.

'Goodbye, old chap. May God richly bless you as you serve him,' he said quietly. He felt the strength of the champion rower's hand as it squeezed his.

'You too, dear friend. Whatever God has for each of us during the rest of our lives, be assured that I will always treasure our friendship.'

Charlie shook hands with Cassels and Hoste and then with Hudson Taylor. 'Learn all you can from John McCarthy. He has a great deal of experience and knows these people as well as any European,' the CIM leader urged.

'I will certainly take you advice, Mr Taylor. He is a man I greatly respect.'

'Be patient with language study. Xianseng Ho is an excellent teacher but, ultimately, mastering the language depends largely on you. It's just plain hard work, so keep at it.'

Charlie knew that the great missionary had tapped into one of his great weaknesses: impatience. He said, 'To be honest, Mr Taylor, I am not finding it easy, but I will do my best.'

'Good man! Keep at it. It's one of the keys to being a successful missionary.' Hudson Taylor turned from Studd and gathered his troops around him.

'Well, gentlemen, the time for departure is close. If I may make one final charge to you four men, remember that you only have the great God to take care of you, no one else, but He is able.'

Turning to the rest of the party he said, 'Let's commit our brethren to the Lord.'

Hudson Taylor knelt to pray on the wooden slats of the wharf and his companions followed suit. The various shipping noises seemed to drift into the distance as the great warrior of God brought his charges before his Lord in prayer.

When he concluded, the Cambridge quartet, McCarthy and Ho embarked upon the little river steamer and, as it left the dock, they stood at the stern and waved to their comrades who were waving back on the slowly disappearing dockside.

****

As the steamer proceeded westward in the warm morning sun, the missionaries stood on the deck and viewed the strange panorama before them. The river was crowded with a vast array of vessels. There were still junks aplenty, but the further they moved down river the more they saw smaller boats such as sampans. Some of these had a covered area at the back to house the boatman and his family on their long journeys along the Yangtze to sell produce in the towns along its banks. There were even cumbersome rafts carrying wood from the west, moving slowly in the direction of Shanghai, where their cargo would be unloaded to be used in the building projects there.

Most peculiar were the long, narrow letter-boats, used for carrying the nation's post. The two occupants of a letter-boat had to lay down in the craft for fear of them capsizing it, and took it in turns to paddle the boat along with their hands, and even at times row with their feet. They moved surprisingly quickly. There were hundreds of vessels, with thousands of people; a vivid reminder of their reason for being in this strange land. It was their task to take the Gospel to such as these boat people.

'It's an amazing sight, isn't it?' John McCarthy said. 'If one wishes to put our task in perspective, we should realise that on those little boats are hundreds, even thousands of people. On the shore are even more. Look at them! Fishermen, farmers, people working on the tea plantations, men, women and children. It's quite possible that among all those thousands that we can see, not one knows the Lord Jesus Christ. That is the task before us.'

'It's quite daunting when put that way, Mr McCarthy.' It was Cecil Polhill.

'One vital task is to teach the Scriptures to those Chinese who are Christians and help them to present the Gospel to their own people,' the experienced missionary said. 'That's probably as important, perhaps even more so, than any evangelism we do ourselves.'

'The most frustrating thing is not being able to speak the language properly,' Charlie put in. 'Teaching, telling the unsaved about Christ... Both are impossible while we continue to mangle the native tongue.'

'True, Charlie, though perhaps not completely so. Most Chinese are extremely polite and will usually give you a hearing whatever mess you make of their language, though they may not understand you properly, of course.'

'Unfortunately I don't think any of our little group is particularly gifted with languages, except Stanley Smith, of course,' Monty Beauchamp observed, in an unusually pessimistic moment. 'And he's not with us now.'

'The point is that none of us can remain dependent for long on anyone else with regard to language knowledge. We all have to master it as best we can ourselves.'

'What's the quick way of doing that?' Charlie asked.

'There isn't one. It's just plain hard work. Listen to Xianseng Ho, practise hard, and take every opportunity to use what you learn. That's the only way, but don't expect instant results.'

A polite cough sounded behind them. They turned around to see who it was. It was Xianseng Ho.

'Pengyou men, xianzai kaishi xuexi,' he said.

The four missionaries knew that it was lesson time again.

After nearly a week and a half on the river they arrived at Anking. Monty Beauchamp disembarked to make the return journey to Shanghai. On his return there he was to discover that there was a change of plan for him, and that he was now to be sent to join Smith, Hoste and Cassels in Shansi, rather than travel with Hudson Taylor.

A further week later the steamer carrying Studd and his companions reached Hankow, where the Han River joins the Yangzte. Here the river was once more alive with frantic activity, with a variety of boats going hither and thither between the banks and the islands. As the missionaries once more took the vantage point on the deck they noticed the tight cluster of little houses on each of the islands, and more still on each bank. They saw a beautiful pagoda crowning one of the little hills that surrounded the confluence of the two rivers. Everywhere they looked they saw people. Once more they became aware of the vast population of the land to which they had been called.

They disembarked and spent a couple of days in Hankow. There had been a practical problem bothering Charlie for the whole of his stay in China so far. He had been unable to find a suitable pair of shoes. His feet were large even by European standards but, when compared with the smaller feet of the average Chinese, they were enormous. No shop in Shanghai had a pair anything like big enough for him. So he decided that he would practise his Chinese on some poor unfortunate local shoemaker, and try to get him to make a suitable pair. He went exploring with Arthur Polhill, and they walked slowly through the Hankow streets looking for a cobbler. The signs above the shops meant little to them, because of their lack of experience at reading

Chinese, but a glance through the doors or windows quickly determined the nature of each shop. At last they found a shoemaker.

The two Englishmen went in. They were greeted formally, but a little nervously, by the proprietor. Charlie addressed the man in his best Mandarin. The cobbler looked back blankly. Charlie tried again, this time with abundant use of sign language. The shopkeeper looked at Studd's feet and noted their size. His mouth fell open in astonishment. He now realised precisely what this strange foreigner was wanting and was horrified. How could he make shoes to fit feet that big? He began babbling at his would-be customers at a furious rate, and Charlie and Arthur hardly understood a word but, with the accompaniment of the man's angry gestures, it was apparent that he wanted them to go. The two missionaries looked at each other, turned back to the man who was still talking excitedly, bowed politely and left.

Outside the shop they looked at each other again and laughed.

'Well, Charlie,' Arthur said, 'Hankow must have more than one shoemaker, so let's keep trying.'

'Indeed,' Charlie responded, with another laugh. 'I'm so desperate I'm not going to give up as easily as that.'

As they continued their exploration of the streets it became apparent, as had been the case in Shanghai, that their Chinese apparel fooled few. Most recognised them for what they were, foreigners in Chinese garb, and stared and pointed at them as they walked past.

It was not long before they found another cobbler's shop and went inside. This time Charlie did his best to explain his needs to the proprietor, with plenty of animated action, and once more Studd had the embarrassing experience of having a shoemaker staring at his feet in disbelief. On this occasion, however, as this man looked back at his two visitors he smiled radiantly, and agreed to do the task. So CT Studd was eventually able to put on his first pair of Chinese-made shoes.

They left John McCarthy in Hankow, but were joined for the next stage of the journey by experienced missionaries Dr William and Caroline Wilson. The Wilsons had been to Hanchung on a previous occasion, and were returning to establish a hospital there. The transport on this final stage was more primitive, as they travelled north-westward along the Han River. No more did they have the semi-luxury of the steamer. Instead they had two partly covered rowing boats, complete with sails for when the weather conditions were right. The boats, though, had ample space. There were three rooms in each, two for sleeping and one for day use. The three Cambridge men and Ho slept in one vessel, and the Wilsons in the other.

The men shared the rowing duties in the two boats. Rowing in the hot temperatures and high humidity, as summer came on, was fatiguing, though they were not reluctant to do it. After all each one had committed himself to serve Jesus Christ whatever the cost. Thoughts of their far away companions kept coming back to them.

'It's times like these we need Stanley Smith. Now, he really can row,' Cecil Polhill said, looking at his blistered hands after one of his stints on the oars. 'Or even Monty Beauchamp or William Cassels; they are good rowers, too.'

'I thought you soldiers were tough,' his brother chided.

'We certainly are,' he said, sticking his chest out. 'But I was a soldier not a sailor.' He grinned.

One night towards the end of May, after they had all bedded down, Charlie was awakened by a rustling noise. He half sat up and listened intently. It wasn't long before he heard the sound again and felt something run across his legs. Before he had time to fully assess the situation a shout came from the next room. 'Rats!'

Charlie heard the further sound of little, scurrying feet, quickly got up, grabbed a match box and lit the lamp. As light was shed on the scene, sure enough, rats seemed to be everywhere. Several were scampering around in the little bedroom that Studd shared with Cecil, and when Charlie shone the lamp outside he could see plenty more.

'Say, one of the pests has grabbed my sock,' came the angry cry from next door. 'Give it back.'

The boat rocked as the sock-deprived missionary chased the rodent to the other end of the craft in futile activity.

Cecil, meantime, had grabbed a stick and began swinging it at every four-legged figure within range but without success. 'They're too fast,' he complained, as he missed again.

The rats scampered; the half-awake missionaries chased and swung. But the rodents were winning the battle. Not one was caught or killed.

'What's going on over there?' William Wilson shouted from the next boat.

'Rats!' Charlie called out. 'Our boat is running alive with rats.'

'You don't seem to be despatching them too well,' Wilson said, watching the frantic action in the lamplight. 'Perhaps you need a change of tactic. You're getting precisely nowhere that way.'

Silence reigned for a moment, except for the still scurrying rodents. Then came the sound of Charlie Studd's laugh. 'I never thought rats were part of missionary life,' he said, sounding surprisingly cheerful.

The others laughed too.

Wilson had a quick word with his wife and clambered from his boat into the other one. 'Why don't we sit down and discuss what we should do?' he suggested.

'If it's all the same to you, Doctor, I'd rather stand,' Arthur said. 'The less I have touching the ground near those brutes the happier I'll be.' He shuddered as he spoke.

Once more they laughed.

'Does anyone have any ideas about how we can get rid of them?' the doctor asked.

'Some type of trap, perhaps?' Charlie suggested. 'Or, bait?'

'I rather think that they'll eat anything, so bait's no problem, but I'm not so sure about the traps,' Wilson said. 'Has anyone any ideas how?'

There was silence again, but the rats still scurried around their feet.

The silence was broken by the musical sounds of pure Mandarin. 'Shouldn't we ask the Lord to take the rats away?' It was Ho.

All eyes centred upon the little Chinese teacher. In spite of their limited knowledge of the Chinese language the three new missionaries knew what he had said.

'We're a fine lot of missionaries, aren't we?' Charlie observed. 'Why didn't we think of that?'

'Well, it's worth trying,' Cecil admitted.

'It's more than worth trying, it'll work. We believe God answers prayer, don't we?' Charlie challenged.

Various sounds of affirmation greeted his comments.

'Then let's pray,' Charlie added. 'Well done, Xianseng Ho. I can see that we have much more to learn from you than Mandarin.'

Ho bowed slightly in acknowledgment.

'Shall we kneel?' Arthur asked, tentatively.

They all looked down at their feet and saw the rats still scurrying everywhere.

'I think the Lord can hear just as well and answer just as sweetly if we stand,' Wilson said. 'Let's pray.'

They began to pray, and continued to do so for over an hour. In the morning the rats had vanished. They did not reappear.

The long, slow journey continued along the Han. The weather grew hotter and at times they had to contend with heavy rain but, in mid-July, they arrived in Flanchung, tired but delighted to have reached their destination.

CHAPTER 13
ON FOOT TO PINGYANG

The walled-city of Hanchung was situated in Shensi province in the north-central region of China, about five hundred kilometres south of the great wall. The church had been established there by CIM missionary George King about seven years earlier, and it now had about a hundred Christians. Xianseng Ho had been the first of them. It was to be the task of the three Cambridge men to base their activities in that church, and to seek to further the Gospel in the surrounding districts.

The day after their arrival William and Caroline Wilson led the little band into the local market place to spread the good news about Christ. Though the new missionaries were still struggling with the language, they were all armed with printed gospels and tracts. So, when words failed them, they at least had some means of presenting the Gospel.

In spite of the difficulties, it felt good to be at last fulfilling the task to which they had been called. As they spoke to the Chinese in the streets, they often found themselves stumbling over words. Frequently their best efforts were greeted with blank looks or giggles, but at least they had the gospels and tracts to fall back upon.

John McCarthy had suggested that after the settling in period in their new home, one of the Cambridge men should accompany a national colporteur on a venture from Shensi province, crossing the Yellow River into Shansi. All three were destined to go on such trips, but Charlie went first. He travelled northwest to Pingyang.

He left Hanchung in mid-October with two colporteurs, named Guang and Wu, who worked for the British and Foreign Bible Society. Apart from any other good this venture may achieve, it would be invaluable with regard to his learning Chinese. Not only were his only companions Chinese but also there were hardly any Europeans living on the five hundred kilometre route.

For the first part of their journey they pulled a cart, loaded high with Scriptures for distribution along the way. Once they entered the more mountainous regions they would have to leave the cart behind and instead carry the remaining Gospels and tracts.

As they went along, Charlie practised his Chinese and at the same time tried to learn about his companions. 'How long have you been Christians?' he asked in hesitant, but not inaccurate, Mandarin. His understanding of the language had begun to show a marked improvement in recent weeks.

'It is more than ten years now that I have known the Lord Jesus,' Guang replied.

'And about the same for me,' Wu said. He was the shorter of the two nationals. 'We thank God for sending people like you to tell us about Him.'

Studd had no difficulties with understanding numbers, so he grasped the meaning of what was said.

'How long have you been colporteurs?'

'About six or seven years now,' Wu responded. 'We began travelling with missionaries Cameron and Piggott.'

Charlie had heard of James Cameron, who was still a CIM stalwart, but did not know of Piggott.

Before they had commenced their journey Studd had noticed that Wu limped, but it was not until they had travelled a few kilometres that Charlie actually looked at Wu's feet, which were largely visible through his sandals. The right one had two toes missing. The missionary found himself wondering what had happened. As they continued on in the sunshine, the relationship between the three men also began to warm. When they stopped for a short rest he felt bold enough to ask about the loss.

'I hope you don't mind me asking, Wu, but what happened to your feet?'

Wu briefly looked down at his feet, as if he didn't know what Charlie meant, and said nothing for a moment. Then one word passed his lips, 'Frostbite.'

Charlie did not understand and said so.

'Snow! Cold!' Wu shivered to demonstrate his meaning and waved his hand knife-like, just above his foot.

Charlie understood.

'It was when we were travelling with Xianseng Cameron and Piggott,' Guang broke in. 'Several of us suffered from it. Me, too.' He extended his left hand and Studd noticed for the first time that there were a couple of fingers missing.

The two men had already made a deep impression on Charlie with their determination to take the Gospel to their own people, but this was further evidence of their courage. As they recommenced the journey, Charlie found himself with a whole new respect for these fine Christian men.

CT Studd was a fit and athletic man – his background in international sport demonstrated that – but even that had not properly prepared him for this arduous trek. Running around the boundary and to and fro along the wicket on soft English cricket pitches, was quite different from marching on stony Chinese tracks. His new shoes, which had served him well enough on short walks in Hanchung, proved inadequate for fifty kilometres a day on this tougher terrain. By the end of the first day, when they bedded down for the night on the boards of a dirty village inn, his feet were badly blistered.

But at least he had the consolation of being able to help distribute Scripture portions to the inhabitants of the village and the other travellers in the inn. Guang and Wu also took the opportunity to preach outside the inn to a crowd, which seemed to include almost the whole population of that village. For the most part their evangelistic endeavours were greeted with enthusiasm. They then tucked in to a hearty meal of rice, which Charlie appreciated as much as did his Chinese friends.

The following day they set off again. Charlie had talked with his two companions about the problem with his feet. They had suggested that he dispense with his shoes and try sandals instead. On that second day Charlie completed the fifty kilometres in sandals but, before they settled down for the night in another little inn, it was necessary for Guang to bathe Charlie's feet, which were noticeably worse than twenty-four hours before.

Sore feet or not, there was no thought of delaying the expedition and on the third day they set off again. The countryside through which they were passing was lush and green after the rains of summer and early autumn. The skies were clear and the sun warm. Charlie found the walking more and more painful. He now had a limp far more noticeable than Wu's. After twenty kilometres of torture he decided to remove his sandals, which had been cutting his feet and toes, and to walk barefoot. By the time they reached their destination that night his feet were worse than ever.

In spite of the pain in his feet, the efforts of the day had made him hungry and he sat down and ate rice enthusiastically with his Chinese colleagues. The other travellers in the inn looked at the trio with suspicion; the presence of Charlie obviously being the cause. Foreigners were not always treated with customary Chinese politeness in major cities and this was even more so in some of the country districts.

After the meal they began their distribution of the Scriptures to the travellers and residents of the town, and the people gathered round eagerly to see what was being given away. It presented Guang and Wu with a good opportunity to tell them about Christ and some listened intently.

The next morning one of the other guests, who was on his way to Hanchung, approached little Wu, desiring to know more about Christ. They spoke to each other for a while and the man responded positively to what Wu said. The trio then prayed with the man and gave him the address of the church meeting place in Hanchung, so that he could link up with the believers there.

Because of the state of Charlie's feet, Guang tried to obtain a horse for the next stage of the journey but was unable to do so. Once more the brave Englishman had to walk over fifty kilometres on his bleeding feet, each step feeling as though a knife was being thrust into them. The following day they topped the fifty kilometres mark again. For much of that distance Charlie walked alone, for Guang and Wu had gone on ahead. Late that day he limped wearily into Sian the capital of Shensi.

The Gospel had not been as successfully planted in Sian as in Hanchung. One Chinese family had caused no end of trouble for the tiny church there and had made it very difficult for anyone converting from the old ways.

There was still a long way to go in their journey to Pingyang but here at least was the chance to rest for a day. They stayed in the home of Charles Hogg, a CIM missionary, who had been based in Sian for about a year. Once more Guang bathed Charlie's feet, one of which was now very puffy and discharging unpleasantly.

Hogg, meanwhile, prepared him some food. When the host brought in the bowl of rice, Guang had already bandaged Charlie's feet and he sat quietly reading the Bible. As Hogg entered the room and put the food before his guest, Charlie smiled appreciatively. As he ate the two men talked. They exchanged a little information about each other, though Hogg already knew a bit about Studd because of his cricketing exploits.

The next day Hogg entered Studd's room to see how he was and found him reading the Bible again. 'How are your feet?' Hogg asked.

Studd put down the Bible beside him on the bed. 'To be honest they are as painful as ever. I have been praying about what to do concerning them.'

'And what do you think should be done?'

'I want you to anoint me with oil.'

Hogg found that request rather perplexing. 'Anoint you with oil? Your feet, you mean?'

'Well, no! My head, I suppose. I have just been reading in James chapter five.' He picked up his Bible again. 'Here's what it says: "Is any sick among you? Let him call for the elders of the church, and let them pray over him, anointing him with oil in the name of the Lord. And the prayer of faith shall", notice it says shall, not may, "shall save the sick and the Lord shall raise him up." Would you do that please?'

'Well, I've never done anything like that in my life before, Studd. I am not a doctor you know.'

'1 know that, but our God is the great healer. He says that He "shall save the sick" and "raise him up", and I believe Him. The way my feet are I don't think there's any chance of me reaching Pingyang without a very long rest. I need His healing if I am to continue.'

Charles Hogg scratched his head as he pondered the problem. 'The thought of it makes me nervous to be honest with you.'

'Please do it, and let's believe that God will heal me.'

Hogg remained silent for a little while and then said, 'Alright, I'll do it.'

He got up and left the room. A few minutes later he returned with Wu and Guang and a little jar of oil. 'I thought three praying might be better than one, so I've enlisted our Chinese brothers in this venture of faith.'

'Good show! Well, I'm ready when you are.'

The three men knelt around Charlie and took it in turns to pray. When they had done that Hogg poured a little of the oil on Studd's head, and they prayed again.

When they had concluded Charlie opened his eyes and said, 'Thank you my friends. Thank you so very much. I think it would be good if I have another sleep now.'

'Yes,' Hogg responded, 'we will let you rest.'

For the remainder of the day Studd rested, hardly moving from his bed. On and off during the day he could hear rain pattering on the roof of the house. It was a good day to be inside. The next day Guang removed the bandages and found the feet had improved but only very slightly.

'I think you had better remain here with Xianseng Hogg. Wu and I will continue on.'

Studd sat up on the bed as if a charge of electricity had been sent through him.

'Never!' he said. 'We have prayed that my feet will be healed. I, at least, believe they'll be healed. So, however they look I'm still going to trust God for the answer. You and Wu get ready for departure and I will join you.'

Although Guang had only known this Englishman for a very short time, he realised that there was no arguing with him when his mind was made up. He left the room, told Wu and Charles Hogg, and prepared to depart.

In just over half an hour the three men were on the road north out of Sian. The two colporteurs had decided to set themselves a shorter daily target, but that still meant that they had to exceed over thirty kilometres each day. Charlie's feet now felt much more comfortable as he tramped along. He had no problems keeping up with his two fleet-footed companions, and as the day came to a close they reached a small town where they spent the night.

The next morning after prayer Guang made a quick inspection of Studd's feet. To Guang's surprise, but not Studd's, the feet were showing a marked improvement. Studd let out a loud 'Praise God!' in English. Guang laughed and echoed it in Chinese.

They set off again, proceeding north-east in the direction of the Yellow River. In the distance on their left they could see the bare, brown mountains at Tongchuan. After another few days they were on the banks of the mighty Yellow River, waiting to cross into the province of Shansi. They had to wait several hours for space on the ferry, for each trip the little vessel made was crowded with carts and mules as well as people. As they waited Charlie found himself in no doubt as to why that river had been so called, for its waters had a dull, but distinct, yellow appearance, caused by an abundance of silt. Eventually, their turn came and they safely crossed the swiftly flowing river.

The response to their evangelistic endeavours, as they passed on their way, was generally very positive. Much of China had been afflicted by a terrible famine in the 1870s and Shansi had been very badly affected. In the northern part of that province it is estimated that a third of the population had died during the famine. Even in the south, the death toll had been quite high. During that terrible time the Christian Church, most notably a number of CIM missionaries, had been prominent in organising relief and this had resulted in the Chinese in Shansi being more sympathetic to Christians, than in the territory west of the Yellow River.

A week after they had crossed the river, on a cool November afternoon, they arrived at Pingyang. The trio made their way to CIM headquarters there. As they entered the little building Charlie was delighted to see the beaming face of Stanley Smith.

'Good to see you, Charlie,' the oarsman said, extending his hand. 'How have you been going?'

'It's great to see you too, Stanley.' Charlie warmly shook the offered hand. 'Not too bad, you know. Up and down, really, I suppose you could say. But, praise to our God for His goodness, that's what I say.'

'Amen to that, Charlie.'

'What a trip we've just had,' Studd continued. 'You should have seen the desire for tracts in the last stage of the journey. The people seemed so hungry for the Word. Hallelujah!'

Smith laughed at his friend's enthusiasm. 'Generally speaking, Charlie, you'll find that's so here in Pingyang, too. They're more open to the Gospel here than in many other parts of the country it seems.'

'What about the others? Are they here, too?'

'No, though they were. Monty and William are in Sichou, about three or four days from here and Dick is in Quwo, a little further away. But Charlie, you must be tired. Let me show you to your room.'

When Charlie got around to examining his feet he saw that they were scarred, and certainly still felt a little sore, but they were much improved on their condition when in Sian. God had been true to His word.

CHAPTER 14
Pastor Hsi

During Studd's, so far, brief stay in China he had taken frequent opportunity to correspond with his family and friends back in Britain. Just after arriving in Pingyang, Charlie wrote a letter to some students in Edinburgh. 'Impossibilities have no real place in the real Christian's vocabulary,' he told them.

> I'm more sure than ever, since coming to China, that the reason why so many Christians get dead and cold is that they refuse to obey Paul's command to rejoice in the Lord always. I'm sure the devil is always trying to keep one from rejoicing in Jesus and especially here in China. I realise now that the joy of the Lord is our strength.
>
> This place is the devil's stronghold, but praise God it won't be for long. If China is to be turned upside down, the missionaries must be turned inside out first. Pray that the Lord will rouse us all to go forth in his might, conquering and to conquer.

In Pingyang CT Studd found someone who, in many ways, was a kindred spirit. Prominent in the Pingyang Church, though with a ministry well beyond it, was Pastor Hsi, who was nicknamed 'Shengmo'. He preached at the first Sunday service after Studd arrived. The Englishman was deeply impressed by the national's earnest manner and, as far as he understood it, his message.

After the meeting Stanley Smith introduced them and over a meal Charlie learned more about the energetic Hsi. At Studd's insistence Hsi told his remarkable story. He was the fourth son in a scholarly Confucian family and he followed in that family's tradition. Yet he possessed not just a fine academic mind, but one which was also very restless. He sought truth in the other philosophical and religious systems of his land. He qualified as a lawyer, acquired considerable medical knowledge (his father was a doctor). He began to investigate Buddhism and also the teachings of Lao-tzu, but in both of them he found himself dissatisfied. As he got to this part of his story Hsi hesitated.

'May I ask what happened next?' the eager Studd urged. He was keen to hear the story of this man of God's conversion, but hovered between his natural impatience and a genuine attempt not to offend.

Hsi fixed his penetrating eyes on the new missionary and smiled slightly before he began again.

'In my early thirties I became quite ill.'

His speech was slower than before and it was apparent that he found this part of his life difficult to relate.

'Some friends of mine advised me to smoke opium in the hope that it might improve my health. I had grave doubts about the advisability of such action but, as my health continued to decline, I was prepared to try anything. I began to smoke it.'

The room was totally silent as Hsi reached this tragic part of his tale. Studd listened intently, determined not to miss a syllable, but afraid to interrupt to ask the meaning of any word that he did not understand. He shot a glance at Mrs Hsi and noticed tears trickling down her cheeks as she recalled what were also very painful memories for her.

Hsi continued. 'Instead of improving my health, it wrecked it. Although immediately after smoking opium I felt better, as the effects of the drug wore off I felt worse than ever. Sometimes I was unable to leave my bed for weeks on end. Then, one day it happened.'

Again he hesitated. His sharp features were animated with emotion and he seemed to be struggling to bring his feelings under control. He looked at his wife, who smiled weakly through her tears. He began to speak once more but a tremor was apparent in his voice.

'My wife thought I was about to die and, as is the custom in our country, she dressed me in my best clothes to prepare me for death. As I grew weaker, I was aware of my surroundings gradually beginning to disappear and my spirit seemed to leave my body. It was as if I had actually died. Then, suddenly I heard a great voice. "Go back!" it said. "Go back!" So I went back. I am not sure that I really wanted to but my spirit seemed to reunite with my body.

'I recovered; if you can call the life I lived for the next few years a recovery. Then about seven years ago, at the time when the famine was at its worst, I heard stories of some foreigners who had come to Pingyang telling of a new religion. At first I was most indignant. You understand that foreigners had not always treated us well and I thought that these men were just more Europeans intent on exploiting my people.

'But these foreigners then did something very surprising. They organised an essay competition on various religious issues and invited the scholars of Shansi to take part. How could I resist? I prided myself on my scholarship, so I sent in no less than four entries under four different names. I won three prizes.' Hsi permitted himself a little laugh as he related his success.

'More importantly, it gave me contact with missionary, David Hill. I had met Europeans before, of course, but this was the first time I had met a missionary. I had been told by many to beware of him – that he was just another foreign devil – so I met him with a mixture of suspicion and prejudice. But this man was different from anyone I had ever met before. One look. One word. It was enough. As daylight banished darkness, so did Xianseng Hill's presence dissipate all the idle rumours I had heard. I beheld his kindly eye and remembered the words of Mencius, a Chinese philosopher: "If a man's heart is not right, his eye will certainly tell it." His face told me I was in the presence of a true, good man.

'He gave me a copy of the New Testament and I began to read it. At first I was just curious but, as I read the Gospels, I realised that they were about someone very special indeed. I became enthralled in the marvellous life of Jesus. As I looked at His life and then compared it with mine, I felt a great shame come over me.'

Studd noticed a tear glistening in the Chinaman's eye.

'I read over and over again the story of our Lord's passion. I prayed over it. I wept over it. And then, one day, as I read I seemed to hear a voice. It was Jesus Himself. He said: "My soul is exceeding sorrowful, even unto death." It was then that it all fell into place. I suddenly realised that He loved *me*, and gave Himself for *me*.

'I was overcome with emotion,' he continued, 'and the tears flowed and would not cease. Yet now they were tears of joy. Jesus had come into my life and made me a new creature. Praise His name!'

The gathering waited for Hsi to continue but it became apparent that he considered he had said enough. Charlie yearned to know more and thought about trying to draw out the little pastor further, but decided against it. The silence was broken by Stanley Smith.

'Such miracles of grace bring glory to our Saviour Jesus. Why don't we spend some time praising His name and praying for more such conversions?' The others agreed and were soon singing in praise.

Later, on their way home through the dusty streets, Smith told Charlie the remainder of the story of Pastor Hsi as best he knew it. He told the fascinated Studd how Hsi had never taken opium from the moment of his conversion, though he had undergone terrible withdrawal symptoms and an intense spiritual struggle.

'It seemed to him,' Stanley said, 'that the Devil was fighting to win him back. It was only through much prayer and the power of the Holy Spirit that he was able to win through.'

'Why do they call him Shengmo?' Charlie asked, shivering in the cold wind. 'It must have a meaning.'

'It does indeed. It means Conqueror of Demons and really it refers to the tale I have just related to you. That is how Hsi viewed his spiritual triumph over opium. It was a victory over Satan's hordes. I also heard that before his wife was converted she was demon possessed and Shengmo was instrumental in casting them out.'

'Amazing! And since then?'

'From what I understand he has been most zealous in spreading the Gospel. He has also set up a number of hostels aimed at helping opium smokers overcome their addiction. There are several such places in the towns and villages surrounding Pingyang.'

By the time Stanley had finished the story, the two of them had arrived back at their quarters. Charlie Studd was elated to have met a man such as Hsi Shengmo and to have heard about his remarkable life. It was a further confirmation of his call to China. Perhaps some of those who would come to the Lord through the ministry of CT Studd in this strange land would have stories to tell like Pastor Hsi.

****

Studd was based in Pingyang for the whole of that winter, evangelising the population with Stanley Smith and their Chinese colleagues. At times, when weather permitted, he travelled in the surrounding districts preaching the Gospel and distributing tracts with Hsi.

The coldness of winter changed to the more pleasant warmth of spring, and then to the heat of summer. In July Charlie went to Taiyuen for a missionary conference organised by Hudson Taylor. Taiyuen was, like most Shansi towns, a strongly Buddhist city, and also a prosperous trading centre, just about to burst forth as a prominent mining town. Plans were in hand to build a railway connecting Taiyuen with other major centres, but for Charlie the only transport was his own two legs, so he walked the 240 kilometres north. As he travelled he admired the beauty of the many fields of poppies, the flowers swaying attractively in the summer breezes. It all looked pretty enough, but within was hidden the deadly promise of its opium cargo.

Apart from the essential practicalities of the conference, it was a great opportunity to meet old and new friends. Though the Polhill brothers had been unable to make it, the remaining members of the Cambridge Seven were all present, as were many other CIM missionaries, as well as men and women from other missionary societies.

As the first day of the conference drew to a close William Cassels was engaged in conversation with John Adamson of the British and Foreign Bible Society, when suddenly Adamson began to stagger.

'Are you alright, old chap?' Cassels asked with concern, reaching out to steady him.

Adamson put his hand to his head and peered back at Cassels with a glazed look. 'I don't feel at all well. Very hot! I'm just not used to this heat.'

'Let me take you to your quarters and I'll get a doctor to look at you.' Cassels took Adamson by the arm and walked him back to the house where he was staying, then went to get Hudson Taylor.

Taylor came to examine the patient and emerged from Adamson's room with a worried look on his face. 'I think it's typhus fever,' he told Cassels and Studd, the latter having just arrived on the scene.

There was silence for a moment as the news sank in.

'Then we'll nurse him back to health,' Charlie volunteered.

'We will indeed,' Cassels added.

'You know, of course, that it's highly infectious and often fatal,' Taylor warned.

'Yes, we know that, but someone has to do it, and we're happy to volunteer and trust God for protection,' Studd said. His friend nodded in agreement.

Through the night and into the next day the two Cambridge men nursed their patient, applying cold packs to try to bring down the fever, and in between times praying for a miracle. But in spite of this his fever remained high, and in addition a new symptom developed. A bad rash appeared on Adamson's face and arms. Hudson Taylor was summoned again and this time the diagnosis was smallpox. Once more he warned the willing nurses of the danger, but they were still keen to continue.

The nursing for the next day or two fell mainly to Charlie, he having persuaded William Cassels to attend the conference meetings. But Monty Beauchamp became another volunteer and, between them, they gradually nursed the Bible Society man through the dread disease, with its terrible skin eruptions, and back on to his feet. The thought that he could have caught the disease certainly entered Charlie's mind, but his faith in God's protection was such that it did not long remain there. In the event, none of the others became sick. Their faith had been once again justified.

CHAPTER 15
'FOREIGN DEVILS'

When the conference had concluded, Studd began the return journey to Pingyang in the company of Monty Beauchamp and Hudson Taylor. The wet season had set in with a vengeance and conditions were appalling. In addition to the driving rain, which soaked everything, the roads and tracks were often reduced to mud paths which made walking a laborious effort. Taylor, who was just recovering from a bad bout of dysentery, had the only horse in the group, but even that animal could do little more than trudge slowly through the mud. Their journey south ran roughly parallel with the Fen River, which they could often hear rushing in torrents when the noise of the falling rain quietened sufficiently.

They were about half way to their eventual destination, with the rain still pouring down, when a new, disturbing, sound greeted their ears just up ahead. A mighty rumble rose above the noise of the pattering rain and, as the three peered ahead, they saw an avalanche of rocks come cascading down onto the road a hundred metres ahead of them. They looked at each other and then, together, looked up at the mountain towering above them on their left. They knew well enough that another such slide could see the end of them, but they had no choice other than to continue on to where the rocks now covered the road. When they arrived there they surveyed the scene.

'Is there any way round it to the right, Charlie?' Beauchamp called to his friend, who had begun to explore the possibilities in that direction.

'It doesn't look like it, Monty. It's no more than swamp this side of the road. I don't think we can make it through that way,' Studd said, wiping the rain from his face with his hand.

'Well, the mountain rules out going to the left,' Monty said, stating the obvious.

'Then the only way is over the rocks,' Hudson Taylor concluded, dismounting from his horse. 'So let's do it.'

The three men clambered over the debris strewn before them, with Taylor leading his unwilling horse. It was a hard climb over rocks made slippery by the rain but they negotiated the hazard successfully. Upon reaching the other side, they sheltered for a brief while under an overhang to catch their breath. Realising that to stay there too long could be dangerous, they soon continued on their way.

The weather had improved by the end of July when they reached Hongtong, which was a day's journey from Pingyang. It was in Hongtong that they were to hold a series of meetings for the Chinese Christians. Word of the pending meetings had been spread far and wide and Christians from much of south east Shansi had assembled for them. By the time the first meeting was held on August 1 there were about a hundred men present and almost as many women. When Hudson Taylor, standing on a specially constructed platform, addressed the gathering he could see numerous onlookers around the fringes of the courtyard. They were not Christians but had just come out of curiosity.

The sight of all those eager faces beaming up at him sent a thrill down Hudson Taylor's spine. This was the fulfilment of a dream, in part at least. Two hundred Chinese Christians in one place at one time. It was only twenty five years ago that there would have probably been only a few more national Christians in the whole of China. He spoke on our Lord's words: My peace. My joy. My glory. The crowd sat enthralled.

Charlie looked about him and wondered, too, as he listened to Hudson Taylor. 'If two hundred now, how many will there be in the year 1900? How many by 1910?' These were indeed exciting times. CT Studd was glad that he was part of it all.

That evening, at a second meeting, with lanterns flickering around the perimeter of the courtyard, the speaker told his audience, '"The Kingdom of God is not in words, but in power." (1 Corinthians 4:20) Therefore I would like to invite any who have experienced that kingdom power in their lives to come up here to the platform to tell us about it.'

The first on his feet was Hsi Shengmo, who told of his marvellous experiences. But he was quickly followed by others, each telling of what Christ had done for them.

On the second day several men and women were ordained to act as pastors in their respective churches and Hsi Shengmo was appointed as the pastors' pastor. Later, 56 Chinese were baptised, some again testifying to what Christ had done in their lives.

The next day Studd and his companions continued on their way to Pingyang. The Chinese Christians returned to their homes and jobs.

****

In August, Studd went on an extensive tour with Hudson Taylor, encouraging the churches and preaching to those who had not heard the Gospel. They returned to Shensi and eventually arrived in Hanchung, where Studd and the Polhill brothers had first based their activities when sent west.

When they arrived, they found the Christian Church there in turmoil. News had just come from the Szechwan province, which was south of Shensi, that there were anti-European riots in Chungking. All the missionaries based there, and many national Christians, had had to leave to escape the people's wrath. Although the Christians in Hanchung did not know it at the time, the riots had initially been directed against Roman Catholic missionaries, but had later spread to include all foreigners. The congregation of the little church in Hanchung was naturally concerned, both for the welfare of their brothers and sisters in Chungking and themselves. That which was happening in one province could so easily spread to another.

Hudson Taylor decided to call the church together for prayer. That evening, nearly a hundred Chinese Christians and missionaries met together to bring the situation to the Lord. Late in the evening Hudson Taylor addressed the congregation.

'Brothers and sisters in Christ, you know well enough the dangers faced by our brethren in Chungking, but I have a particular fear that the church there might well cease to exist unless we take some action. We know our people have been scattered but to what degree we don't know. Do any still remain in Chungking? Or have all fled to surrounding areas? I want two missionaries to go to Chungking, assess the situation and, if possible, reorganise the church there. It will be dangerous, so I will only send volunteers. Is anyone prepared to go?'

A number of hands went up around the room. One of them belonged to Charlie Studd. Taylor looked at the response and assessed it for a few moments. 'We need one experienced missionary. Mr Studd, you can fill that post. And, one new man.' He hesitated as he thought the problem through a little more. 'Mr Phelps, you can go with Mr Studd.'

Charlie was delighted to think that he was now in the 'experienced' category after only eighteen months service. In spite of the danger, he was elated that he had been selected for this demanding task. As the gathering broke up he went to introduce himself to Fred Phelps, who had arrived in Hanchung only a few weeks before and had been in China little more than six months.

The next day they set off. Within three days they were well into Szechwan and that night sought lodging in a small town called Pauling. They tried several inns but the response in each was exactly the same: No foreign devils! Though there were no actual threats made, there was an undercurrent of hostility that made it apparent that their presence was not appreciated by the residents. However, one farmer just outside town let them have a room. The room's solitary, ever-open window overlooked the farmer's pigsty, so the air was foul but they were grateful for the man's kindness. Charlie reflected that in this respect they were better off than their Lord. He had 'nowhere to lay his head'. Their night's sleep was restless and broken. Dawn seemed a long time coming.

They continued on their way the following day but as the days went on, and they came closer to Chungking, the attitude of the populace became much more hostile. Although they were dressed in Chinese clothes, they were easily identifiable as Europeans.

A couple of days' journey from their destination, they stopped in one small town and were quickly approached by an aggressive crowd. The mob began waving sticks at the two Europeans and shouting, 'Death to the foreign devils! Death to the foreign devils!'

Charlie looked at the menacing rabble and had no doubt they meant what they said. 'I think we'd better make a strategic withdrawal, Fred', he said to his companion. 'Just take it nice and slowly.' With that they began to gradually walk away from the crowd, keeping half an eye on their antagonists' reaction.

The Chinese kept up their threats and steadily stalked their quarry. Charlie found himself bathed in sweat, even though it was not that warm.

'They don't seem to be losing interest, do they?'

'No, they don't. Shall we make a run for it?' Phelps asked.

Before Studd could answer, the decision was made for them. With a scream, the mob charged at the two Englishmen.

'Let's get out of here!' CT started off as fast as he could. Phelps followed a step or two behind.

As Charlie ran hard, desperately fighting for breath, he found himself glad of his sporting background. His athleticism and fitness helped him maintain a good pace. Fortunately Phelps, too, was fit and able to keep up with him. The crowd continued the chase, throwing stones as they went. Some of the missiles caught the two missionaries glancing blows, but they were not serious enough to impede their progress. It soon became apparent that the two foreigners were fleet of foot, and one by one the chasers lost interest. CT Studd and his companion escaped to fight another day.

From then on they continued their journey only at night, hiding up during the day in case of further trouble. Travelling through the unknown terrain at night, though, was not without its dangers, but they managed to sneak into Chungking and begin their search for the British Consul, whom they assumed was still in the town. As they conducted their clandestine search they noticed that many buildings, particularly European ones, had been damaged, in some cases even destroyed, by fire.

Hudson Taylor had given them directions to various sites where they might find help and eventually they found the Consulate. When they entered, dirty and dishevelled, the Consul's mouth fell open in disbelief.

'Where did you two come from?' he eventually spluttered in amazement.

'From Hanchung,' Studd replied. 'We're missionaries with the China Inland Mission. My name's Studd and my colleague here is Phelps.'

'You must be mad coming here. Weren't you aware of the danger?'

Charlie laughed. 'Yes, the journey was a bit hot but God protected us. You see we had to know what had happened to the church here, and to help if we could, so the trip had to be made by someone.'

'I see. Anyway, my name's Bourne,' the Consul said, rising and extending his hand. 'It's good to see some friendly faces. I can tell you that there haven't been too many of them in this part of the world during the last couple of months.' He ran his fingers nervously through his shock of white hair. 'Please take a seat. You both look exhausted. I'll get you some refreshment.'

The refreshment came and, as they ate and drank, the Consul made it clear that the two men could not stay. He told them that he was the only European allowed to remain in Chungking but he could guarantee them a safe passage to another part of the country. He insisted that they leave the next day. However, Charlie had not travelled hundreds of kilometres to be foiled in his objective. He was determined to stay.

The Consul invited them to dinner and later over the meal he agreed that one of them could remain. The next day Phelps departed with some reluctant Chinese officials. Studd stayed behind.

During the next three weeks he remained based at the Consulate, only daring to venture forth at night. He visited all the dozen or so addresses he had been given but all but two of them were deserted. Those Christians who remained were terrified of being discovered as believers in a foreign religion, and even more disturbed by Studd's presence. In the hurried conversations he had with them, he learned that all the missionaries had had to leave for fear of their lives, and many Chinese Christians had done likewise when the mobs turned on them. Several Chinese believers had been beaten or publicly flogged, because of their association with foreigners.

While hiding in the Consulate Charlie had plenty of time to read the Scriptures. One particular passage that attracted his attention was Luke chapter 18, about the rich young ruler. He had a suspicion why he found it so striking. The words of Jesus, which closed the encounter, stuck firmly in his mind. 'Yet lackest thou one thing: sell all that thou hast, and distribute unto the poor, and thou shalt have treasure in heaven; and come, follow me.' (Luke 18:22)

He, CT Studd, was or, at least, would soon become a very rich man, for the considerable inheritance which his father had left to him was due to be his upon reaching the age of twenty five. As he had now reached that age, he knew that if he had still been in England the fortune would already be his. He had no idea about how or when he would receive it while in China. He had told Hudson Taylor before leaving England that he intended to give it away. This passage of Scripture, so strongly applied by the Holy Spirit, seemed to confirm the correctness of that intention. Yet it was all so academic. In theory he was a rich man, but in practice he hardly had a penny.

A few days after he had read that Scripture, the post arrived. This was a remarkable occurrence in itself, when one considered the prevailing anti-European climate in that city and its surroundings. Among the letters for the Consul were two for Studd: one from a banker and one from a solicitor. They advised him that he had inherited £29,000 (millions of pounds in today's values). During the next day or two he laid those letters before the Lord and prayed for guidance.

When he was firmly convinced in his mind what he was to do, he approached the Consul. 'Mr Bourne,' he called, as he met him on the stairs in the Consulate. 'I need your help.'

'Certainly, my dear Studd. Do you want to leave Chungking?'

'Well, no! At least, not yet. It's something else altogether. That post I received the other day advised me that I have just inherited a considerable amount of money. And, you see, I want to give it away. So, I need your –'

'Give it away?' Bourne interrupted. His voice and face expressed his astonishment. 'Surely not all of it?'

'Well, yes, all of it. You see, when I dedicated myself to the Lord's service here in China I decided that, when it came, I would give this money away at His bidding. And now that I am about to do so, I need the signature of a government official to authorise it. I'd be grateful if you would oblige.'

The Consul's face gazed back at the missionary in astonishment. 'But, you can't do that, Studd. It's madness.'

Studd fixed his eye determinedly upon Bourne. 'It's my money,' he said with force. 'Indeed, I believe it is now God's money, so I respectfully request that you comply with my wishes.'

Bourne looked back at Studd and stroked his moustache gently as he thought the problem through. 'You are right, of course. It's your money but I would like you to think it over a bit longer before you make a decision that you might later regret.'

'My mind's made up.'

'It may seem so, but I'll not sign until you have had more time to think about it. If you still feel the same way in two weeks, I'll sign.'

'If that's your decision, then I will accept it. Thank you, Mr Bourne.' Studd turned on his heels and returned to his room.

Two weeks later Studd approached the Consul again with his request and the Consul kept his promise. Charles Thomas Studd then, calmly, gave away his fortune. The beneficiaries of his generosity were carefully chosen. He gave £5,000 to DL Moody, which was used to help establish the Moody Bible Institute; £5,000 to George Muller, the founder of numerous orphanages in England; the same amount each to Mr Holland, who worked among London's poor, and to Commissioner Frederick Booth-Tucker, the leader of The Salvation Army in India. The gift to the Indian Salvation Army was most appropriate, bearing in mind that Edward Studd's fortune had been largely made in that land. Smaller amounts were also given to William Booth (The Salvation Army's General) and Dr Barnardo for his work with homeless children, and to others.

While he remained in Chungking, Studd did his best to encourage those Christians that remained, but he gradually came to realise that there was little he could do in the short term. Frustrated by his inability to do anything concrete to re-establish the church there, he took Bourne's repeated offer of a safe passage and returned to Hanchung.

CHAPTER 16
Priscilla

While Charlie Studd was gladly serving his Lord in China, unknown to him, something was happening in Ireland that was to make a significant change to his way of life. Priscilla Livingstone Stewart had become a Christian and believed that she was being called into missionary service.

Priscilla was born in Lisburn on 28 August 1864. Her parents were staunch Christians, and it was not unusual for them to show hospitality to evangelists and other Christian workers visiting their town. As the red-headed Priscilla grew into her teens she became fervently opposed to all things Christian. The regular experience of having these 'Holy Joes' in her home greatly angered her. Her temperament proved as fiery as her hair, and any attempt that these visitors made to speak to her of the things of God was firmly rebuffed.

On one such occasion an English evangelist was visiting them and he noticed Priscilla's cold attitude towards him. She returned scowls for his smiles and grunts for his kind words. He questioned her parents about the situation and they advised him about how difficult their daughter was, and how antagonistic to Christianity. So he, brave man, decided to speak to her about Christ.

For most of the weekend of his visit she had successfully avoided him, staying in her room as much as possible, but he eventually caught up with her.

'Miss Stewart,' he called, 'may I have a word with you?'

Priscilla turned in answer to the call, glared at the man, but said nothing.

'Miss Stewart, I really believe that you need to get your life right before God. You need Christ. Will you let me help you find him?'

Priscilla bristled. Her face flamed with passion and anger at this unwanted intrusion. 'No thank you very much,' she spat out. 'I don't want your religion. Keep it to yourself.'

'But –' The evangelist tried to break in.

'I suppose you want me to end up with a face as long as a fiddle like everyone else round here,' Priscilla continued with venom, giving the man no opportunity to speak. 'Understand this. I don't want your God. I don't want your Jesus. I don't want your religion. I will never love your Jesus, nor call him Lord and Master. I am in control of my own life and I intend to keep it that way, so there.' With that she turned haughtily and stormed off.

Some months later she went to stay for a while with a friend who belonged to The Salvation Army. There was something about this young lady that Priscilla found extraordinarily attractive. The rebellious Priscilla felt much more at ease with this friend than with her own family and many of its Christian acquaintances. But she resisted her friend when approached about attending the Army meeting hall.

One Sunday afternoon her friend returned home from a meeting, feeling rather unwell. Later, when her father asked about accompanying him to the evening service at which he was speaking she declined, being still unwell.

'Why not take Priscilla with you instead,' she suggested.

If the comment had come from anyone else, Priscilla would have been furious but from her friend she took it calmly.

'A wonderful idea!' the father said. 'Do come, Miss Stewart.'

Priscilla looked at her friend, then back to the woman's father. 'Alright! I'll come,' she agreed quietly.

This was to be the first time that she had attended a Salvation Army meeting and the thought of it made her very apprehensive. She knew well enough that Salvationists were evangelistic up to the hilt. She feared that a zealous soldier would corner her and try to convert her. She went mentally prepared for battle in case anyone dared to challenge her.

As she entered the building she noticed that most of those arriving at the citadel were decked out in blue uniforms. These had gradually become standard wear as the Christian Mission, founded by the Rev. William Booth in London, had transmuted into The Salvation Army. She also observed a couple of soldiers leading a boisterous group of drunks into the hall.

Even before the service commenced the hall was noisy. Once worship began the din was terrific. A small brass band played tunes, familiar and unknown. 'Hallelujah Lassies' swung their timbrels vigorously in support, and soldiers shouted 'Praise the Lord!' and 'Hallelujah' to just about everything said or done.

As a guest of the speaker Priscilla viewed the proceedings from a seat on the platform. She would dearly have loved to be in a less conspicuous spot but meekly sat where she had been placed. All the time she dreaded that someone would point a finger at her and ask, 'Are you saved?' It was to her immense relief that nobody did. The worst she experienced was that someone thrust a leaflet into her hand just as she was leaving the hall.

She held the leaflet tightly in her hand all the way home but did not become really aware of its existence again until after she had returned to her friend's house, and retreated into the guest room that had been allocated to her. As she collapsed upon her bed, exhausted and miserable, she noticed the piece of paper she was clutching. She smoothed it out and looked at it.

It was a tract written by General William Booth telling of a dream he had had. Graphically illustrated, it told how the General had dreamed of a terrible shipwreck. The victims of the disaster had to swim in the sea, desperately seeking salvation from the fierce elements. A parallel was drawn between the shipwrecked mariners and sinners who were lost on 'the sea of life' and needed salvation, which could only be found in Jesus Christ. She read it through, then screwed it up, threw it to the floor and then drifted off into a restless sleep.

A few days later she returned to her family and her life continued in opposition to Christ. She lived for the moment. Her life became an endless round of dances and parties. Her attractiveness and vivacious personality made her very popular with other young people, male and female alike.

One night she attended a grand ball. She had looked forward to it for weeks and she was not disappointed. Invitations to dance with her were frequent and enthusiastic. She was thrilled to be the centre of so much attention from the young men of the town. In between dances she sat smoking cigarettes, surrounded by a host of admirers. She eventually arrived home from the dance at 4 am. She went to her room and fell on the bed, without changing. She was exhausted but happy; her mind was in a euphoric haze.

She then descended into the mists of sleep.

Priscilla held the tennis racket tightly in her hand. As her partner stayed back, she rushed the net as quickly as her long skirts allowed, and played a winner past a despairing lunge from one of her opponents. Another point; another step closer to victory. She laughed in triumph and prepared to serve again. As she was about to do so, she became aware of a dramatic change going on around her. Whereas before the game had been a private contest between four friends played in isolation, now, suddenly, there was a crowd and a none too friendly one at that. She hesitated in her serve, listening to the rumbling discontent from the courtside. She looked at the faces which were all staring at her, waiting, she felt, for her to make a mistake.

Suddenly, before she had time to regain her composure, a figure emerged from the crowd and hovered in the sky above them all. Priscilla found herself pointing to the man, whom she instantly recognised. She cried out in astonishment, 'Look! That's the Son of God.'

The suspended figure looked back at her and said in a loud voice, 'Depart from me, for I never knew you.' The voice, the words, sent a shiver down Priscilla's spine and she dropped the racquet. Gradually the vision of Christ became cloudy and He, and the crowd, vanished. Priscilla turned to her tennis partner and heard herself say, 'Never mind, we are all going together.'

But next, the court and her tennis companions vanished and in their place was fire, glowing brightly, and burning intensely. The heat was unbearable. She found herself gasping for breath. And, Priscilla Stewart was entirely on her own. 'What a terrible place. How can I escape it?' she wondered desperately.

She awoke and found herself bathed in sweat and shaking in terror at the sights she had seen. She looked around her room in relief, taking in each familiar object in an attempt to ease her fears. 'It was only a dream,' she thought. 'It must have been the lobster I ate at the ball last night.'

Three months later she was visiting an aunt with some other young people, when the after-dinner conversation became centred upon the subject of dreams.

'I think dreams come from God,' one young man suggested. 'Or, perhaps, in some cases the Devil.'

'Nonsense!' Priscilla retorted tartly. 'God has nothing to do with dreams.

When I was at school and studying hard I often dreamed. I would study, then go to bed, and though my body slept my mind remained active in a dream. It was just too much study. Other times I eat something that disagrees with me and I dream again. Usually then it's a nightmare.' As she said this she pulled a face and waved her arms about spookily. The other young people laughed.

The youth persisted. 'But that doesn't necessarily mean they are not from God. Maybe a nightmare can be a warning.'

'I don't believe it,' the young firebrand responded. 'Just recently I had a very bad nightmare. Coincidentally, I happened to dream it the night after the ball, when I had been feasting on lobster and other rich food. You see. It was the food that did it. God doesn't come into it.'

The debate continued until it was time for the others to go home. Priscilla was due to spend the night with her aunt. After the others had departed she helped her to clear away the remains of supper. As they did so her aunt's curiosity got the better of her. 'What was your nightmare about, Priscilla?' she asked.

Her niece was a bit taken aback by the question and mumbled, 'I'm sorry, but I don't want to talk about it.'

'Please tell me,' her aunt persisted. 'I'd like to put your theory to the test.'

Not one to ignore a challenge, Priscilla began to tell her aunt about the dream of the tennis match, the subsequent encounter with Jesus and the vision of Hell. As she told it, Priscilla found herself beset by unusual doubts. She wondered how much it really did support her own argument. Could this dream possibly be a message from God after all?

Her aunt, however, was in no doubt. 'My dear girl, if anyone has ever had a warning from God in a dream then it's you. Can't you see it?'

Priscilla felt uncomfortable. The problem was she *could* see it. For years she had been boldly speaking against anything Christian, but now her mind was in a turmoil and full of uncertainty about her previously held convictions. For once she was speechless. Her head hung down miserably.

'Give your heart to the Lord Jesus,' her aunt urged. 'You have been favoured with as clear a message from God as I have ever heard. It must be a warning. You need to believe in Him.'

The rebel heart began to melt; the rebel's knees to bend. Priscilla knelt on the hard kitchen floor beside her aunt and begged God to help her. As she confessed that she had never before trusted in God but now she wanted to, she became aware of another presence in the room. She was convinced it was Satan. He reminded her forcefully of all the times she had defied God and mocked Christians and, in particular, those times when she had rashly stated that she would never accept Christ as Lord and Master. But, suddenly that evil being departed. Instead, she experienced another presence; one that was compassionate and good.

She heard Him say, 'Child, what is it you want?'

In desperation she answered, 'To get to God but I can't.'

Then, in her mind she saw Jesus hanging on the cross, His wounds bleeding profusely. She asked, 'Why are you there?' As she gazed upon the terrible vision the answer came. 'He was wounded for our transgressions; he was bruised for our iniquities. By his stripes we are healed. Indeed, Priscilla, by my stripes you are healed.' Suddenly, the picture departed from her mind. She became conscious of her surroundings again.

She saw her aunt still kneeling, tears flooding down her cheeks. As Priscilla rose slowly to her feet, her aunt did likewise. As the older woman looked at her niece she knew that something dramatic had taken place. 'What have you seen? Tell me what you have seen,' she asked eagerly.

'I have seen Calvary,' Priscilla replied slowly, 'and forever Jesus will be my Lord and my God.'

She joined The Salvation Army and frequently took part in the bold processions through the streets, braving the fusillades of rotting fruit, stones and bad eggs that the local trouble-makers hurled at them. Within two years of her conversion the twenty-two year old Priscilla Stewart was on her way to China, determined to convert that nation's entire population.

CHAPTER 17
In Partnership

A few months later Studd made a return trip to Shanghai. In the nearly two years that he had been labouring in the northern parts of China he had become quite proficient in speaking Chinese, but the dialect spoken in Shanghai was sufficiently different for him to decide to concentrate his evangelistic labours there working among Europeans at the newly founded Mission to Sailors. During the early part of the evening, he and other helpers would tour the docks to invite men to attend the mission. When there, the sailors were presented with the Gospel. The singing at these meetings was usually accompanied by Charlie on his banjo, strumming favourites from Sankey's *Songs and Solos*.

One day John Stevenson, the deputy director of CIM, entered the mission building accompanied by two young European women. The three walked straight up to Studd and Stevenson did the introductions.

'Mr Studd, may I introduce these ladies to you. This is Miss Jennifer Burroughs,' he said, pointing to a rather prim young woman, with mousey-brown hair done up in a bun. 'And this is Miss Priscilla Stewart.' He indicated the red head. 'They are our most recent missionary arrivals. Ladies, this is Mr Charles Studd.'

The two women extended their right hands and Studd gently shook each in turn. A strand of hair fell down across Jenny Burroughs' forehead as she bowed her head slightly.

'Welcome to China, ladies,' Studd said. 'I look forward to serving the Lord with you.'

'Thank you, Mr Studd,' Priscilla Stewart responded in a lilting, Irish accent. 'I hope we have many opportunities to do so.'

'You're Irish?'

'Yes, Mr Studd,' a note of defiance sounding in her voice. 'From Lisburn.'

'Oh!' was the only response Charles could muster, as her blazing eyes seemed to pierce his being. He was not often embarrassed but this was an exception.

'Well, ladies, I will leave you in Mr Studd's care,' Stevenson said. 'He will show you the ropes.'

For the next two weeks the two women worked alongside Studd. At the end of that period Stevenson approached him again. 'May I ask what your opinion is about our new arrivals?'

Studd paused for a moment to think. 'Miss Burroughs? She's a relative of Dick Hoste, I understand. She's fine. She'd appear to be admirably suited to the work here in China. But, I am a bit concerned about Miss Stewart. She is a dedicated lady but her health does not seem at all good, and that affects the amount of work she does. Have you seen her walk up stairs? She has a real struggle to make it.'

'Yes, I have. It's quite a concern. She seems to have heart trouble, so we're not quite sure what to do with her at the moment. If there's no improvement in her condition, we may have to send her home.'

'That would be a great shame, for she is clearly set on missionary work. She seems determined to convert the whole country,' Studd said with a broad smile.

'A bit like you when you first came,' Stevenson responded. 'Anyway, we'll leave it a little longer and see if she improves.'

A few days later they were all at a meeting led by Studd, when he decided to read part of the letter he had received from Commissioner Frederick Booth-Tucker in India, thanking him for the £5,000 gift. The letter told of the efforts and hardships of the Salvation Soldiers as they took the Gospel to the Indians, and the success that they were having in spite of opposition. There was absolute silence as he read and his hearers were deeply moved, not least Priscilla Stewart.

From that time Priscilla took a more active part in proceedings and frequently spoke at the meetings. Her messages were full of fire and converts were frequent. In addition her health took a turn for the better and, instead of wearily trudging up the stairs, she was able to bound up them two at a time. Thoughts of sending her home vanished from Stevenson's mind, but new thoughts began to enter Studd's. With only one sister and an education at an all-male school and a male-dominated university, Studd had had little experience of the opposite sex.

His life, up until the time he decided to go to China, had been dominated by sport and his thoughts had turned to young ladies far less often than other men his age. But Priscilla Livingstone Stewart could not be ignored. She was good-looking, vivacious and, most importantly, burned with the same evangelistic zeal as him. He found her most attractive. She, too, felt drawn to him. He later claimed that he had not even noticed her good looks and that he was surprised when someone had mentioned the fact to him. Rather, what had attracted him was her zeal for Jesus Christ.

In the middle of the year, though, she was sent to Takutang in central China along with Jenny Burroughs. There they joined another two ladies from CIM. Charlie grieved the loss, though he recognised the necessity of the break. He had never felt this way before. He had been separated from close friends and relatives many times, but no previous separation had caused this depth of feeling.

There was no doubt: Charlie Studd was now in love with 'Scilla Stewart.

In spite of being essentially a man of action, Studd had carried on an extensive correspondence with a variety of people since his arrival in China. Now most of his letters flew in one direction, westward to Takutang.

Soon after Studd's return to Shanghai he had received a most welcome letter. It was from his brother, George, telling him that he intended to visit Shanghai on his way to Japan and Australia. George's health had again been poor. This trip was his way of escaping the rigours of another British winter and, hopefully, of recuperating in the warmer climes. Charlie was always good at reading between the lines and sensed from the letter that all was not well spiritually with his brother, so he encouraged some of the other CIM staff to pray for him.

When George's ship arrived Charlie was on hand to greet him. It was a great reunion for them both. Charlie took his brother back to his room to stay and decided to remain largely silent on spiritual matters.

George had continued his cricketing career for the two seasons after Charles had gone to China but, because of his legal studies and declining health, he had then decided to cease playing at the highest level. But, wherever the English travel, cricket goes with them. Shanghai had its own cricket club, and that club did not miss the opportunity of enlisting George Studd into their team. He played in several games and in one of them nearly reached a hundred. Charlie saw this innings and viewed the occurrence with fond memories but no regrets.

After that game George was besieged by expatriate Englishmen wishing to meet him and to enquire about their homeland. As the crowd eventually diminished one rather pompous man cottoned on to George and would not let him go.

'What happened to that brother of yours? CT, I mean. Not the other one,' the man said, gruffly. 'CT was extraordinarily good, but he just seemed to vanish.'

'Well, actually, he's here in Shanghai.'

'In Shanghai!' the astonished man exclaimed. Then, he leant forward with his face uncomfortably close to George's. 'Why don't we see him at the cricket club then?'

George received a strong whiff of the man's alcohol-laden breath. 'I suppose you could say that he has other fish to fry.'

'Other fish to fry? What do you mean?'

'He's a missionary here.'

'A missionary!' the questioner exploded. 'What on earth for?'

'To tell others about Jesus Christ.'

The man once more pushed has face close to George's. 'What a darn-fool thing to do. A waste of a good cricketer, if you ask me.'

'He's here at the ground today if you want to meet him.'

'Here today?'

'Yes.'

For the first time the man backed away. He stared at George as though the cricketer had something wrong with him, snorted and then mumbled through his moustache, 'I'm not keen on meeting missionaries.' He then rapidly vanished from the scene.

George breathed a sigh of relief and did a little chuckle to himself. But this encounter began to make him think. Charlie had given up everything to follow Christ, but what had he done by comparison? Nothing!

During the next few days George met many of Charlie's colleagues and was greatly impressed by their quiet sense of contentment whatever the circumstances. He asked his brother to explain the secret.

'I don't think it's a secret. At least it shouldn't be,' CT said. 'These men and women have given their all to Jesus Christ. That is the reason for their peace and contentment. Do you remember what the Apostle Paul said? "I have learned, in whatsoever state I am, therewith to be content." (Philippians 4:11) Why was he able to say that? Because, he had given his whole life, not just part of it, to Christ. He was willing to be abased and therefore he experienced the uplifting of the Holy Spirit. He was ready to suffer need, so therefore he knew Christ's strengthening. George, do you remember when you were ill nearly four years ago?'

'Yes, sort of, though most of it is very hazy.'

'It was that experience and your simple faith that made me give my all to Christ. Yet, somehow, you seem to have gone backwards since then.'

George fixed his eyes on the floor, unable to look at his brother. 'You're right, I know'. For a few moments there was silence and then he dared to look up at Charlie. 'What must I do to get back my first love?'

'Capitulate to Jesus and trust him for everything,' CT challenged.

Again there was silence for a moment, broken by another question from George. 'But how can I do that?'

'George, it is a matter of the will. You must hand your will over to the Lord. You must determine that in every area of your life you will seek His will and not your own.'

George looked up thoughtfully. Signs of the anguish he was in were etched on his face. 'I will!' he said suddenly in a moment of triumph. 'I will. Pray with me Charlie. Pray with me now.'

The two brothers went down upon their knees and Charlie prayed for his older brother. When he had done that, George followed it with a heartfelt prayer of commitment to God. A few days later George wrote to their mother.

'I have felt the Spirit striving within me, and I felt such a hungry, unsatisfied craving that I could not rest till I had given myself up. Now I can't tell you what peace and joy the Lord has given me in believing.'

George decided to cancel his intended trip to Japan and Australia and remained in China. Within a few weeks he went inland with Charlie to Shansi.

While on this trip Charlie fell ill with typhoid. This time the nursing fell to George. Whereas Charlie was successfully nursed back to health, other CIM missionaries were not so fortunate in those final months of 1887. Several of them died from typhus or typhoid. A short time after Charlie's recovery, George returned to England.

While he was recovering from his illness, Charlie found more time to write to Priscilla. He expressed his love in page after page of scribbled prose. Letter after letter found its way to her, including, eventually, a proposal of marriage. He confessed later that he knew very little about her apart from her spiritual condition, but that was enough for Charlie Studd.

This proposal presented a problem to Priscilla; one greater than such proposals might normally cause. It was a rule of CIM that missionaries have at least two years of experience on the field before they be allowed to marry. Therefore, if she said 'Yes' to her suitor, she would probably have to leave the mission. Studd, of course, had served his two year probation.

Priscilla Stewart did some soul-searching and then put pen to paper in reply. When Studd received her letter he opened the envelope with trembling hand. As he read the words before him, he was mortified. Priscilla had said, 'No.'

But CT Studd was not a man who readily took 'No' for an answer. His immediate impulse was to continue his letter bombardment and to try to win her over, but he recognised the need to take the matter to the Lord once more to seek His guidance. For eight days he fasted and prayed. At the conclusion of that period he was more certain than ever that it was God's will that she become his wife. Once more he resorted to the pen.

'You have neither the mind of God, nor the will of God in the matter, but I have,' he bluntly told her, 'and I intend to marry you whether you will or not, so you'd better make up your mind and accept the situation.'

It is said that there are some proposals that a girl cannot refuse. Few would have expected this to be one of them. The letter had all the character of an irresistible force destined to encounter the immovable object: the stubborn and headstrong will of Priscilla Livingstone Stewart.

He kept sending her letters. On another occasion he wrote, 'I only get more and more convinced about it, and I cannot doubt it is of the Lord, for you know how I've spent the time since receiving your letter: everything else has been laid aside, occupation, sleep and food, and I've sought His face to know His will. He has led me straight forward and day by day He speaks to me and gives me encouragement and emboldens me to ask definitely for you.'

Eventually the Irish lass began to soften. Her subsequent letters seemed less resistant to the idea of marriage and, on October 5, she wrote to Studd accepting his proposal.

When he received that letter Charlie Studd felt he could have jumped over the moon for joy. Not that his joy was brought about by purely selfish motives. Certainly, he wanted her. He needed her and in a way he had never needed anybody before, for he was passionately in love with her. But, he also believed firmly that it was the Lord's will that he marry Priscilla, and her acceptance meant that the Lord's will was being done.

From then, as one would expect, the tone of his letters changed. They became softer, more affectionate and more romantic. But, all the romance was inseparably tied up with their work for God.

'I just want to beseech you, darling,' he told her, 'that we both make the same request every day to our Father, that we give each other up to Jesus every single day of our lives to be separated or not just as he pleases. I love you for your love of Jesus. I love you for your zeal towards Him. I love you for your faith in Him. I love you for your love of souls. I love you for loving me. I love you for your own self. I love you for ever and for ever. I love you because you will always be a red-hot poker making me run faster.'

On Boxing Day 1887 Studd received an envelope in a writing that he did not recognise. He opened it and settled down to read it. Stanley Smith, who was working with him at that time, saw his friend's colour change as he read its contents. Studd's face was ashen. Smith hurried over to him. 'Is everything alright, old chap?' he asked in concern.

Charlie's face slowly looked up from the pages of the letter. He tried to refocus his eyes on his friend's face in front of him but the mist of tears hindered him. 'She's ill, Stanley', he blurted out in his distress. 'She has pneumonia.'

'Oh, no! My dear friend, I am sorry.'

'Why, Stanley? Why would God let this happen to her? What if she dies?'

Smith knew well that deaths from pneumonia were common enough in those days and he was no better at answering that age old question 'Why?'

than anyone else. 'The Lord must have a purpose in all this, Charlie,' was all he could suggest.

Studd was not listening. 'Why?' he asked again. 'Why?'

The two friends sat together for a long time. Neither uttered another word. For Smith the time dragged agonisingly but Charlie had ceased to have an awareness of the passage of time and even his surroundings.

Suddenly Studd burst out, 'I must go to her. First thing in the morning I'll go to her. But now, Stanley, please pray with me. I know that our God has power over life and death, and I am prepared to accept His will whatever it may be, but whatever the outcome we must commit my darling Scilla to God in prayer.'

'Most surely, Charlie,' Smith agreed, and the two friends knelt down and poured out their hearts to God.

Though at this stage Studd did not know it, his fiancée had caught pneumonia after kneeling in the snow at an open-air meeting praying for the Chinese, while Pastor Hsi preached the Gospel. That brave, if foolhardy, act would do all the more to convince Studd that he was marrying the right woman. To him, selfless dedication in the cause was the only way to go.

The next day Charlie said farewell once more to his old Cambridge companion. 'The Devil has been slamming me something awful of late, Stanley,' he said. 'He's a selfish fellow, too, for I don't believe he could abide me in hell.'

Smith laughed. 'I'm sure you're right, Charlie. You'd make it too hot even for him.'

Though his heart was still heavy, Charlie smiled back at his friend. 'Goodbye, old chap. Hope to see you soon.'

'Bye, Charlie. I'll be praying for you both.'

Charlie departed from the scene with a cart he had hired for the trip. The southward journey took three days. By the time he arrived, to his great relief, Priscilla was well on the way to recovery. Studd remained only a short time in Takutang, just long enough to make sure that his beloved was completely well. He then departed on another journey with Stanley Smith who had followed him to Takutang. On this trip it was Smith's turn to fall sick. He caught typhus, and once more Studd took on the role of nurse. Smith, like George Studd before him, could testify that Charlie nursed his patients with the gentleness and care that only the best of nurses showed. If sometimes CT Studd could be rather severe, he was more often compassionate and kind.

Once he was sure that his companion was well enough, Studd returned to Takutang to see Priscilla. He could hear wedding bells.

Priscilla, now fit once more, was delighted to see him, and talk of an immediate wedding began in earnest. They both agreed that it was desirable, but for their marriage to be legal (and moral in some eyes) it had to be carried out by a British Consul or some other such official. They would have to travel to Tientsin on the coast, north of Shanghai, to have the ceremony performed, but this presented a problem. Neither Victorian propriety nor Chinese sensibilities could approve of an unmarried couple travelling together, unaccompanied, the hundreds of kilometres to the coast.

Pastor Hsi, though, had the solution. 'I can perform the wedding ceremony,' he suggested.

'That wouldn't be accepted legally in our country, Shengmo,' Charlie said. 'In British eyes our marriage would not be official.'

'But, it would be in God's eyes, Xianseng Studd,' the Chinaman persisted.

'You can't argue with that, Charlie,' Priscilla put in enthusiastically. 'That, after all, is the most important thing.'

'It certainly is,' Charlie said with a triumphant laugh.

'If Pastor Hsi conducts a Chinese wedding service here, we could then travel to Tientsin for a British ceremony.'

'That's the answer then. Praise the Lord!' the delighted Priscilla cried out. After a moment's thought she said, 'When do we get married then?'

'Why not tomorrow?' her prospective groom replied.

'Tomorrow?'

'Why not?'

'Then tomorrow it is,' she said. 'That's if Pastor Hsi agrees.'

A big smile creased Hsi's face. 'Tomorrow it will be.'

News of the wedding spread rapidly through the little Christian community in Takutang, and the next day the building which housed the four missionary ladies buzzed with activity. The ceremony was to be conducted out of doors. Some of the Chinese Christians assembled decorations and gaily coloured lanterns for the procession that would lead the bride to the wedding place, while others prepared for the feast that would follow.

Charlie Studd was unusually nervous. 'The Demon' Spofforth had not made him more so, nor the mob he encountered on his way to Chungking. This was different. It was new; to some degree, the unknown. But he was excited, too. He met with Hsi Shengmo a little while before the time appointed for the service. Charlie was dressed in his usual clothes, but hatless and barefoot.

Shengmo was shocked. 'But Xianseng Studd, you can't dress like that for your wedding. This is a special occasion.'

'Why not?' Charlie enquired. 'The clothes are clean aren't they?' He looked down at himself.

'Yes, but you have no hat.' Shengmo looked at Studd's feet. 'And, no shoes. You must have a hat and shoes for your wedding.'

'If you say so, Shengmo, but it's a bit late for me to go and get them now. What do I do?'

'I will lend you mine.' With that Pastor Hsi hurried off and quickly returned with his own hat and a spare pair of shoes.

Charlie slapped on the hat and bent down to squeeze his large feet into Shengmo's small shoes. After that the two men joined in prayer. Then, from not far away, came the sound of great excitement. Shortly after they heard the noise, the first sight of the procession came into view. Priscilla was surrounded by excited Chinese and no less enthusiastic missionaries. She rode in state in an old cart, madly decorated with spring flowers of many hues, while women carrying lanterns and flags escorted her on both sides and behind.

When the procession reached Charlie and Shengmo, Priscilla alighted from her carriage. She was escorted to her fiance's side by Jenny Burroughs and the wedding proceeded. What followed was a Christian wedding, Chinese-style. As far as Charlie and Scilla were concerned this was the real thing.

During the ceremony the tightness of his borrowed shoes gave Charlie no choice but to bend down and remove them. Shengmo gave the missionary a disapproving look but continued on without stopping.

After the ceremony had concluded the feasting began. Many Chinese had grown used to going without since the terrible days of the famine. Although food had been more available since, it had not always been in great abundance. Yet on this day there was no shortage. All ate to their hearts' (and stomachs') content. This was a day to celebrate.

Although Studd had recently given so much money away, he was still not short of funds. Just before the wedding he had been sent the remainder of his inheritance: £3,400. Impressed by the biblical warning, 'But if any provide not for his own, and especially for those of his own house, he hath denied the faith, and is worse than an infidel' (1 Timothy 5:8), he handed this amount over to his wife.

Priscilla decided to send the full amount to General William Booth, for the work of The Salvation Army. Charlie Studd had married the right woman.

The following day Mr and Mrs CT Studd began their journey to Tientsin, where their vows were confirmed.

CHAPTER 18
In Lungan

The Studds were now both just associate members of the CIM but as keen to spread the Gospel as ever. They were determined to go to a town where no westerners lived and either no Church existed or, at the most, a very small one. They eventually settled in Lungan, a town in eastern Shansi, about 150 kilometres from Pingyang.

The missionary James Cameron, who had been associated with Bible Society colporteurs Guang and Wu (Studd's companions on his first trek) had visited this town on one of his tours, but had established no actual work there. In more recent times Stanley Smith had based his activities in the town and a small church now existed, though Smith had now gone to another field. Charles and Priscilla had also previously visited there.

The people of Lungan were mainly animists. Their lives revolved around a fervent belief in spirits, though there was also a substantial Muslim population. As in many such towns and villages, the people were extremely suspicious of foreigners and it was apparent from the beginning that the Studds would not be well received.

The Studds' first problem was to find a place to live. All enquiries were at first fruitless and even one as hardy as CT Studd was a bit reluctant to live on the streets with his new wife. Eventually, they ran across a bad tempered old man, who made his dislike of them very plain.

'I have no house for you,' he said gruffly when Charlie had made his purpose known.

'But we heard that you had several houses for rent. Could we use one please?' Studd asked with great politeness. 'We have some money for the rent.' Studd showed the little money they had.

'I have no house for foreign devils. No house!'

'But we won't harm it and we will pay you.' Charlie showed the money again.

'I tell you, I don't have a house for you. Go away!'

Studd considered his position for a moment but, strongly suspecting that the man was lying and painfully aware of their own need, he kept pleading.

'We're desperate. How can my wife sleep on the streets? She hasn't been well and to do that might kill her.'

Priscilla stood behind her husband, in Chinese style, quietly praying as the bargaining went on. The man thought for a moment and then a wicked smile crossed his face. 'I have a house for you.'

Studd was taken aback by the man's sudden change of heart. Indeed, at first he wondered if he had misheard him. 'What did you say?'

'I have a house,' the man repeated, the same ugly smile on his face.

'Then we'll take it,' Studd quickly responded, before the man had a chance to change his mind. 'Where is it?'

'I'll take you to it. But first the money,' he said, his right hand appearing from under the folds in his gown.

Studd handed over the required sum and he and Priscilla followed their landlord to their new home. The man insisted that they walk ten paces behind him, for he did not want it to be seen that he was having any association with the foreigners. As they walked along passers-by cursed them. The looks of hatred they witnessed made them realise that their task would be neither easy nor pleasant.

They reached their new home and neither was surprised to see that it was in very poor condition. It was, in fact, a dilapidated two room building, without doors. Its floor was very unevenly bricked and, apart from a brick bed at one side and an old boiler in the middle, was unfurnished. To his credit, Studd's thoughts did not return to the luxurious Tedworth House of his childhood. To have a roof over his head – any roof – was good enough for him.

The Studds thanked the Chinaman, who once more smiled back at them with the same unnerving look. 'Spirits!' he said mysteriously.

'I beg your pardon?' Studd said. 'I don't understand.'

'Spirits!' the man repeated, along with the smile. 'This house is possessed by spirits.'

This time both Charlie and his bride understood. They looked at each other and then cautiously at their new home.

'How do you know?' Charlie asked.

'I know,' the man said, with a disturbing little laugh.

'Well, thank you anyway for letting us have this house,' Charlie said. He made a little bow, ignoring his landlord's gloating. 'As for the spirits, we believe in the good Spirit who triumphs over all evil ones so I don't expect we'll come to harm, but thank you for the warning.'

The man departed, laughing away to himself, well satisfied with his afternoon's business.

After he had gone the Studds spent a few minutes surveying their new home. It did not take long, as there was not that much of it. They then set about making things more liveable. Charlie began washing down the dirty, white-washed walls, while Scilla sorted out their meagre possessions. The bed had no mattress, so she used a quilt they had been given for that purpose. They had no other bedclothes, except one blanket, so it was just as well the weather was now getting warmer.

As Charlie busied himself with the walls, his activity was suddenly interrupted by a piercing scream from his wife. He looked in the direction of the bed where she had been working, and saw her standing erect with a horrified look on her face. She pointed at something on the floor.

'It came from under the bed!'

It took Charlie a moment or two in the dim light to recognise the object of her fear but, as it crawled towards him, he realised that it was a scorpion. He was standing barefoot, his shoes beside him. He quickly made a grab for one of them, moved determinedly toward the creature, and flicked it toward the door. The arachnid landed just inside the door and Charlie hurtled after it. He gave it another flick with the shoe, propelling it through the doorway. Once more he followed it, grabbed a piece of wood outside the door and proceeded to pound it to pulp in the dirt.

Charlie went back into the house and rushed over to his distraught wife. He threw his arms around her and held her close. She was trembling violently. Charlie, too, had been shocked by the incident. As he held Priscilla he was not sure how much of the trembling was hers and how much his. His breathing seemed laboured, too, which was surprising after what had not been a great deal of effort.

He stroked her hair and gradually she regained her composure. 'No bare feet from now on, Charlie Studd. Put your shoes on!'

Her husband was not always good at taking orders but this was one he was happy to obey. 'Yes, my love,' he said. 'Are you alright now?'

'Yes I'm fine,' she replied, a little indignantly. 'There are not many things that frighten me but I can't stand those creatures.'

Charlie released his hold on her and put on his shoes. Turning to his wife again he said, 'Let's thank the Lord for that deliverance, Scilla.'

'Yes, of course but I'd rather not kneel.'

Her husband laughed. 'I think I'd rather stand, too, at the moment.' They stood and prayed with heads bowed. Priscilla could not help but open an eye every now and then to make sure that no other vermin were coming their way.

Later that evening they recalled what their landlord had said about their home being haunted. The incident with the scorpion had pushed his words out of their minds until then.

'I'm not sure how seriously we should take his words,' Charlie said thoughtfully. 'Though, he certainly seemed to believe it.'

'"Greater is he that is in you, than he that is the world." (1 John. 4:4) I believe we have nothing to fear, Charlie.'

Once more they prayed, committing themselves to God. This time, in the light of a flickering lantern, they dared to kneel beside their bed. They then lay down. The thin quilt gave little relief from the hardness of the bricks beneath them but soon they fell asleep in each other's arms.

They awoke with a start. It was still night, but a noise had disturbed them both. They cast a quick glance at each other and then surveyed the scene in the little house by the light of the still burning lamp.

'There it is!' Priscilla shouted, pointing towards the door. 'It's a rat.'

Charlie leaped from the bed and dashed in the direction of the doorway. The rodent beat him through the opening and sped into the night. For a moment he peered into the darkness outside, and then turned and re-joined his wife. She was sitting on the side of the bed. He sat down beside her.

'Funny ghost!' he joked.

She laughed. 'Yes, I didn't know they had four legs.'

They lay down once more, but sleep would not come this time. Before day dawned they were both up and praying for God's blessing on their work in Lungan. When dawn finally came they had a quick breakfast and then set about erecting a door to keep out further unwelcome visitors. During the next few days they made contact with the little group of Christians in Lungan and familiarised themselves with the town. Each time they left their home, whether it was to go to market or to preach the Gospel, they were greeted by abuse from their neighbours.

****

In the first couple of weeks in Lungan, Charlie experienced further trouble with his breathing. It was asthma, though he did not know that at the time. The boiler in their home insisted on belching smoke into the house and this caused him considerable distress. He was thus forced to make modifications to the contraption so that the smoke exited from it through a hole in the roof, rather than straight into their living area. After that his health improved.

Charlie and Priscilla got to know the dozen or so national Christians quite quickly. All had become Christians during or since the time Stanley Smith had stayed in the town.

The leading figure was Liu Kezhong, who had become a Christian less than two years before the Studds arrived. He was a merchant in his thirties with a wife, also a Christian, and four young sons. Unusually tall for a Chinese, though slightly shorter than Studd, he was an imposing figure, who had assumed leadership of the church after Smith had moved on.

He was the most educated of the little band and had exhibited considerable Christian growth during his short time as a follower of Christ. His occupation, which had suffered because some of his business associates had severed contact with him over his new found faith, took him to various parts of Shansi and beyond. This was useful in keeping in contact with Christians in other parts but hindered the development of the church in Lungan. Liu was delighted that the Studds had decided to base their activities in his town, for he could see that they could give it the stability that his travels prevented.

Some weeks after they had settled in they had a visit from Jennifer Burroughs. She arrived late one afternoon, when Priscilla was preparing the evening meal.

'Ni hao,' the slender visitor greeted her friend, as she peered through the open doorway of the Studds' home.

Priscilla turned in surprise. 'Jenny!' she cried with delight. 'What are you doing here?'

'I've come to join you.'

'Join us? We hadn't heard you were coming. Oh anyway, don't just stand outside, come in.'

Jenny entered the house. 'You didn't receive a letter from John Stevenson in Shanghai?' she asked.

'No!' Scilla responded. 'But we've had suspicions that some of our mail wasn't making it. We're not as popular here as we might be,' she said with a wry smile.

'I know what you mean.'

'Charlie is out distributing tracts, but he should be home fairly soon. I'll prepare some more rice for you.'

'Thanks, Scilla. I must say I'm hungry after the walk.'

'Where are my manners?' Priscilla spluttered. 'We don't have much to sit on, but you can use the bed or the floor, whatever suits you. Make yourself comfortable.'

The visitor sat down on the bed.

Within minutes Charlie arrived home. He burst through the door, embraced his wife and kissed her affectionately, without noticing the new arrival.

Priscilla responded to him, but then pushed him away. 'Look, Charlie! Look who's here.'

She pointed in the direction of the bed.

Her husband turned. 'Miss Burroughs! What are you doing here?' he asked excitedly.

'I'm your new helper, Mr Studd,' she replied, rising from the bed. 'Mr Taylor and Mr Stevenson both wanted me to join you but it appears that Mr Stevenson's letter advising you about it didn't arrive.'

'That's great news. So you're permanent then?'

'As permanent as anyone is.'

Charlie smiled. 'And how's your cousin, Dick? Where's he now? I've lost track of him.'

'When I last heard, he was stationed in Hongtong working with Pastor Hsi.'

'He's as on fire for the Lord as ever, no doubt?'

'Yes! You know Dixon. Though, I did hear that there had been a disagreement between him and Pastor Hsi. But Hsi Shengmo's not always easy to get on with.'

'So I've heard,' Charlie responded, 'but we've never had any problems with him, have we Scilla?'

'No, though he is fiery,' his wife replied. 'But the Church needs a bit of fire, so I wouldn't criticise him for that. Anyway dinner is ready, so let's eat. No silver service I'm afraid, Jenny, but you can have first choice of chopsticks.'

Jenny smiled and selected a pair from those offered her.

After the meal Charlie rigged up a makeshift screen for their new helper to sleep behind. The next morning he constructed a more permanent arrangement in their house, for there was nowhere else for their new colleague to stay.

Often in the weeks they had already spent in Lungan, the young married couple had discussed with each other what strategy they should use to reach the citizens of their new town. After the practical arrangements of settling Jenny Burroughs into their home had been made, they shared their thoughts with her.

'You're familiar with The Salvation Army, I assume, Miss Burroughs?' Studd asked.

'Yes, indeed,' she replied. 'I'm not aware that they had a church near my home in Norfolk but I saw them in action a few times when I was visiting London.'

'Well, Scilla and I thought we might try some of their methods here. You know, parades through the streets, bands, that sort of thing.'

'But the Christians here don't seem keen on the idea,' Priscilla put in. 'We're not sure why. I don't think it's because they're ashamed to be recognised as Christians for they already are, and suffer for it.'

'In spite of that we thought we might try it and three makes a better parade than two,' Studd said, with a smile. 'So are you with us?'

'But what shall we do for a band?' Jenny wondered out loud. 'I play the piano a little but that's not going to be much help.'

'I still have my trusty banjo,' Charlie said, reaching out for his well-used instrument. 'We thought that you and Scilla could play the cymbals. We have two pair. It won't have the effect of a brass band or a 'Hallelujah Fiddle', but it will at least have a Chinese flavour.'

Jenny smiled. 'That settles it then. I'll join you. When do we go out?'

'Why not this afternoon? It doesn't look like being too hot. We could launch our attack on the market,' Charlie suggested.

The two women agreed enthusiastically and later that afternoon they ventured out into the local market, instruments at the ready. On their walk to the market place, they were greeted by the usual scowls and curses from the Chinese, but when they began their noisy parade in the busy trading place the opposition intensified. Now their neighbours' chorus of curses was accompanied by a fusillade of stones and rotting vegetables. In spite of the opposition, when they reached the far end of the market they immediately wheeled around and boldly made the return journey, with banjo strumming and cymbals clanging. All three had been the target of direct hits, but the bruising stones and rotten vegetables did not stop them.

When they had completed the second length of the market they halted and Charlie began to preach, as the two ladies stood on either side of him with eyes closed, praying. In just a few minutes a large crowd had gathered menacingly in front of them, continuing their taunts and still throwing whatever came to hand. Studd proceeded with his message undeterred. The sound was so threatening the two women opened their eyes to see what was going on.

As the crowd continued to grow, Jenny became rather concerned. 'This is looking very dangerous,' she said to Priscilla. 'I think it's time we withdrew.'

'Charlie doesn't like admitting defeat, Jenny. He thinks it is bad for the Gospel.'

'But even our Lord made some strategic withdrawals on occasions. I think we should do the same.'

Scilla thought for a moment and then tugged on her husband's gown. He turned around. Without saying anything she indicated with a movement of her head that they should retreat. Charlie looked into her face, then at the crowd. Without another word he picked up his banjo and slowly walked from the scene, ushering the two women before him. More projectiles followed them but, mercifully, the crowd did not give chase.

The following day, soon after they had eaten breakfast, there was a commotion in their street. As Studd and the two women peered through their doorway to see what the fuss was all about, they witnessed a noisy and angry procession making its way towards them. At its head, carried in a sedan chair, was the local Mandarin. Dressed in ornate robes with the opaque white stone of office on his cap, he was the district magistrate. He had come to make his displeasure known. As the crowd came to a halt outside their home, the bearers lowered the chair and the Mandarin stepped slowly from it.

As the man walked towards the three missionaries, they were left in no doubt as to his mood. His face told them that he was furious. The trio bowed and remained silent, waiting for the Mandarin to speak.

'Foreign devils will not parade in the market.' He seemed to spit out his words but the 'not' was clear enough to let it be known that he would tolerate no disobedience. 'Foreign devils will not parade anywhere,' he continued. 'If there are any more such disturbances you will be driven out of Lungan. Do you understand?'

Studd bowed again before speaking. 'We were only trying to –'

'No more parades!' The Mandarin's interruption was almost an explosion. 'Do you understand?'

'Yes,' Studd said, bowing again. 'But –'

'I will not tolerate any disobedience,' the magistrate said once more, his face leaving no doubt that he meant what he said.

'Yes, sir,' Studd replied respectfully.

The Mandarin, convinced he had made himself clear, stepped towards his entourage, mounted his chair, and was then carried from the scene.

Studd was shocked at the aggressiveness of the encounter and, as he watched the Mandarin depart the scene, he began to tremble. The women, too, were clearly upset. He ushered them back into their home. For several minutes they all sat silently on the floor, then Priscilla rose from her place and began to make some tea. When she poured the hot liquid it became apparent that she, too, was trembling, for the tea slopped over the edges of the cups. She took a cup each to Charlie and Jenny, returned to the stove for her own and then joined the other two back on the floor. They sipped the tea in silence.

After what seemed an age Scilla spoke up. 'What do we do, then?'

'I'm not sure,' Charlie said, after a moment's hesitation, 'but we won't stop preaching the Gospel, I promise you that.'

When they had finished their tea they heard the sound of other visitors outside. They looked at each other but knew that it was too quiet for a return of the Mandarin. They heard a gentle knock. Charlie stood up and went to the door. He opened it and was greeted by the solemn faces of Liu Kezhong and another member of the local Lungan church, Xianseng Zhang. He invited them in.

After initial greetings the two Chinamen explained their mission. 'Xianseng Studd,' Liu began, 'we would be most pleased if you would not hold any more parades.'

Studd was taken aback at this request coming from his Christian brethren but he decided to hear Liu out.

'You see, such incidents only inflame the local troublemakers and increase official opposition to the Lord's work,' Liu continued. 'We're not ashamed of our faith, Xianseng Studd, but we believe we should present it to our people in a less aggressive way.'

'We are barely tolerated as it is, Xianseng Studd.' This time it was Zhang. He was short and bespectacled. 'Such tactics will certainly bring bad trouble down on our heads, without any guarantees of winning souls. We respectfully ask that you don't try this method again.'

Studd turned his eyes from the two Chinese and looked at his missionary colleagues. He could see the embarrassment on their faces. He remained silent for several minutes as he considered the problem. His inclination had been not to give way to the intimidation of the Mandarin but this was a whole new dimension on the problem. He sensed that his two Chinese brothers may well have had a fear of persecution and, though he never could abide cowardice, to some degree he sympathised with them in that. He had heard of some of the terrible beatings inflicted upon Chinese Christians by disapproving Mandarins. But it did not seem to be just that which had made them approach him in this way. They appeared to believe that not only would other methods cause less trouble, they might also be more effective.

Eventually, he spoke. 'Brothers, we have much to learn from you. We will do as you ask. But we must not slacken our efforts in taking the Gospel to the lost. The only thing we will change will be the method.'

For the first time since they had entered the Studds' home that day the two Chinamen smiled. They bowed. 'Thank you, Xianseng Studd,' they said in unison.

'You will excuse us if we go now,' Liu said. 'We have things to attend to.'

Charlie bowed back and the two visitors left.

After they had gone Charlie took a deep breath. 'I think we still have much to learn about these people,' he said, as much to himself as the two women.

When Hudson Taylor heard of their Salvation Army style innovation some time later he wrote to express his concern. He felt that such methods, in an area where Christianity was so strongly opposed, would only engender unnecessary antagonism and achieve little, if anything, of value. But the Studds had already learned that for themselves.

Some weeks after the parade through the market, a new strategy was formulated. They decided to build a little chapel for worship and also a hostel for opium addicts. The work on the former started almost immediately but for the latter they needed the advice of Pastor Hsi.

A month or so after the parade Priscilla set out on her own trek. She went to a neighbouring town, in a rickety, horse-drawn cart, to encourage the church there. No missionary or other westerner resided in that town, so her arrival on the scene caused a furore. She pushed her way through the jostling crowds that harassed her as she searched for the local pastor's home. Eventually she found it.

She knocked on the door and, when it was opened, her host hurriedly pulled her into the courtyard surrounding his home and closed the door with a bang. The crowd took that gesture as an insult and congregated outside the building demanding that the door be reopened. Though the crowd's mood was not excessively hostile, it was still a disturbing situation. The pastor was reluctant to agree to their request for fear of their intentions.

However, Priscilla suspected that non-compliance with their demand might make the situation worse. 'Open the door, Pastor Tsu,' she urged, bravely.

'But that will put you in danger, Furen (Mrs) Studd.'

'I think we'll be in more danger if we don't. Open the door and I will speak to them.'

The Chinese pastor thought the problem over for a moment and then stepped towards the outer door and opened it.

'Where is the foreign devil?' someone in the crowd shouted. It was taken up by others.

Priscilla appeared in the doorway and the crowd suddenly went silent. She decided to make the most of the opportunity. 'You ask, "Where is the Devil?" I've never seen him, he is not here. I have come to bring you good news. Why do you curse me?'

The crowd began to move slowly towards her but its mood had now moderated. The people now seemed motivated by curiosity rather than fear or anger. 'Why are you that terrible colour?' someone asked. 'Did your parents starve you?'

'What's wrong with your hair? How did it become that colour?'

Priscilla did her best to answer those questions and the many that followed. By the time their curiosity had waned she had their confidence and was bold enough to preach a brief Gospel message.

She stayed a week with Pastor Tsu and as people frequently gathered outside his home wanting to see the red-haired, European woman, she regularly made an appearance and preached the Gospel. When the week concluded she returned to Lungan, followed for the first part of the journey by some whose fascination with her still remained.

CHAPTER 19
'IN LABOURS MORE ABUNDANT'

Liu Kezhong's business travels made him the obvious choice as the one to contact Hsi Shengmo about the hostel for opium addicts. He went off with an invitation for the fiery evangelist to pay them a visit. While they were awaiting his arrival, work continued on the chapel and evangelism proceeded in a more subdued form. This quieter presentation of the Gospel did not end all opposition; the Studds' neighbours seemed all too ready to voice their hatred. The antagonism was apparent every time they dared venture outside the walls of their home.

Then, almost by accident, they hit upon an idea. They invited the locals into their home. They let them poke into every nook and cranny in the house and examine all their possessions. From then on the opposition was less fierce, but it did not abate entirely. They seemed to be generally, tolerated, though certainly still not accepted.

Autumn was approaching and Scilla had suspected something for a number of weeks; now she was sure. One day, when Charlie had returned from a trip to a village just outside Lungan, his wife sat him down for a meal and broke the news to him.

'Charlie,' she said quietly, 'I'm with child.'

Her husband looked up from the food bowl in front of him. Rice spluttered forth from his mouth as he stuttered, 'Wh… Wh… What did you say?'

'I'm going to have a baby, Charlie.'

Studd gulped down the remainder of his mouthful. He quickly got up, moved next to his wife and put his arms around her.

'Darling, that's wonderful news,' he enthused. 'You're alright, though?'

She blushed. 'Yes, Charlie, I'm fine.'

'We will have to decide where the baby will be born. There's no doctor we can rely on here, so we might have to send you elsewhere for the birth. Pingyang, perhaps, or Shanghai ...' His mind was racing.

'It's still months away, Charlie, so we don't have to decide that now. We'll commit it to the Lord and let Him choose.'

'Yes, of course.'

'Oh, and there's some other news, too. Xianseng Liu returned today. He said Pastor Hsi will be here next week.'

'Hallelujah!' Studd shouted. 'It really is a day of great news isn't it? Our God is really good to us, eh, Scilla?'

'He is, indeed.'

****

Early the following week there was a knock at the door. As Priscilla opened it she was greeted by the familiar smile of Hsi Shengmo.

The pastor greeted her. 'Good evening, Furen Studd.'

'Charlie! Jenny! Shengmo's here,' Priscilla cried out in delight. 'Come in, Shengmo, come in. It's wonderful to see you.'

The little man entered their home and bowed again in greeting. Charlie by this time had stood up. He bowed in return. 'Welcome to you, Shengmo. We're just about to eat, so you've arrived at a good time.'

Hsi laughed a little. 'So it seems,' he said.

They all sat down in readiness for the meal. 'Shengmo, would you ask the Lord's blessing on our meal?' Charlie said.

Shengmo nodded his assent. His steady voice then sounded out words which seemed vaguely familiar to Charlie, though he could not quite place them.

> *Our bodies are yours, yes wholly yours;*
> *Our spirits own you for their Lord.*
> *Within your hand we lay our all,*
> *And only ask that we may be,*
> *Whene'er you need our service, Lord,*
> *Alert and ready for your use.*

Though Charlie had not recognised the words as such, Hsi had just prayed the chorus of a hymn he had written.

During the meal they discussed plans for establishing a refuge for opium addicts. Hsi, as an ex-addict himself, had set up such hostels in many towns throughout Shansi province, and was only too happy to help the Studds do so in Lungan. He told them of his successes and failures, and of those who had come to the Lord as a result of the ministry. He advised them on the building requirements of such a refuge and asked them whether they intended to cater for women addicts (who were fewer in number) or just men.

The next day, after morning prayer, they drew up both a plan for the buildings and a strategy for the running of the refuge. The day after that Pastor Hsi left them but promised to return when the buildings had been completed, to aid them in the early stages of establishing the hostel.

Within a week the construction of the buildings was underway and by late autumn they were ready for their first intake. The early inmates were drawn from the vicinity surrounding the mission. The opium addicts were not hard to find but most proved difficult to persuade to enter the refuge. Rumours about the evil practices of the 'foreign devils' were common. Those addicts who were approached with offers of help usually rejected them for fear that they might never leave the refuge alive. But, one by one they came in their varying degrees of devastation. They were men with sallow complexions and emaciated bodies; their faces showing only despair; each hoping for release from their addiction but, at the same time, longing for their next dose of the life-taking drug. Here before the missionaries was agonising proof of the Chinese proverb: It is not the man that eats the opium, but the opium that eats the man. It was as though this terrible drug was eating away its victims; body, mind and soul.

The local Christians gave their support to the work and, as the cold days of winter ran past with intermittent snow, the early discouragements gradually turned into rays of hope. Some of the inmates, in their more lucid moments, were only too happy to listen to stories from the Bible, and dared to ask questions about this new, strange religion. Some, also, showed a genuine desire to escape their habit, but the drug's pull was immensely strong and the struggles, therefore, intense.

As the new year approached the Studds had to face another problem. Should Priscilla go to Pingyang for her confinement, or have the baby at home in Lungan? They had prayed together about the matter since the time that Scilla had told her husband of her pregnancy. In Lungan they could count on no medical aid save their own minimal nursing knowledge. If she went to the hospital in Pingyang, with travelling time, she would probably be away for three months. Could the needs of the mission allow her to be away for that long? Also there was the principle of identification with the local Chinese. If the Chinese women had their babies without running away to a hospital, could a Christian missionary do less? They finally decided that Priscilla would stay.

The time for the birth drew close and Priscilla found herself getting more and more tired. Reluctantly, she had to shed much of her work load. One morning she was resting on the bed when she felt a pain in her back. She thought little of it at first, as aches and pains had been a common part of her experience in recent weeks, and this one went soon enough. But it was not long before it returned, then vanished again. When the feeling returned once more she began to wonder if this was the early signs of labour and considered if she should call Jenny Burroughs from the refuge. Before she could decide the pain subsided again. She continued to lie on the bed, offering a silent prayer to God.

It was not long before the pain returned and this time extended to other parts of her body. *This is it*, she thought, but remained on the bed. Next time the pain occurred she rose from the bed and hobbled into the refuge next door. She found her colleague and gave her the news. Jenny quickly ushered her back into the house, where once more the pregnant woman lay down.

'I'd better go and fetch Furen Liu,' Jenny said. 'She said that she would help, and she has had four children herself.'

'Thanks, Jenny.'

'Will you be alright?'

Scilla smiled. 'I don't think it's due quite yet. Oh, and Jenny, you had better let Charlie know.'

'Yes, I'll do that.' With that she disappeared through the doorway.

It seemed like an age to Priscilla before the front door opened again. This time it was Furen Liu.

'Xiaojie (Miss) Burroughs told me the baby is coming, so I have come to help,' she said gently, her voice soothingly musical.

'Thank you, Furen Liu. May the Lord bless you for coming.'

Before the conversation could get any further Charlie burst through the door, hotly pursued by a breathless Jenny Burroughs. He fell on his knees beside his wife. 'How are you, darling?' he asked with concern.

'Fine, Charlie! There's not much happening yet.'

'Oh!'

'It will probably be some time before the baby comes, Mr Studd. Why don't you go back to work,' Jenny suggested, 'and we'll let you know as soon as the baby arrives.'

'No! I'm staying.'

'But –'

'No buts, Miss Burroughs. I'm staying.'

Jenny thought of stating that this was women's work, but the look on Studd's face and the tone in his voice made her decide against it. She looked at Scilla, who nodded her assent to her husband's stand.

'I've nursed people before, Jenny Burroughs, and you will not stop me aiding my own wife at this of all times.'

Jenny knew there was no point in arguing and recognised that the decision was not really hers anyway.

'Well, if you're staying, Mr Studd, you'd better make yourself useful. Make your wife as comfortable as you can, and then sit beside her and hold her hand. She will need that when the pains become bad.'

Charlie fussed around his wife for a while and then settled down beside her.

The labour pains were still infrequent and, after about an hour, Charlie was called from his wife's bedside by a worker from the refuge. About half an hour later he burst through the door once more.

'Hallelujah!' he called out enthusiastically. 'Stanley Smith has just arrived and he has promised to pray next door until the baby is born. Isn't that great news, Scilla?'

'Yes, Charlie, I am grateful.'

Studd sat once more by his wife and grasped her hand again. For a time the pains were no more frequent than before, the afternoon slowly turned to evening, but then the pains started coming more frequently and with a greater intensity. Scilla's brow was covered in beads of perspiration, though it was getting quite cold in the house. Each time the pain surged, she moaned and then let out a piercing cry as the pain reached its peak. At those times her hand gripped Charlie's so tightly that he thought she would crush it. Charlie had no previous experience of witnessing the pains of childbirth, and to see his beloved in such agony stabbed at his heart. In between each contraction he comforted his wife with words gentle and soothing, but each time the words were then shattered by another cry, seemingly worse than the one before.

Jenny and Furen Liu busied themselves in preparation for the baby's reluctant entry into the world. Jenny's hair insisted on continually falling over her forehead as she bent over her friend's writhing form. Each time she stood erect again she brushed it back with the rear of her hand, her worried frown clear for all to see in the light of the lanterns. Furen Liu seemed more in control. At least she had the experience the others lacked.

Scilla was exhausted. The stress and pain of childbirth was having its effect. Again the pain surged and once more she cried out. This time she articulated a prayer of desperation. 'Oh, Lord, help me!' she screamed. None of them were aware that it was now well into the night. Time seemed to have no meaning.

Eventually, the baby's head appeared and then the perfect form of a tiny girl slowly entered the world. The slippery, little bundle of new life was placed in the arms of its weary mother. Scilla looked at her daughter and then at her husband, and smiled weakly. Charlie uttered an almost breathless 'Hallelujah!' as the tears of relief and joy flowed down his cheeks.

Jenny sat down on the hard floor for a moment of respite. It had been a long, difficult day. Furen Liu stood weeping in the background. At first the others did not think much of it but, as her tears continued to flow, Jenny became concerned and went over to her.

'What's wrong, Furen Liu? Now is the time for rejoicing. You know that the Bible says that when a child is born the mother rejoices because a man is born into the world. Surely we should do the same.'

'But, you see, that's the problem. It isn't a man, it's a little *girl*.' Furen Liu's voice quavered as she uttered the last word.

Jenny understood immediately. Chinese society placed little value on women. In that part of the world female babies were often exposed to the elements to die of cold or starvation or even to be eaten by wolves.

'Furen Liu!' Jenny's voice conveyed her shock. 'You don't think the Studds would...' She was unable to finish the sentence.

'Oh, no, Xiaojie Burroughs. I know they wouldn't. It's just...' She hesitated, as she tried to bring her emotions under control. 'Before we believed in the Lord, I gave birth to a little girl, too.'

Furen Liu showed no intention of continuing, but Jenny thought of the Liu's four boys and guessed the fate of the girl. She put her arms around the still sobbing Chinese woman. 'I had better take you home. It has been a difficult day for all of us.' The two women left the Studds' house and disappeared into the night.

The day after Grace Studd had been born, Priscilla's condition deteriorated, rather than improved. She received the best of care from her husband and friends, but continued to grow worse. A missionary nurse arrived on the scene a few days after the birth and added her ministrations to that of the others, but still there was no improvement. Each day Priscilla seemed to get worse. Charlie Studd was most certainly not one who valued this life above eternity but he, naturally enough, began to be concerned about losing the woman he loved, which from a human standpoint seemed more and more likely each day.

The nurse told him that there was little chance of recovery and that, even if she did get better, they ought to head straight back to England, for she could not be expected to survive in China for long. This spurred Studd to action. Once more he followed the injunction and claimed the promise of James chapter 5 verses 14 and 15, which he had last used on his horrific march with Wu and Guang, when his feet were in such a terrible condition. He anointed his wife with oil and prayed over her.

The next day there was a marked improvement in her condition and she quickly regained her health and strength. Once more CT Studd's faith in his God had been vindicated. An immediate return to England was never seriously considered.

The next year Scilla gave birth again, this time to a boy, but, tragically, little Paul Snowball Studd died the following day. Within, Scilla was broken-hearted, but so determined was she not to give her husband cause to worry and to set an example of Christian hope to her neighbours, she shed no tears and refused to mourn. In her Bible she recorded the birth of her son and penned the words:

'Tis my happiness below,
Not to live without the cross,

> *But my Saviour's power to know,*
> *Sanctifying every loss.*

The children came yearly after that: Dorothy in 1891, Edith in 1892 and then Pauline. It seemed to the Studds that God's gift of four girls, and the love that they were able to shower upon them, demonstrated to their neighbours, more than words could do, the great value that each child has, whether male or female.

CHAPTER 20
'In Stripes Above Measure'

The droughts of the 1870s had left their mark on the consciousness of the people of Shansi, and when the rains had not come by the middle of one summer there was a great deal of nervousness about another drought. The Muslim section of the population of Lungan took it rather stoically but the animists, the larger portion of the community, were already praying to their ancestors and gods for the rains to come.

Summer continued on. It remained hot and dry. Scarcely a drop of rain had fallen the whole wet season thus far. Crop failure was almost certain and the prospects of a hungry winter faced them all. The citizens of Lungan decided to try one last, communal effort to bring the desperately needed rain. They imported a rain god from a neighbouring region and decided to parade it through the streets allowing the sun to shine on the idol's head, which, with the associated burning of incense, it was supposed, would bring the needed downpour.

The day before the proposed ritual, placards appeared all over the city advising that on the following day all citizens should have the outer doors of their houses closed and that they should burn incense to the rain god.

There was never any possibility that those in the small Christian mission could go along with these demands, for it would be a complete denial of all they stood for. On the day of the procession their doors remained open and they burned no incense.

For some time the Christian community had been getting blamed for every little mishap in the town and the people had not been slow to blame them for the pending famine. Now these 'foreign devils' and their associates were blatantly refusing to appease the rain god. Was it any surprise that after the procession the sun still shone from a cloudless sky? It was clearly the fault of the Christians.

From the middle of the day a noisy crowd had begun to congregate around the mission buildings and, as time went on, the gathering grew and the mood worsened. Charlie viewed the scene from within with increasing concern. Priscilla, who was sick in bed, fired questions at her husband, trying to ascertain the seriousness of the situation. Charlie maintained his watch, did his best to answer her questions, and tried to formulate a plan should the worst eventuate. Anticipating trouble, Charlie had already instructed his Chinese helpers and the inmates to leave the complex, and they had taken little Grace with them. Jenny Burroughs was also away on mission business in another town, so they were the only ones left in the compound.

Suddenly, the mob converged in an angry swell upon the little chapel and began to tear it down. Charlie rushed to his wife, picked her up in his arms and dashed from their house into the courtyard of the complex. He placed her down.

'I will go to get the Mandarins. They must put a stop to this,' he said, concern etched into his face. 'God protect you, my dear.' With that he scaled the wall and ran off in the direction of the nearest Mandarin's residence.

When he arrived there he learned that all the Mandarins had left the town. None had wanted to be guilty of supporting a riot, but neither had they wanted to be seen favouring the missionaries, so they took the easy way out and vanished.

Studd rushed back in desperation, afraid of what he might find on his return. As he ran his fears were fuelled by the sight of smoke coming from the direction of the mission. He quickened his pace. His heart beat quickly; his breathing was laboured. He prayed as he ran, entreating God to spare his wife. He arrived back at the mission complex and, to his astonishment, the crowd was quietly dispersing. He saw that the smoke was coming from their home but, ignoring that, he charged into the courtyard. There was Scilla on her knees, praying.

He ran over to her. 'Are you alright, Scilla?'

The trembling woman opened her eyes. 'Yes! I think so. What happened? One minute they were all screaming and shouting, then it went quiet.'

'I don't know but stay here, Scill. Our home's on fire I'm afraid. I must try to put it out.'

Once more he dashed off, this time in the direction of the smoke. To his surprise there was already someone beating out the flames. It was one of the addicts. Studd joined him in extinguishing the fire and it was not long before they had put it out.

'Thank you! Thank you!' was all Charlie could say, as the two men, their firemen's job done, sat down outside the house exhausted.

The Chinaman gave a slight smile. 'Xianseng Studd, you are helping me, so I thought I'd try to help you.'

Studd smiled grimly and nodded.

Eventually, they stood up again and surveyed the damage. One wall had been badly burned and a new roof would have to be constructed, but the remainder of the house seemed sound. The Church had been more severely damaged and would have to be completely rebuilt.

The two men went into the courtyard where Priscilla sat waiting. 'The house is repairable, darling. But we won't be able to sleep there tonight,' Charlie said. 'We had better spend the night in the refuge and work out what to do in the morning. Praise God, for such a deliverance.'

The final phrase was said with great feeling. Studd picked up his wife once more, and carried her into the quarters which normally housed the addicts. Their Chinese helper followed them.

When Charlie had found somewhere suitable for his wife to lie down, his thoughts turned once more to the astonishing deliverance they had just experienced. He turned to his Chinese companion. 'Wang, what happened out there? Why did the riot cease so suddenly?'

Wang gave a rather wan smile. 'Amazing as it may sound, it was just one of the local teachers that called the mob to order and persuaded them to continue taking the rain god in procession through the streets. You see, Xianseng Studd, we Chinese have a great respect for the scholars amongst us. When he spoke to them, they listened. When he told them to continue the march, they did.'

'Hallelujah! Can you see the Lord's hand in that, Wang?'

'Yes, Xianseng Studd, I think I can.'

During the next few weeks the work of rebuilding went on. Priscilla's health began to improve and Charlie took time to get to know Wang better. His story was a disturbing one. He came from another town in Shansi where he had frequently committed adultery and had also murdered a man. It seemed to Studd that Wang had broken every law that God had made. He was totally dependent upon opium and, before coming to the refuge, had contemplated suicide. But, the refuge had given him some hope. True, he had at times vanished from the mission complex for a day or two and returned in drug-induced stupors, but, particularly since the riot, he had shown both an increasing keenness to be cured and a genuine interest in the Gospel.

He paid close attention to the Bible stories that the Studds told at the devotional times, and began to ask questions as to their meaning. At the end of one meeting, Wang went up to Charlie and asked, 'May I speak with you, Xianseng Studd?'

'Certainly, Wang, what can I do for you? Why don't we sit down?' Charlie indicated two chairs and they both sat down.

Wang came straight to the point. 'Can Jesus save anyone?'

'Yes, anyone! Anyone at all.'

'A murderer?'

'Yes, we have told you about the thief on the cross. He was a murderer and our Lord saved him.'

'An adulterer?'

'Certainly! What about the woman taken in adultery in John's Gospel?'

'An opium addict?'

Studd smiled slightly. 'Well, I don't know of any opium smokers in the Bible, but you know Pastor Hsi. He was an opium addict. Look at what Christ has done for him.'

'But, Xianseng Studd, can He do it for me?' There was desperation in the man's question.

'Why not? If He can forgive others, if He can save their souls, why wouldn't He be able to do that for you? He loves you every bit as much as them. The Scriptures say that Jesus came "to seek and save that which was lost". (Luke 19:10) Without him you are lost. He came to seek and to save you. There's another Scripture which says, "Whosoever believeth in him should not perish, but have everlasting life". (John 3:16) It doesn't say "This one!" or "That one!" It says "Whosoever!" And that means anyone, whether he is a murderer and adulterer or whatever. Anyone that believes in Jesus will receive eternal life.'

Wang listened intently and, when Charlie stopped, he remained silent, weighing the words carefully in his mind. Charlie let him take in what had been said. After a couple of minutes Wang looked Studd in the eye and the missionary could see the man's eyes moist with tears.

'Xianseng Studd, would you pray for me? I want to become a Christian.'

Studd felt a thrill go through his whole body. 'Indeed!' he said. 'Let's kneel down.' The two men knelt together and Charlie prayed that Christ would save his companion. When he had finished Wang, too, said a halting, but sincere, prayer beseeching God's forgiveness.

Then he began an intense struggle to quit smoking opium. Wang was determined never to smoke it again, but the drug had such a strong hold over him that his whole being seemed to crave it. The Studds had medicines designed to lessen the agonies of withdrawal, but in reality they were of little use in alleviating the problems associated with it. An all-pervading tiredness seemed to encompass his whole body, yet he could not sleep. He drank much, but was always thirsty. Though the weather was still quite warm, he was continually shivering. His body ached. His eyes and nose streamed water. He was smitten with severe depression. His desire for the drug was intense, yet he did not give in. Now there was a new power at work within him. Christ had not only forgiven his sin but had come to him to help him combat sin.

The Christians in Lungan met for prayer to seek his deliverance, praying that the Holy Spirit would give Wang the power to overcome the terrible addiction. Yet, for a time, his plight seemed to get worse. It was as though Satan was fighting furiously to regain hold of that which had been his. Wang's depression deepened. Even though he could not sleep, terrible visions came to him.

At times it seemed to Wang that the Devil would retake him. *Oh for peace and rest*, he thought. He knew that rest could be found in an opium pipe but he realised, too, that such rest was only for a little while, and the opium would then drag him down once more.

In the end, release came almost suddenly. The strong desire for the drug subsided. God's peace and joy flooded his being and gradually he was able to slip into a beautiful, deep sleep. When he awoke it was clear to everyone that Wang was a new man. He was still weak from lack of food and sleep but a new desire seemed to control him. He wanted to tell others about Christ.

Before he had even regained health and strength he was telling the Studds, Jenny Burroughs and anyone who would listen that he wanted to go back to his home town to tell them about the Saviour. He listened even more intently to the Bible stories. When they gave him a New Testament, he devoured its contents avidly, determined to learn as much as possible about his new found faith.

When he had recovered, Wang set off for home, knowing that the old Wang would not have been well received by his ex-neighbours, and suspecting that the new Wang would be even less popular. As he walked the miles to his destination he memorised passages of Scripture and prayed for the people he knew there. Upon arrival he called upon his family who promptly rejected him. He then visited some old friends who did likewise.

Disappointed but not really surprised, he found his way to the town square and carried out the next stage in the plan he had formulated on his trek home. He began to preach to the townspeople, who were about their daily business. It was not long before a crowd had formed. The people were curious. Many recognised him as the troublemaker who had left town in disgrace some time before. He now seemed so different, yet he was still causing trouble; this time by talking about foreign gods.

If Wang knew the danger he was putting himself in, he did not show it. He fearlessly proclaimed his new-found Lord. But gradually, as the content of his message became clear, the mood of the crowd changed. Some of the gathering began to shout abuse but were unable to drown out his enthusiastic preaching. Frustrated by their inability to stop him his antagonists emerged from the crowd, grabbed him and marched him off to the Mandarin.

They arrived at the Mandarin's palatial residence and stated their business to an official there. They were all then ushered in to a beautifully decorated room, and told to wait for the Mandarin to summon them. Wang realised that it was unlikely that he would be well received by this local magistrate and knew that his punishment could be most severe. As he waited, he prayed, and found a strange sense of peace coming over him.

After what seemed an age the big doors at the opposite end of the room swung open, another official emerged and beckoned Wang and his captors into a large adjoining room. The men on either side of Wang grabbed him roughly, pushed him through the doorway and threw him to the ground in front of the Mandarin. Wang knew well enough that he had better stay where he was but he moved into a kneeling position facing the magistrate. From his humbled situation, though, he could still see the stern face of the bespectacled magistrate.

The Mandarin sat on a chair behind a large wooden desk, both of which were on a small platform a little above the level of the remainder of the room. On either side of him sat two officials, whose faces looked no more friendly than their leader's.

'Who is this?' the Mandarin barked.

Wang's accusers bowed and one said, 'His name is Wang, oh Mandarin. He has been a troublemaker for many years.'

'And what are the charges?'

'He has been proclaiming Christ, a foreign God, Mandarin. He seems to have been bewitched by the foreign devils.'

The Mandarin sat silently for a moment. His face grew even graver. He then addressed Wang. 'What do you say about this charge? Is it true?'

Wang remained in his kneeling position, not even daring to look up. 'Yes, Mandarin,' he responded tentatively. 'I have become a believer in Jesus Christ. He has saved me from my sins and made me a new man, and I want to tell others about Him.'

The Mandarin paused once more and looked at his associates on either side of him. Then returning his attention to Wang again he pronounced sentence.

'You are as bad as the foreign devils themselves. You are sentenced to two thousand strokes of the bamboo.'

Wang heard the Mandarin's words but they had a kind of unreality about them. *Two thousand strokes? Two thousand strokes!* he thought. He had seen such punishments inflicted on others. He knew that few survived and, for most, it was a long, painful death. He considered protesting but he knew it was useless. Instead, he silently prayed to his Lord for strength to endure this savagery.

Once more he was grabbed by his accusers and this time dragged into the courtyard outside the Mandarin's residence. There he was strung up and two men approached him, each armed with a bamboo rod. Wang heard them coming up behind him and braced himself for the onslaught.

The first blow came down fiercely on his back. Wang gasped at the pain, which seemed to radiate from the point of impact to his whole body. Another blow fell on him, this time from the other side. He cried out in agony. Once more the bamboo lashed his back and again, and again. The pain seemed to increase with each blow as his back became more bruised and torn. Mercilessly the two torturers continued the punishment; blow upon blow fell on the brave man's back. His agonies grew more intense. He cried out to God in prayer. His back became more and more tender, but gradually his mind became numb to his suffering. For more than an hour they beat him. By the time they stopped he was senseless and barely alive. They untied him and left him to die.

Some of Wang's old companions had heard of his sentence and arrived on the scene just as the punishment was ending. As the crowd of witnesses dispersed, they moved towards the inert form of their old friend. They looked at his battered body, the back a mass of red pulp. As they gently picked him up he uttered a weird, unearthly groan. They took him back to the home of one of them and for the next two days nursed him as well as they could. When he regained consciousness he asked them to take him back to Lungan, where there were now more experienced medical staff. His friends complied with his request and he returned to Lungan on a springless, horse-drawn cart over the rough roads, every bump causing more suffering.

When the little party arrived at the mission complex, the Studds, who were not unaware of the brutality of many Chinese punishments, were shocked at the physical condition of this new convert. Not only was his body mangled, but his mind was frequently wandering and his speech was incoherent. For the next few weeks Wang was lovingly nursed by Charlie and Priscilla and the other mission staff. Special prayer times were held on his behalf. Gradually his bodily strength returned and with it full control of his mind.

'I'm going back,' he declared one day.

'Back?' Charlie was stunned. 'What do you mean, back?' He suspected he already knew the answer.

'Back home, to preach the Gospel again.'

Studd was a brave man but even he was taken aback by the apparent foolhardiness of the idea. As he thought about the possibilities, he hesitated between dissuading Wang and encouraging him. 'Do you think that's wise, Wang?'

'I have no choice, Xianseng Studd. My people need the Gospel. Who will take it to them if I don't?'

Charlie sighed resignedly. 'I suppose you are right. But, you don't go until you are fully well. Is that understood?'

'Yes, Xianseng Studd,' Wang replied with a weak smile.

After a further two weeks, they were unable to restrain him any longer and Wang set out on his next journey home. On his arrival he adopted the same strategy as before, preaching in the town square. Once more a crowd gathered, but this time they listened with some awe to a man who, it seemed, had come back from the dead. But, it was not long before some officials appeared on the scene and, for the second time, Wang was roughly escorted to the Mandarin.

Inwardly, the Mandarin was shocked to see the accused kneeling before him again, for he had assumed he was dead, but his face showed no emotion. He asked for Wang's name, though he already knew it, and then asked what the charges were.

'Wang is speaking about a foreign god again, Mandarin,' was the reply.

The magistrate was stunned at such audacity. It was some time before he spoke again. Everyone in the hall remained silent, none daring to speak. Then the Mandarin addressed Wang. 'Is this charge true?'

'Yes, Mandarin,' Wang said boldly. 'I am preaching about Jesus Christ, the Son of the one true God, who made this world.' Wang knew that such a confession would probably result in another savage beating.

Once more the Mandarin was shocked into silence. He was disturbed by this turn of events and did not know how best to deal with it. Eventually, he turned to his associates, back to the accused and pronounced his verdict.

'You will be sent to prison until I decide what to do with you.'

Wang was dragged off to gaol and was consigned to a small, dirty cell. He sat on the floor and considered his position. It was not long before he was on his knees praying for guidance, protection and another opportunity to preach the Gospel. While he was praying he had become vaguely aware of the sound of activity on the other side of his cell's wall. When he finished praying, he rose to his feet and peered through a small window, which looked out upon the street beneath. To his astonishment a large crowd had gathered and, when he was spotted at the window, fingers pointed in his direction and the crowd hummed with excitement.

The converted drug addict looked down at the people before him and it suddenly dawned on him that here was an answer to his prayer for another preaching opportunity. He began to speak through the little window in a loud, clear voice, telling of the good news of Jesus Christ. The hubbub outside subsided rapidly as the crowd became aware what was happening. Wang was able to speak at length without hindrance. The next day the same thing occurred: the crowd gathered and Wang preached.

Later that day the cell door was flung open and the gaoler walked in. Wang looked up in surprise.

'You're free,' the gaoler barked.

'What did you say?' Wang was not sure he had heard correctly.

'You are free to leave prison. The Mandarin says you are more trouble inside than outside.'

Wang chuckled a little to himself and then out loud he exclaimed, 'Hallelujah!' He picked up his things and followed his captor through the prison's corridors and out to freedom. From then on Wang was never short of an audience and, though officialdom still disapproved of his activities, it was decided to leave him alone.

When the Studds next heard from him they were relieved to hear about his deliverance, and delighted to be told that he was already forming a small group of believers around him.

CHAPTER 21
'A Thorn in the Flesh'

Like their Chinese neighbours, the Studds suffered the deprivations of the famine that followed that rainless summer. They had no inexhaustible supply of money to purchase provisions from far afield. All their financial resources had long since been given away. They trusted in God to supply their need, and money for food and other supplies often came at unexpected times and in strange ways.

At one stage in the succeeding long winter it seemed as though God had let them down. Their supplies were all but exhausted and, because of the inflated prices of the scarce food items, they had completely run out of money with which to buy more. As was their practice at such times Charlie and Priscilla knelt together in prayer to take their problem to God. They did not badger the Lord with a laboriously long prayer, for they recognised that He already knew their predicament, but for a quarter of an hour or so they poured out their hearts to God, expecting an answer.

Their financial needs were most commonly met through the arrival of the fortnightly postal deliveries. When the next mail arrived they tipped out the contents of the bag with enthusiasm. They looked at the various envelopes and, where possible, guessed the senders' names, then opened each letter and avidly read the contents. When the last letter had been read they realised that they had received no money. There had been plenty of news and good wishes, but nothing to provide for their immediate needs. They looked at each other. Both had unusually downcast expressions.

Charlie got up from where they were sitting and picked up the mail bag again. He tipped it upside down and shook it vigorously. At first nothing happened. Then, at last, another envelope appeared and fell to the floor. The Studds looked at each other and smiled tentatively. Charlie picked up the fallen letter and examined the envelope.

'I don't recognise the writing, Scilla. I wonder who it's from.' He was almost afraid to open it.

'Well, open it, Charlie. Don't keep me in suspense,' Priscilla chided.

Charlie opened it and took out two pieces of paper. He examined them and handed one over to his wife. She realised immediately that it was a cheque, and felt tears of joy welling up in her eyes as she looked at it.

'It's from a man named Frank Crossley. I don't know him. Do you?'

'Never heard of him,' Priscilla said, choked with emotion.

'Listen to this, Scilla. He says: "I have for some reason or other received the command of God to send you a cheque for a £100. I have never met you. I have only heard of you and that not often, but God prevented me from sleeping tonight by this command. Why He should command me to send you this I don't know. You will know better than I. Anyhow, here it is and I hope it will do you good."'

Studd handed the letter to his wife and took the cheque back, looking at it as though it was the most amazing piece of paper he had ever seen. His face suddenly lit up.

'Hallelujah!' he exclaimed. 'Our God is wonderful, Scilla.'

'He is, indeed.'

Charlie fell on his knees and his wife knelt down beside Him, and together they burst out in praise to God.

****

As their years in China continued, Studd's health frequently became a source of concern. His asthma attacks occurred more often and his general condition grew progressively worse. In March 1893, after nearly eight unbroken years in China, he became so seriously ill that Scilla nearly despaired of saving him. His breathing was so bad that it seemed each breath might be his last.

One afternoon he gasped to his wife, 'James . . . five, fourteen, Scilla.'

'What was that? I don't understand,' she said, bending over him and wiping his brow.

'Call . . . the elders . . . and anoint me . . . with oil. And pray for me.'

This time Scilla understood. She called together Liu, Zhang, their wives and a couple of other members of the church and they carried out Charlie's wish. He was anointed with oil and the little group knelt by his bedside to pray for him.

He showed no improvement that night but the next morning he was considerably better. His breathing was much easier and his general condition had improved. But from then on Priscilla found herself thinking seriously about the possibility of returning to England. Though her husband's health was much better at the moment, it seemed to her just like another swing of the pendulum. For a while he would be well, then he would decline into sickness again, and each bout seemed to be worse than the one before. She found herself thinking, *If this most recent attack has nearly killed him, will the next be his last*?

Early in April she decided to suggest to him that they return to Britain. She did not expect that her comments would be well received and they were not.

'The Lord has not told me to go home, so I won't,' was his immediate response.

'But, Charlie, maybe the Lord is telling you exactly that through your health,' she gently suggested.

'Scilla, don't you see? God has placed me here in Lungan and I could not possibly leave it without a direct message from Him, and I have not received such.'

'But next time you have an attack it might kill you. Why don't we just go home and rest for a while so that both of us can fully recover our health, and then we can return here at a later date? You desperately need to slow down for a while.'

'Scilla, if I'm going to have a short life, all the more reason for me to live fast and do more. Remember, every man is immortal till his work is done.'

Priscilla sighed in frustration but she knew her husband well enough to realise that he would not be persuaded to do what he believed was against God's will, so she left the matter there. A month later a cheque came from Charlie's mother in London for the express purpose of paying their fares home. She had heard of his deteriorating health and had decided to remove every stumbling block to her son's return.

Yet, still Charlie was unmoved. He still waited on the voice of God. During the remainder of that year his health fluctuated but the bad times rarely interfered with his heavy workload for long. But, in 1894 the voice was heard. CT Studd came to believe that his Lord was calling him back to England.

It was a sad day when they packed their meagre possessions, dressed their four daughters for the long journey ahead and said farewell to the people of Lungan for the last time. On the first, brief stage of their trek they were accompanied by an entourage, comprising most of the members of their church. Even Wang, who had come from his town to say goodbye, joined the procession. For most of that part of the trip little Pauline cried continually, while the older children sat solemnly in the cart provided for them, confused and saddened by the apparent finality of the event. When the time came for the accompanying group to return to Lungan the full impact of the separation hit them all. Both the Studds and their Chinese friends shed tears. They all suspected that this was the last time they would see each other in this life.

As Charlie called them to their last prayer together, he reminded them of a similar event 1,800 years before, when the Apostle Paul had said farewell to the Ephesian elders at Miletus.

Lifting his hand he repeated Paul's words. '"And now, brethren, I commend you to God, and to the word of his grace, which is able to build you up, and to give you an inheritance among all them that are sanctified." (Acts 20:32) I pray, Lord, that thou wilt give these thy children a special portion of thy blessing and keep them for eternity.'

Goodbyes over, the group of Chinese Christians returned to Lungan, except for two young men who accompanied the Studds on the remainder of their journey to Shanghai. Weeks later, the Studds met Hudson Taylor and formally handed the mission complex over to the CIM.

Upon the wharf-side in Shanghai, Charlie, Priscilla and the children said their final farewells to their two Chinese companions. The children cried and their parents could do little to comfort them, for they too were crying. The two young men were also in tears. The Studds mounted the gangplank with heavy hearts, not knowing whether they would ever return to China.

As they leaned on the ship's rail to wave goodbye, a fellow passenger, who had witnessed the scene, came up to Charlie and said, 'Well, Mr Studd, I can see you didn't come out to China for nothing.'

Charlie looked the man in the eye and replied, 'We certainly didn't. We came out to China for something very worthwhile indeed and God has richly blessed.'

PART THREE

THE WORLD

CHAPTER 22

INTERLUDE

The Studds arrived home towards the end of 1894. Charlie's mother was only too glad to host the family at Hyde Park Gardens, and even provide a nanny for the girls. Not that doing so was by any means a task devoid of problems. Although her home had plenty of room for the family of six, and even more if need be, the four little girls spoke only Chinese and were used to eating only Chinese food. They turned the house upside down.

On one occasion a feud between the girls and the nanny resulted in a rebellion led by Grace, the eldest, which saw the four sisters locking themselves in the bathroom. It was only after vigorous persuasion from their mother that they unlocked the door and faced the consequences of their actions. Pauline, the youngest, at first refused to eat the English meals, and only did so, eventually, out of necessity. Life was now so different for the whole family; not just the language and the food, but the whole lifestyle. Dora Studd took every opportunity to spoil each member of the family, particularly the girls, and often experienced her son's displeasure for doing so.

Kynaston, too, was pleased to have his brother back home and took great delight in pampering his four nieces. George, though, was in America. A couple of years after his return from China he had gone to the USA and commenced working with a Christian Mission in the slums of Los Angeles.

Charles and Priscilla had extensive medical check-ups. Apart from his asthma, Charles had no major problem, but his wife was diagnosed as having a heart condition which put any thoughts of a return to China in the near future out of the question.

For a while Charlie contented himself with numerous speaking engagements throughout Britain, but in 1896 another call came to him. Soon after Charlie had gone to China, Kynaston had visited America to help promote the work of the Student Volunteers: a movement which had been inspired by such as the Cambridge Seven in England, and had been fostered by DL Moody and his associates. Its aim, simply put, was to inspire the young students of America to volunteer for missionary service. It was this group that, now, invited Charlie to follow in his older brother's footsteps to encourage the youth of America to commit themselves to missionary endeavour.

For eighteen months he toured the USA, speaking at Universities, Colleges and Churches, counselling literally hundreds of students concerned about their souls, lack of spiritual power, or missionary call. For that whole period Priscilla remained in England, frequently asking him in letters to let her join him. Each time he said 'No!' afraid that the presence of his wife might both slow his pace and inhibit the students coming to see him. On several occasions he received word that Priscilla was ill and, whilst this deeply disturbed him, it did not hinder his resolve to see his American tour through to its conclusion. The last few months in the USA were marred by his own sickness. He again suffered from asthma and other ailments and even spent some time in hospital before returning once more to England.

Even though he was kept busy by further speaking engagements in his home land, he continually experienced a sense of frustration. To him this was not his real task. He, CT Studd, was a frontline soldier but it seemed to him that his current work was fit only for a 'Chocolate Soldier'. He yearned to go overseas again. This time his dream was to go to India, the land where his father had made his fortune.

It was at this point that William Vincent, Edward Studd's friend, entered the story once more. It was now nearly a quarter of a century since Vincent had been converted in Dublin and had later taken Edward Studd to hear Moody and Sankey. He advised Charlie that some expatriate Englishmen in India were looking for someone to conduct some evangelistic meetings near the district where Edward Studd once lived and worked. If Charlie was prepared to go, he would pay all the necessary expenses. It all seemed too much of a coincidence to be anything other than the hand of God so, early in 1900, he packed his bags once more, left his family and headed off for Tirhoot in Northern India.

If Charlie had a plan at this stage it was, simply, to do what was required in Tirhoot and then return to England. But, as always, he was open to any obvious leading from his Lord and Master. Whilst conducting the proposed meetings, he received an invitation from the Union Church in Ootacamund (popularly nicknamed 'Ooty'), near Madras (now Chennai) in Southern India, to be its pastor. The Union Church was the spiritual home of a variety of noncomformists among the British Raj in Ootacamund. His congregation would thus be mainly expatriate Britons.

Now, this did not sound like the kind of task one would expect a pioneer like Studd to accept. At first he had strong reservations. The idea of his being tied just to one place, and that amongst his exiled fellow countrymen, did not sound like the call of God to him. But, after further discussions, it was agreed that he become the Pastor of the Union Church, but that he also would be allowed to devote one-third of his time to evangelise in the surrounding districts.

He arrived in Ootacamund, which was more than 2,000 metres above sea level, at the end of May, and Priscilla and the children joined him in October. From the point of view of marriage and family life the six years spent in Ooty proved to be the most idyllic in his experience. From his perspective, though, pastoring a church which was technically British was not ideal. But, within that church and on his excursions further afield, he had plenty of opportunities to evangelise, and that well pleased him.

His wife and daughters were all delighted to be seeing more of him than they had done at any time since their stay in Lungan, and even he appreciated that. For the only time in his life he found himself being paid a regular salary, a fact which made him nervous (was he no longer trusting God alone?), but it greatly relieved Scilla.

The time spent in Ootacamund seemed perfect for the development of the four girls. They enjoyed the company of other British children and, as time passed, the older girls came to appreciate the attentions of the young men. All four daughters were strikingly attractive.

As his work was mainly amongst the British, members of the Army, planters and some government officials, it gave him opportunity to socialise in traditional British ways, something he had done little of since his Cambridge days. He took up riding again, had a try at golf, and, inevitably, returned to cricket. The club he played for made a number of tours and often played against Army teams. CT Studd would play cricket in the daytime and then evangelise among the soldiers in the evening. In spite of the fact that he had only rarely held a cricket bat since he retired from the game, his old skills came flooding back. In one period he made two double centuries, creating what was then an Indian record. A number of his daytime opponents would later look back at this time as when they had become Christians through the ministry of Mr Studd.

He also encouraged his daughters to become horse-riders but, instead of starting them off on easy mounts, he placed them on spirited ponies, which frequently bucked them off. On the occasions when he took them for carriage rides he insisted on driving up hills with fearful gradients and then down the other side. He thought it was a way to toughen up his girls, to prepare them for missionary service. He had no time for softness and genteelness as far as his offspring were concerned, even if they were female. To Grace, Dorothy, Edith and Pauline it was all a great adventure, full of fun and excitement, and they loved and admired their father for it.

The girls were provided with a governess, or more accurately three, over the period of their Indian sojourn, for each governess in turn found the Studd children difficult to handle. Edith Studd later reflected, 'We had nearly driven three governesses nuts, learning nothing ourselves but probably teaching them a thing or two.'

But amidst all the happiness of family life there was a major problem. Charlie's health was once more in poor condition. The high altitude proved to be no friend to him and he frequently awoke at night gasping for breath.

In 1906 it was decided to return to England but, before leaving, it was agreed that his four daughters would be baptised. Studd had some time before come to accept that baptism was for believers only. None of the Studds' daughters had been baptised as infants and, now that they were all genuine believers, it seemed a good idea for them to be baptised together without further delay.

As no baptistery existed Studd decided to construct one. He excavated a flower bed, purchased a zinc-lined bin to place in the hole and, as the day of the baptisms was cold, organised a team of Indian boys to fill it with hot water. The work of filling the receptacle proved harder than expected because it leaked. While the early part of the service continued inside the Studds' house, the boys continued to carry saucepans and pots of steaming water and pour it into the bin, which just refused to be filled.

The service was attended by numerous missionaries including Amy Carmichael. Charlie had instructed them to ask his daughters questions about their Christian experience, to see if they were suitable candidates for baptism. The questions satisfactorily answered by each, the happy father then baptised his daughters one at a time, pushing them under the still warm water.

During Studd's time in India he also helped establish a Christian school in Ooty: Hebron School. Today that school is a very successful and well-respected establishment. It is co-educational and caters mainly for boarders.

Once again CT Studd and his family returned to England, to London, to Hyde Park Gardens, to be greeted by a welcoming but ageing Dora Studd.

CHAPTER 23
No 'Chocolate Soldier'

'In peace true soldiers are captive lions, fretting in their cages'
CT Studd (*The Chocolate Soldier*)

The two years after this return to England were not happy ones for Studd. Certainly he was in demand, dashing from one speaking engagement to another, for this organisation and that. Many saw his value as a stirrer of men and used him to present his simple but challenging messages to a wide variety of people, assembled under a host of different umbrellas. Studd realised that this task was important but he was like a captive lion, fretting in a cage. He felt like a 'Chocolate Soldier', yet he knew that he was an 'altogether Christian', one who dared to take the Gospel to anywhere and to anyone; to fly in the face of danger and hardship, and to overcome opposition. But, here he was stuck in England trying to fan spiritual embers into flame, often, it seemed, without success. He prayed that God would give him the opportunity to return to the frontline once more and, for a while, his thoughts returned to India.

One day, while visiting Liverpool, an advertisement for some meetings caught his attention. It read:

CANNIBALS WANT MISSIONARIES!

He smiled at the cleverness of it but, whereas some who saw it might have been rather concerned about the reason for which cannibals wanted missionaries, CT Studd suspected he knew and decided to go along to find out the details. He attended one of the meetings. The speaker was German missionary, Karl Kumm, who had trekked across Central Africa to spread the Gospel.

Dr Kumm was an imposing figure, tall, broad shouldered, with a bushy, rather unkempt, beard. As Kumm rose to speak, Studd thought that his appearance was not unlike that of cricketer WG Grace, and, like Grace, though in a different way, he seemed to radiate boldness.

'Christian friends,' he began, 'I vont to challenge you tonight vith the needs of darkest Africa. In that vast continent there are many tribes who live in the depths of heathenism. They have never heard of God's love, of His saving power in our Lord Jesus Christ. Thousands of people, indeed, millions, destined for Hell. Souls vithout hope in this vorld or the next. Who cares about this? It seems no one cares.' His deep, mellow voice sounded out his despair.

'True, Christian missionaries from both your country and mine have gone to some parts of that land, yet in many other areas, particularly in Central Africa, the Vord of God has not been proclaimed. And while ve are inactive the Muslims are not!' Those words were emphasised with great force. 'The Islamic religion has a firm grip upon Northern Africa, and it is gradually, but steadily, sweeping south.' He waved his hand in an extravagant sweeping motion. 'It is taking its Gospel, which is not a Gospel, to more and more and more precious souls. And vot do ve do? Not'ing! Vot does the Christian Church do? Not a t'ing!'

Studd had already received the message and understood it. He was filled with a deep sense of shame: personal shame for his own withdrawal from the missionary scene (even though enforced by ill-health), and collective shame for a church that had become complacent.

'Why have no Christians gone?' Studd asked God in his mind.

Back came the answer, 'Why haven't you gone?'

'Because, the doctors won't permit it.'

'Am I not the Good Physician?' was the challenging reply.

Studd turned his attention to Kumm once more. He hung on every word that he spoke.

'Vot ve need is men and vimen of dedication and bravery to enter Africa and set up a chain of mission stations in areas as yet untouched by the Gospel of Jesus Christ.'

He then went on to outline some of his proposals in greater detail and concluded with the challenge, 'Then who vill go for Christ? Vill you?' His finger pointed to the left. 'Vill you?' He pointed to the right. 'Who vill go?'

His voice rose in pitch. 'Even tonight, thousands vill die vithout Christ. You cannot say, no! Vill you go?'

As the sound of Kumm's voice died away, the hall became totally silent. In that silence CT. Studd answered Kumm's question; indeed, God's question. He said, 'I will go.'

After the meeting he spoke to Kumm, told him of his resolve and arranged to meet and discuss the matter in more detail at a later date. But first there was a greater problem: his family. He knew that he would have to go without them. Of the two eldest daughters, Dorothy was already married, and it did not look as though Grace would be far behind her, so they presented no great difficulty. Edith and Pauline were still finishing their schooling and were independent enough not to be greatly distressed by their father disappearing into the African jungle. They, too, would naturally remain behind.

But, what about Priscilla? With her weak heart he knew that he could not take her with him, and he also realised that this type of venture would mean separation not just for months but for years. It would be hard to break the news to her but his mind was already made up. He had heard God's call. Not even the love he had for his wife could stop him. He decided that he would tell her as soon as he returned to Hyde Park Gardens.

Priscilla, not surprisingly, was shocked. 'Oh, Charlie!' she burst out. 'How could you? How could you?' Her voice rose in pitch as she spoke.

Charlie thought of reminding her that when they first were married that they both agreed to accept any separations that might arise from doing the Lord's work, but decided that now might not be the best moment.

'You know I can't say no to God, Scilla, and I am convinced that this is His will.'

'But, Charlie, you may be away for years. That's if Africa doesn't kill you first, which with your health it may well do. You really must rethink this.'

'No, Scilla, my mind is made up. I must go.'

'How could you do this, Charlie? Don't you ever think of me?'

Those last words stung but did not dent his resolve. 'I'm sorry, Scilla, but I must go.'

At that Priscilla stormed off to their bedroom, fell on the bed and cried until she could cry no more.

When Dora Studd heard the news she, too, was reduced to tears. Edith and Pauline were somewhat bemused by it all but knew well enough that when their father had made up his mind there was no changing it.

Studd realised, though, that this could not be a solo effort. He needed support. He accepted the offer of some friends to act as an organising committee, something he had no great appetite for himself, and began planning his departure. The members of the committee, under the leadership of William Bradshaw, agreed to support him up to the hilt, including with finance, but only if his doctor passed him fit enough to take on the arduous task of evangelising in the disease-ridden African jungles.

He agreed to see the doctor. The doctor examined him and made his report to the committee. Bradshaw then advised Studd that the doctor was not entirely happy with his health but that the committee were still prepared to back him providing he promised that he go no further south than Khartoum. They were afraid that the conditions in Central Africa would kill him.

Charlie Studd could make no such promise. He had to have the freedom to travel wherever he believed God was leading him. He refused to accept that limitation. The committee then withdrew its backing.

Ironically, his first attempt to leave the country for Africa, in the company of Karl Kumm, was thwarted by illness. He was on the point of leaving when he suffered a severe bout of malaria and had to postpone his departure. He later said, 'It was the only time that God agreed with the doctors.'

But some time afterwards, shortly after his fiftieth birthday, towards the close of 1910, he considered himself fit enough to go. He departed on a trip to northern Africa, intending to gauge the needs and to formulate how best they might be met. On the first night after leaving England he retired to his cabin and heard God speaking to him. 'This trip is not merely for the Sudan. It is for the whole un-evangelised world.'

But, how can that be? Studd thought. *I have no money and no support. Even my wife doesn't believe in what I am doing.* Then the thought came: *Faith in Jesus laughs at impossibilities.*

The whole trip took six months. On one ten-week trek, with two other missionaries, the conditions were so bad that twenty-five of the twenty-nine donkeys they took with them died, in spite of Studd's tender nursing. Studd's health remained good throughout this arduous journey, though upon his return to Khartoum he once more fell ill with malaria. During his time in the

Sudan he talked to various Christian leaders in different parts of that land, and determined that his target country would be the Belgian Congo, south of the Sudan.

He returned to England and began another whistle-stop tour to advertise the need for world mission, particularly in this case the Congo. He went back to Cambridge and spoke at the Guildhall, which was packed. CT Studd had never been one to mince words and on this occasion he used in his address the substance of what was to appear later in printed form as *The Chocolate Soldier*.

'Every true Christian is a soldier of Christ,' he began. 'A hero par excellence. Braver than the bravest. Bold and fearless.' His audience loved this. Such military analogies could always be guaranteed to stir pre-World War 1 listeners. 'Battle is the soldier's vital breath, and today what I am calling you to is nothing less than war against Satan's hordes.

'But the otherwise Christian is a chocolate soldier, dissolving in water and melting at the mere smell of fire. Sweeties they are! Bonbons! Lollipops!' He spat the words out with obvious contempt. 'Each clad in his soft clothing, a little frilled white paper to preserve his delicate constitution. The Christian Church is full of these chocolate soldiers. Many of you are chocolate soldiers.'

The mood of his audience changed discernibly. Who was CT Studd to talk to them like this? After all, their being at this gathering proved they were prepared to back him in his venture of faith. Why should he pick on them?

He continued on. 'God never was a chocolate manufacturer and never will be. God's men are always heroes. You can trace their giant foot-tracks throughout the pages of Scripture.'

He then proceeded to tell of Noah, Abraham, Moses and other great biblical saints, comparing their bravery with the cowardice of the Bible's 'chocolate soldiers', such as the ten spies who gave a bad report of the promised land.

Most of his listeners were feeling quite uncomfortable. They were not used to being addressed in this way. But, some were getting the message. They realised that Studd was right. If the world is to be won for Jesus Christ, then it would take dedication and heroism, not complacency and an unwillingness to dare.

'Last June, at the mouth of the Congo, there awaited a thousand prospectors, traders, merchants and gold seekers, waiting to rush into these regions as soon as the government opened the door to them. If such men hear so loudly the call of gold and obey it, can it be that the ears of Christ's soldiers are deaf to the call of God, and the dying calls of men? Are gamblers for gold so many and gamblers for God so few?

'We Christians, too, often substitute prayer for playing the game. Prayer is good, most certainly good, but when used as a substitute for obedience it is nothing but blatant hypocrisy. Today, God is calling you to dedicate your life to Him in the evangelisation of the world. He wants you.' His finger stabbed out to the right. 'And you.' He pointed to the left. 'Commit yourself to taking the Gospel to the Congo, to the rest of Africa, to the world. He is calling you to give up being a chocolate soldier and become a militant Christian. Dare to take the Gospel of Christ to the heathen, whatever the hardship and risks, and be sure there will be such. Trials and tribulations always await those who take God's call seriously.'

He stopped and looked around his audience. 'I think I know what some of you are thinking. Here I am Lord.' He paused. 'But, send my sister.' The joke was not lost on the congregation but scarcely anyone laughed. 'No, ladies and gentlemen, this is not the response God wants.

'When the great Isaiah received the call from God, what did he say? "Here am I; send me." Send me! Not somebody else, but me. It is all very well to pray to the Lord of the harvest to send out his labourers, the Bible tells us to do that, but what about you? God is calling you to take His Gospel to the heathen. Not someone else. You! What are you going to do about it?' Each time he emphasised the, 'you'.

The challenge had been made but what would be the response? Studd realised that there were those who were not too happy about some of the things he had said. The thought, *But I don't care a brass button about what many of them think*, went through his mind. But others were deeply moved by his words and passionate conviction. Over twenty came to see him after the meeting and gave their names as people willing to accept the call to Africa. Among them was a tall, slim young man with a shock of red hair: Alfred Buxton, the son of one of Studd's Cambridge contemporaries, Barclay Buxton, who had gone to Japan on missionary service at about the same time as Charlie had gone to China.

Alfred Buxton was different from Studd in almost every way. He was thirty years Studd's junior, quiet, with a cool, calm demeanour, and a willingness to listen to the views of others. But, both shared the same blazing fire: the desire to see the world won for Jesus Christ. According to Edith Studd, the young Buxton had, 'the truest of grey eyes that looked straight at you.' And she should know. She made sure she got close enough to look. Alfred and Edith already knew each other at this time, indeed they were corresponding, and a romance was blossoming but this was put on hold because of the likelihood of his departure to Africa.

It was not until 1913 that Studd and Alfred Buxton finally left England. When CT Studd had departed to go to China 28 years before, he had been treated like a hero. Now the attitude to him, even within the churches, was different. Charlie Studd had lost much of his popularity. Many regarded him as a fanatic; one who neglected his wife and family. But it did not matter to Studd what people thought about him and his actions, as long as he believed that what he was doing was the will of God.

CHAPTER 24

AFRICA

In the popular thinking in Britain at that time Africa was the 'dark continent'. Though certainly a mystery, it was not as great a one to the British as China. However, to the Victorians and Edwardians it was still a world of strangeness: a place full of superstition, heathen religion and abominable practices, all shrouded under the cloak of impenetrable jungle. Death by disease or savage cannibals awaited the unsuspecting traveller.

The Belgian Congo (now Zaire) is set in Central Africa and almost entirely landlocked. The mighty Congo River marks its northern border and, so dangerous is it in parts with its rapids and swamps, hemmed in by dense jungle, that it was not successfully navigated from source to mouth until as recently as 1974.

When the Portuguese first arrived at the mouth of the Congo in the fifteenth century the great kingdom of Kongo held sway on both sides of the river. But, in the next hundred years or so, the desire of the Portuguese for slaves resulted in war between the two powers and the eventual decline of that African kingdom.

From early in the seventeenth century a substantial portion of the territory inland was the home of the Bakuba: a loose federation of about twenty tribes, originally under the great chief Shamba Bolongongo. Shamba was a gifted and efficient leader, and it is claimed he had many supernatural powers. By the end of that century the Bakuba had spread their influence to most of the region, forcing other tribes, such as the forest pygmies, out of their traditional homes.

In the nineteenth century the territory on either side of the Congo River was divided between two colonial powers: the French controlled the northern part, while the Belgians ruled the southern. Not that controlled and ruled are necessarily the correct words, for much of these enormous regions, particularly what eventually became the Belgian Congo, had never been visited by Europeans. The harshness of the interior had been an adequate discouragement to would-be explorers.

It was not until David Livingstone, and later Henry Stanley, ventured into those areas that that part of Africa began to open up. Strangely, Livingstone had originally intended to go as a missionary to China but, because of the Opium War, was redirected to Africa, where he first arrived in 1841. Like Studd, Livingstone was a pioneer. He did not want to preach the Gospel where it was already being preached. He wanted to take the good news of Christ to those who had never heard it. So, with a mixture of religious zeal and explorer's curiosity he entered unknown parts.

On one of his courageous exploits, in 1869, Livingstone ventured into the eastern parts of the Congo, just west of Lake Tanganyika. It was during this journey that Stanley was sent in search of him and, in the 1870s, Stanley, himself, engaged in some heroic exploration in that region and further to the west and north. In the early 1880s King Leopold of Belgium, using Stanley's knowledge, laid claim to this vast part of central Africa. It was ratified as a colony under Leopold's personal control at the Berlin Conference in 1884-85, but his administration of it was inefficient and at times most brutal. The region eventually became an official Belgian colony in 1908.

Following Livingstone and Stanley, numerous Europeans ventured into the territory seeking fame and wealth. Also, Roman Catholic missionaries entered the Congo in abundance but few Protestants followed Livingstone's example. It was this land that CT Studd and Alfred Buxton intended to enter and their aim was to establish a chain of mission stations throughout the land.

CHAPTER 25
NO SACRIFICE TOO GREAT

'If Jesus Christ be God and died for me, then no sacrifice can be too great for me to make for him.' CT Studd

Shakespeare said, 'Parting is such sweet sorrow.' When Studd and Buxton left their respective loved ones there was plenty of sorrow, but a sorrow etched with heartache rather than sweetness. Both Charlie and Priscilla knew well enough that when they farewelled each other on January 13 1913, it would be years before they would see and touch each other again, if ever. For Charlie this was difficult enough, but he at least had the firm conviction that he was doing God's will. It was much harder for Priscilla. Right up until close to the time Charlie was due to leave she was still unable to share that belief.

Then, mercifully, conviction came. A few days before her husband was due to leave, Priscilla was travelling in a train reading a book. Her heart was heavy and she found it difficult to concentrate on it. At one point the book gave two Scripture references which she decided to look up when she arrived home.

Upon arrival at their new home in Norwood, purchased by Dora Studd, she found that everybody was out and the loneliness caused her to slip still further into a mood of despondency. She lit a fire in the living room and sat down in front of it but the warm glow gave her no comfort. Her mood sunk even lower and she began to cry and cry, as if she would never stop. As she sat there in tears the thought suddenly came to her about the two Bible references.

She rose from her chair, wiped her tears away with a handkerchief and found her Bible. Nestling back into the chair, she opened the well-worn book at Psalm 34 and through her still tear-moist eyes read: I will bless the Lord at all times; his praise shall continually be in my mouth.'

In a moment her mood changed. She felt herself gripped by the power of these words. 'I will,' she thought. 'That means determination. It means grit... courage. "I will bless." I should be making the Lord happy and that won't be done by weeping like this.' The thoughts came rapidly. 'The verse says, "I will bless the Lord at all times". That means now. Now is not the time for weeping, it is the time for blessing the Lord.'

She continued to read. Verse four hit her with force. 'I sought the Lord, and he heard me, and delivered me from all my fears.' Then verse 6: 'This poor man cried, and the Lord heard him, and saved him out of all his troubles.' The last three words seemed to stand out boldly. *If God could deliver David from all his troubles*, she thought, *then why not me? Why not Charlie?* She read on and looked also at the other Scriptures. By the time she had finished reading, her tears were gone.

Charlie, Alfred and the other three men going with them were leaving under the auspices of the Africa Inland Mission (AIM), though in Studd's case it was not without some misgivings. He was a little uneasy about the control that organisation might exercise over their work in Africa.

After the farewell meeting, the night before departure, a member of the audience accused Studd of deserting his family. It was not the first time that he had suffered such a charge, nor was it to be the last, but this time it particularly stung. He felt anger rise within him, which he could barely control. He looked the man directly in the eye.

'When God's Son came to Earth He sacrificed everything for us. What have *you* done for Him?' Studd's accusing emphasis on the 'you' and his penetrating glare, reduced the man to mumbling incoherency.

As the man stammered in embarrassment, Studd continued. 'If Jesus Christ be God and died for me, then no sacrifice can be too great for me to make for Him.' His antagonist departed in confused silence. This phrase, uttered in a moment of stress, was to become his watchword. It had entered his mind as a message to him from God.

The day of departure had been dreaded by all. They knew it would be difficult. That January Monday morning was cold and dreary, adequately reflecting their mood. Priscilla and most members of the family had decided to say their goodbyes in London, where the missionary party boarded the train bound for Dover. Charlie had never liked farewells and he felt awkward and unusually melancholy as he awaited the train's departure time.

He stood holding Scilla's hand, but neither of them seemed to know how to articulate their thoughts. Though Priscilla had come to accept the necessity of separation, this was still an agonising moment to be endured, rather than rejoiced in. She was determined not to cry; at least not until the train had left the platform.

In that strange way that happens at such times, each second seemed like an age, yet each minute hardly a moment. They both strongly desired this painful goodbye to end, yet could hardly bear the thought of its resulting separation.

'All aboard!' the railwayman called.

Charlie turned to his wife, looked into her eyes and grasped her tenderly. He held her and kissed her, knowing that he may never have another such opportunity. 'Goodbye, Scill. I love you.' The words sounded so inadequate, almost as if someone else was saying them.

'Goodbye, Charlie. You know I love you, too. God take care of you.'

He let go of her. Their fingers touched for the last time and Charlie climbed into the carriage. The whistle blew, the mighty engine stormed into life, and the train drew slowly away. Charlie peered through the little window and saw his beloved waving her farewell. Edith Studd and Barclay Buxton (Alfred's father) had decided to travel with the little party as far as Paris. Edith and Alfred had become engaged, though unofficially because of the likely lengthy separation. The parting for them was no easier and, in some respects, was harder.

Edith wanted to follow them to Africa, but both her father and her fiancé had forbidden it. It was too dangerous, at least initially, and it was essential that Alfred concentrate on the missionary task, rather than the needs of a wife. When they had established a bridgehead and had carried out some consolidation, then it might be considered but not before. How long might that take? Well, it was unlikely to be less than two years, and probably longer. Two years separation! How could she endure it? For Alfred, he would at least have the adventure of travel and danger. She would have little of value to while away the weeks and months of loneliness.

As the train left the Paris railway station Edith saw the two familiar faces framed in the carriage windows. It seemed to her that one was too old, the other too young but, even in the depths of her misery, she believed that she would see them both again.

Before the party had arrived in Africa Studd resigned from AIM. When they reached Mombasa in Kenya, where they disembarked, a cable from the mission awaited them, seeking to clarify the position of each member of the party. Had only Studd resigned, or had all of them done so? This forced each of the five to consider where they stood. Alfred Buxton decided to align himself with Studd and, therefore, also resigned. The other three members of the group expressed their intention of remaining under the AIM umbrella.

Now CT Studd felt free to pursue that which he believed to be the Holy Spirit's leadings. He had already formulated what he called his 'five smooth stones' of missionary policy, with which anyone who joined forces with him must agree. They were:
1. Absolute faith in the Deity of each Person of the Trinity.
2. Absolute belief in the full inspiration of the Old and New Testament Scriptures.
3. Vow to know and to preach none other save Jesus Christ and Him crucified.
4. Obedience to Christ's command to love all who love the Lord Jesus sincerely without respect of persons, and to love all men.
5. Absolute faith in the will, power and providence of God to meet our every need in His service.

He then formed his own organisation named the Heart of Africa Mission (HAM), which was built firmly and squarely upon those stones.

CHAPTER 26
Guess Who's Coming to Dinner

In March the two companions went by train inland to Nairobi. The cooler temperatures of the high altitude Nairobi were a great relief after the oppressive heat of the coastal city of Mombasa. But, whatever the conditions, Studd and Buxton had come to proclaim the word of God. Charlie preached several times at different churches in Nairobi, while they made the necessary preparations for their trek inland.

This done, they went by a variety of trains and steamers to Masindi in Uganda, through frequent torrential rain, finishing the last leg of the journey by motor car. They were now on the fringe of European involvement in Africa. To the west lay Lake Albert and, beyond that, regions that were only just being explored by white men, including much of the eastern portion of the Belgian Congo.

Their time in Masindi was not happy. There, Alfred was the first of the pair to experience the ravages of fever, African style. His senior partner nursed him back to health. Next, Alfred received a cable from England. He opened it in haste, eager to receive news from home, yet a little nervous about what it may convey. It was from his father. It read: 'Cannot consent you two going interior alone.' As Alfred scanned its brief message his face fell.

Charlie was watching and knew immediately something was amiss. 'What's wrong, young fellow?' he asked gently.

Alfred handed him the telegram but said nothing. Charlie read it and scowled. 'It seems to me you have a decision to make, Alfred.'

'Yes it does, doesn't it?' the crestfallen young man muttered.

Though they were not to know it until later, the cable had been triggered by some letters to the Buxton family from missionaries in Africa, who expressed grave doubts about what they called 'Studd's wildcat scheme'.

For the next twenty-four hours Alfred considered the problem. Should he continue into the jungles of Central Africa, or obey his father's instructions and turn back? He discussed it with Studd. To the experienced campaigner it was a simple case of black or white. Was Buxton going to obey God or man? Studd told him of the number of occasions that he had to disregard the advice of Christian men and women, who, to him, were counselling contrary to the will of God. The young Buxton was in precisely that same position. Studd asked him outright, 'Will you obey God or man?'

Alfred prayed the matter through and slowly came to the same conclusion as his companion. To refuse to continue their venture of faith would be direct disobedience to his Lord and Master. He knew that he must take the Gospel to the people of Central Africa whatever the risks. He cabled back: 'Must go on. Fear nothing. Psalm 105:12-15.' (Which reads: 'When they were but a few men in number; yea, very few, and strangers in [Canaan]; when they went from one nation to another, from one kingdom to another people; he suffered no man to do them wrong; yea, he reproved kings for their sakes; saying, "Touch not mine anointed, and do my prophets no harm."')

In their plan to move westward they gathered around them a little team of national porters and, with a brave sense of the absurd, acquired two bicycles to use when the terrain permitted. The next stage of their journey was to the eastern shore of Lake Albert, which marked the border between Uganda and the Belgian Congo.

But, as so often with decisions made in faith, that act was quickly tried in the fire. The first night out from Masindi they pitched their camp and settled down for the night. It was not long, however, before they were rudely awoken. At first Charlie thought it was a dream. It felt as if he was being eaten alive, little bit by little bit. He quickly came to his senses and realised that the source of his suffering was real enough. He was covered in insects which had decided to use him as a midnight snack. He leaped out of the tent and violently dusted the offenders off, as best he could. He then went to the camp fire, grabbed a blazing stick and returned to his tent to discover the identity of his tormentors, and to see what could be done about them.

As he peered through the flap in his tent he immediately recognised his attackers as ants: thousands of them. While he was investigating the problem he was rather careless with his makeshift torch. It touched the flap. The tent quickly caught fire and Studd stepped back in horror. By the time he and the rest of the party, already aroused by the noise he had been making, moved to deal with the inferno, it was too late. The tent and all it contained was destroyed.

In spite of the setback they continued on and eventually arrived on the eastern banks of Lake Albert. As they gazed across the wide stretch of water to the hills beyond its western bank, like Joshua on the banks of the Jordan, they felt their promised land beckoning to them from the other side.

The next day they crossed the lake on the steamer, leaving their porters behind, and finally set foot on the territory of the Belgian Congo. The crossing was pleasant enough, apart from the unnerving sight of the crocodiles cruising in the shallows on either side. For two men who intended to camp the following night on the western bank of Lake Albert, those gigantic amphibians presented a real concern, but at least they had arrived. Not that they were the first white men so to do. The steamer had been busy enough over the last year or two ferrying Belgian officials and European traders across this stretch of water. Not far from where they now stood was the Belgian Post, at which they would have to receive official approval for their entry. Nor, even, were they the first Protestant missionaries to venture this far. Some members of AIM had preceded them six months earlier.

They pitched their remaining tent. As they worked, they were plagued by hundreds of mosquitoes, with their infuriating, high-pitched hum and disease carrying stings. When the two men prepared their evening meal of porridge, flies swarmed around them getting in their food and their mouths as they ate.

They decided to spend the night outside the tent, under mosquito nets. Before retiring they prayed together and then stoked the fire to discourage the crocodiles or any other creatures from coming too close. They drifted into sleep, with the jungle chorus of mosquitoes, flies and crocodiles singing them a loud, discordant lullaby. It was not long before they awoke. The rain was coming down in torrents, so they were forced to take shelter in the tent.

The next morning the two Englishmen reported to the primitive Belgian Post and, making their request in schoolboy French, managed to acquire the necessary authorisation to go ahead with their plan. The Belgian authorities were more cooperative than expected but they warned them of the dangers ahead.

'Messieurs,' a tall Belgian official said, 'ahead of you are many fierce tribes and some of them are cannibals. Only a few weeks ago one man from our country was captured by one tribe, stripped, beaten and sent back here naked. Another, hunting elephants, was killed by a poisoned arrow. Others have just disappeared. We can only guess what's happened to them.'

Studd and Buxton may have only had a poor level of French but, with the Belgian's accompanying extravagant gestures, they were left in little doubt of what was being said.

'We know the dangers, monsieur,' Studd said in his broken French. 'But we believe that our God will protect us and, if not, we are not afraid to die.'

'The people you talk about are those we are most keen to take the Gospel to.' It was Buxton this time.

The official shrugged his shoulders. 'Well, you can't say you haven't been warned,' he said, stamping the papers in front of him.

'Anyway,' Studd continued, 'we think they may be more interested in our bicycles than us.'

'Bicycles?' the astonished Belgian asked.

'Yes, we intend to ride them where possible and carry them when it isn't,' Charlie replied.

The official shook his head and muttered under his breath about the craziness of the English. He handed over the completed papers. 'You will need native guides, too, messieurs. We will provide them for you. But, be warned, they will be reluctant to enter certain areas and you, if you have any sense, will heed their advice.'

Studd took the documents. 'Thank you, monsieur. You are most kind.'

When the guides had been provided, Studd and Buxton first went to make contact with the AIM missionaries in Mahagi, a few miles from Lake Albert. After amiable discussions, and having no shortage of country to divide between them, it was agreed that the newcomers would go to the west and the south, as the AIM, so far, had only been working in the north. Their immediate destination was Kilo, a small town not far from the southern tip of Lake Albert. It was known to have a Belgian presence but no church.

They began their trek but it was not long before they had the frightening experience of becoming separated from their guides. They were lost in unexplored African jungle. They decided to press on in the general direction they had been moving in; up and down hill after hill; through the heat and the rain, all the while hoping that they would meet up with their porters again.

They often had an uncomfortable feeling that they were being watched and, from time to time, encountered small villages. For the most part their bikes were useless, being burdens to bear, rather than vehicles of transportation.

At one stage they had walked and cycled for hours when suddenly they came across a tribesman with a basket slung over his shoulder. In one hand were a bow and some arrows. It was not clear who was more taken aback by the encounter, the two white men or the one black. The national looked at them nervously having heard, no doubt, that white men were not to be trusted.

Studd and Buxton, though, had noticed that in the basket were maize cobs and other food. They had not eaten for most of the day and they saw the answer to their immediate need in that basket. They decided to approach the tribesman slowly, smiling as they came.

The black man watched them cautiously and, when they began to get close, started to back away. Charlie grabbed his companion's arm to stop him going further forward, then with an energetic piece of amateur theatricals he made their need clear. The tribesman understood. He looked at his basket, then back at his strange, new acquaintances.

'If we want some food from him, I suppose we ought to give him something in exchange,' Alfred suggested.

'Yes, you're right of course, old chap. But what?'

Buxton smiled. 'You're always going on about not caring a brass button, why not try some of those,' he said, indicating the buttons on their trousers.

'Why not, indeed?' he said with a little laugh. 'I always thought trousers had too many of the wretched things, anyway.'

Studd reached for the knife at his side, and gently withdrew it. The African watched nervously. Studd proceeded to cut some surplus buttons from his garments, and then replaced his knife. He held the buttons at arm's length. The black man looked at them with interest as they glistened in the sunlight that filtered through the trees.

'Come on my friend,' Studd said gently. 'We won't hurt you. It's a fair exchange isn't it?'

The tribesman began to approach them slowly. When he was sufficiently close he peered intently at the shining objects in the white man's hand.

'They're yours, old chap, in exchange for some food,' Studd said, pointing to the basket with his other hand.

The black man reached out and took the offered trinkets with delight, examining them closely.

'Now, your part of the bargain,' Studd said, indicating the basket once more.

For the first time the African smiled, showing his teeth, which were filed to a point in the fashion of cannibals. He clutched the buttons in one hand and lowered his basket to the ground, indicating to the visitors that they could help themselves.

The two missionaries grabbed some cobs of maize and some sweet potatoes. 'Thank you! Thank you, so very much!' Studd said, smiling.

The black man looked at the two Englishmen, then back at the buttons. He said something which may well have been, 'Thank you, too', and quickly vanished amongst the trees.

'Well, Charlie, the Lord does provide in some mysterious ways, doesn't He?'

Studd laughed again. 'He does indeed. I never expected a cannibal to provide us with food. Hallelujah!'

They pitched camp, using their only tent, and ate the unexpected bounty. Sleep came quickly once more, in spite of the zing and the nip of the persistent mosquitoes and the monkeys chattering in the trees.

They set off early next day and tramped through the undergrowth in what they presumed was the correct direction. At least they were moving south, so they were reasonably optimistic that they would meet up again with their guides, who they assumed were looking for them. The only sign of human life they experienced that morning, though, was the distant sound of drums, spreading unknown news from place to place.

In the middle of the afternoon they became rooted to the spot. Barring the way ahead of them was a group of fierce-looking tribesmen, armed with bows and arrows and, like the man previously encountered, with their teeth filed to a point.

To the two white men, this looked as though it might be a sudden end to their missionary endeavour. Here ahead of them were the cannibals they had come to convert, or so they assumed, but it seemed highly unlikely that they would get any opportunity to present the Gospel to them. The missionaries feared that these warriors had other, rather final, plans for them.

The black men moved closer and surrounded the two Englishmen. Studd and Buxton prayed silently to God. 'Is this the end? If so, let it be quick.'

One of the Africans addressed them animatedly and pointed with his spear in the direction they had previously been going. The circle of warriors opened and the two white men were left in no doubt that they were expected to walk through the gap provided. Left with no option they did so, and found themselves continuing on their way, but now accompanied by jabbering tribesmen, especially curious about the strange wheeled contraptions that these peculiar white men insisted on carrying with them.

They soon arrived at the tribal village situated in a clearing in the jungle. There to greet them was their friend of the previous day, still holding his collection of buttons. Upon seeing him, Studd and Buxton felt a little more relaxed. He still seemed friendly enough. He pointed to a big open fire, above which hung the carcass of an antelope. Their friend made gestures to them indicating that dinner would soon be served. It quickly became apparent that the two missionaries were honoured guests, rather than items on the menu.

As Charlie and Alfred settled down to eat with their new found friends, they could not help reflect that if they were to have dinner with cannibals, there certainly was no better way than this. They stayed the night with their hosts, not without a little nervousness, but came to no harm.

The next day, after parting with a few more buttons, they set off once more in the presumed direction of Kilo and, after giving up hope of linking up with their guides again, suddenly encountered them. The remainder of the journey to Kilo passed without further mishap.

CHAPTER 27
The Heart of Africa

Studd and Buxton came to know Kilo better than they had intended; not that there was that much to know about it. It was the home of a Belgian official and a number of other Europeans, most of whom were on the search for gold and, of course, numerous Africans. The missionaries had planned to make it the initial base for their activities in that region but not remain there. But they were, however, forced to stay for three months, while awaiting their main supplies. They pitched their tents at the back of the town store, which was run by a Greek man. Conditions were primitive; the weather hot and wet.

Inevitably, it seemed, Studd became stricken with fever. Buxton nursed him back to health but it was not long before the older man once more fell ill. This time the fever was much worse than the earlier bout. Buxton cared for him, dosed him with such medicines as they possessed, but this time there was no improvement. CT Studd appeared to be dying.

It was a depressing time for the younger man. Here he was in an alien environment, with his friend and only Christian contact for miles around slipping rapidly, it seemed, towards eternity. Outside their tents the rain teemed down, flooding the surrounding ground, so that eventually the water seeped even into their shelter. Buxton felt so alone. At times even God seemed far away. Frequently Studd was delirious, and only occasionally coherent.

In one of Studd's lucid moments once more James chapter five came to his mind. '*Call for the elders*' he thought. *Elders? There's only one Christian here and he's barely twenty-one. Never mind, he'll do.* '*Anointing him with oil. What could we use for oil*? *Why, kerosene, of course.*

He told his companion the plan. Alfred was desperate enough to try anything. He brought the container of kerosene over to his friend, dipped his finger in it, and anointed the ailing man. He then knelt down on the wet floor of the tent and pleaded with God to restore Studd's health.

The next morning the missionary pioneer had remarkably improved and in the succeeding days continued to do so.

But more troubles were at hand. While Studd had been at his worst a letter had arrived from Priscilla. When he was well enough to open it he learned that his beloved wife had collapsed and, for a while, had been in a serious condition. Though the letter did advise that she was 'daily feeling a wee bit better', it still conceded that her heart was 'not much to boast of'. However, unknown to Charlie, by the time he had received the letter there had been a further improvement in his wife's condition.

In addition he received a letter from England advising him that the committee, which had been formed to back his project, was considering resigning because of his split with AIM. He was furious. He wrote back, 'Tell the committee I'm not the man who has only gone to look and see, to pioneer and select stations; I've come to do the real job and fight for God against the devil.' CT Studd intended to continue waging war against the hosts of the evil one, even if it meant fighting on alone.

But, good news came too. Studd had become a grandfather. His daughter Dorothy, married to the Rev. Gilbert Barclay, had given birth to a daughter, Ann.

While still marooned in Kilo he received the first issue of the Heart of Africa Mission (HAM) magazine, produced by Priscilla. He was delighted with it, except that it contained so many photos of himself that he had reservations about sending it to anyone, in case it gave the impression that this new work was 'Studd's mission'. Even though he was prepared to continue on alone, he hated the idea of any work being labelled 'his', for he knew it was God's. While he was still convalescing he began to think about the future direction of HAM. If Africa, why not the world? Asia, like Africa, desperately needed the Gospel, he knew that well enough, and so did South America. What was needed was a mission that embraced the world.

The awaited supplies arrived in August and Studd considered himself strong enough to venture forth into more dangerous regions. Buxton, however, was not so sure. He knew his companion had been very close to death and wondered whether they should delay their expedition a little longer.

Charlie would have none of it. 'I have a sound backbone, a hot heart, and faith in the Lord. That's more than enough to see me through,' was his response to Buxton's concerns. Whatever doubts Alfred still retained he kept to himself. He knew there was no arguing with his companion when he was in that mood.

Like the explorers before them they assembled a team of national porters, numbering about seventy, and set off in a north-westerly direction, intending to reach Dungu. For four days the party struggled through the difficult terrain. At times the two missionaries were able to use their bikes but, for the most part, they had to struggle up and down hill, through the dense Ituri Forest, frequently slipping on the rain-soaked jungle floor. Occasionally the sun was sighted peeping through the gigantic trees which formed a canopy above them but for most of the time they trudged on in semi-darkness.

Their porters told them the area was the home of pygmies: descendants, no doubt, of those who had been forced from their homes by Bakuba tribesmen centuries before. But Studd and Buxton never saw any of them. The pygmies, though, must have been well aware of the interlopers in their territory. The missionaries made it hard for them not to know, for they insisted on singing Sankey hymns at full volume to cheer them on their way.

When they reached a Belgian post at the end of the fourth day, the porters, who had already shown much reluctance to work, refused to set camp and also made it clear that they would not go any further. While Studd had been sick, Buxton had spent the time in between his nursing duties learning the local language, Bangala. He now did his best to encourage the reluctant bearers to continue the trek. He was unsuccessful. For a frustrating two weeks they remained where they were. They could not persuade their men to go on, nor, for some time, could they obtain any others to replace them.

Eventually, replacements were found, and the journey was continued. After another week, through friendlier terrain over which the bicycles were more useful, they arrived at Arebi, a military post, and established camp there. They then pressed on to Dungu, and arrived on October 8.

Once again they were faced with disappointment. The AIM, in spite of the agreement made between its representatives and Studd, had decided, after all, to establish a station in Dungu, and had four missionaries already there.

Studd was angry but he was never interested in fighting with other Christians; there were too many in need of the Gospel for that. He made it clear that he strongly disapproved of their act and then decided to look for another centre to base his own outreach.

While in Dungu they made friends with Count Ferdinand de Grunne, the chief Belgian official there. This imposing, giant of a man treated them with great kindness. He allowed them to use one of the government huts for the duration of their stay, and was very helpful in sharing his knowledge of the whole district. After discussions with him, they selected Niangara to the west as their new base and pencilled in another centre, Nala, as a likely spot for a second mission station. The Count also encouraged them to continue with their learning of the Bangala language, which proved to be the lingua franca of that area.

Late one afternoon, as they were about to commence their evening prayer time before moving on to their new base, the sky became heavy with dense, black clouds.

'Looks like we're in for a storm, Charlie,' Buxton said, surveying the heavens.

Before Studd could respond rain fell down upon them in torrents. They hurried into their temporary accommodation but were already soaked to the skin. They dried themselves off as best they could and, through a little window, watched the rain pour down.

'Well, there's no point in wasting time, Alfred. We were about to spend some time in prayer, so let's do so.'

A loud clap of thunder pronounced the 'Amen!' to that suggestion and the two men began to pray. The noise of the storm outside was so loud they could barely hear their own voices but they were comforted by the thought that this noise was no barrier to God.

The rain pattered noisily. The thunder roared. Suddenly, there was a terrible bang, the ground they were kneeling on shook, and bits of the roof fell down upon them. The rain, which had previously just leaked through in one or two places, now came cascading through the thatched roof. The lamp went out.

'Are you alright, Alfred?' Charlie shouted in the darkness.

'I think so,' the stunned Buxton called back. 'We must have been hit by lightning.'

'Quickly! Move our stuff into the drier parts of the hut. Get it off the ground.'

'But, Charlie,' Buxton cried out urgently, 'the roof's on fire!'

Studd looked up. 'Don't worry about that. The rain will douse it.'

Buxton cast another look above him and was unsure his companion was right. Before either of them could think further, a figure appeared in the doorway gesticulating wildly. It was one of the Belgians. 'Get out! Get out quickly, before the house burns down!'

In spite of the rain the fire was catching hold. Without another word the two Englishmen began to rapidly salvage their possessions, taking as much as they could out into the wet. By this time a crowd of excited Africans had gathered outside watching the developing conflagration.

Then Count de Grunne, wrapped only in a towel, appeared on the scene. He grabbed Charlie by the arm. 'Is everybody safe, Monsieur Studd?'

'Yes, nobody is hurt, thank God. But we've lost some of our equipment I'm afraid.'

It suddenly dawned on Studd that there was a box of cartridges in the burning building. When the fire reached them there would be a highly dramatic firework display, and a dangerous one at that.

'What about the cartridges? Did you get them out?' he asked Buxton.

'They're still in there! Get everyone out of the area immediately.'

The two Englishmen and the Count started urging the Africans to move out of range. Some, sensing the urgency in the Europeans' manner complied, but others needed extra persuasion. Before they had all cleared the open area in front of the house, the shells began to explode in rapid fire shooting in all directions. Those tribesmen who had been reluctant to move before quickly scurried for cover.

Studd and Buxton watched the display from behind one of the other houses. 'Guy Fawkes Day's come a bit early this year, Alfred,' Charlie joked.

His companion laughed, in spite of the seriousness of the situation. 'So it would seem.'

They both ducked as another load of cartridges exploded. It was not long before the unintended display concluded and shortly after that the fire was extinguished by the rain. They returned to their possessions, still lying in the wet outside the burned out hut and, with the help of some of the Africans, ferried them to a drier spot.

As it turned out not too much was lost. After five or six days in Dungu they began to make their way to Niangara by canoe, a journey which took three days. They had then arrived in what had been called, 'The very heart of Africa'. It was from there that their work in Africa was to radiate.

CHAPTER 28
MISSION ESTABLISHED

In Niangara they once more experienced the kindness of the Belgian officials, who loaned them a government house and, with the help of Count de Grunne, they successfully negotiated the purchase of a large piece of land on which to establish their mission.

At first Charlie thought that God could not have done better than send them to Niangara. The town was ideally situated in a densely populated area, surrounded by a variety of tribes, most of which had, at least, a little understanding of Bangala. The difficulties of the past few weeks could all now be viewed as overseen by the Lord's providence. *How great is our God*, Studd thought.

However, there was some opposition from the local chiefs about their erecting mission buildings in that region. One in particular, Baragweni, fiercely opposed them. So, after gaining just a toehold in Niangara, the two Englishmen decided to press on to the south-west. They hiked for five days, eventually arriving in Nala. Nala was like a dream come true. It was an abandoned Belgian post and, consequently, much of the building work which they had expected to be necessary was already done. They just had to commandeer the empty buildings and use them for mission purposes. Mosquitoes were fewer there than in other parts they had visited, food was plentiful, and people abounded. It was as close to ideal as one could expect for European missionaries trying to establish themselves in the African environment.

When they arrived back in Niangara they were delighted to learn that the African chiefs – even Baragweni, whose objections had previously presented an obstacle to them – were now cooperative. Studd was able to obtain land concessions in Niangara and Nala and, later, Poko and Bambili, further to the west. Gradually they learned the ways of the Congolese tribes among whom they were working. Polygamy and adultery were normal. Some of the chiefs had many wives. The women were frequently cruelly treated. Spirit worship abounded and cannibalism, though it was officially outlawed by the Belgian authorities, was still practised by some tribes.

By April 1914, in Niangara, they had built their own rather unimposing house, which they nicknamed Buckingham Palace, and were generally accepted by the local population. True there had been no conversions yet but opportunities for presenting the Gospel were increasing with time. They even had been able to speak to Baragweni and his tribe about Christ.

If the situation on the battlefront was encouraging, the news from home base was little better than disastrous. Mail came infrequently and not always in order. One letter arrived from Priscilla telling him the disturbing news that she had been so ill that she had nearly died. His heart went out to her. But, the letter went on, after Lord Radstock, a member of the HAM Committee, had prayed for healing she had shown significant improvement, though she was still not really well.

Later a letter arrived from her doctor advising Studd that his wife was so ill he must come home immediately. A glance at the date at the top of this letter indicated that it had been written before Priscilla's, so was now out of date. Charles Studd could not help but think that the Lord must have His hand even in the postal service. This letter's late arrival had saved him having to make a very difficult decision.

Then, he received the terrible news of the death of Radstock's son and Studd's son-in-law, Martin Sutton (Grace's husband). As Sutton was also chairman of the HAM Committee this left Priscilla, partly bedridden, to soldier on with little help, amidst the agony of family bereavement.

Such worries, on top of his own struggle coming to terms with conditions in Africa, would have driven most people to despair but Studd was not a quitter. His faith in God was real, his determination strong. Yet he was not unrealistic. He knew that the job ahead would be long and difficult. But, he believed, the great thing was that God was on his side. Studd mused, 'It is grand to be launched into a fight when you know you have not a mortal chance of winning, for one knows He will win it for you.'

One day Studd and Buxton were working in the mission compound when an African helper, Shamba, came rushing up to them, screaming, 'Mamba! Mamba! Mamba!'

The two missionaries looked up at the man, saw a strange mixture of fear and awe on his face, and tried to grasp what he was saying.

'Mamba! Mamba!' he repeated. 'Come at once.'

He signalled them to follow him. The man rushed off in the direction of the 'Palace', but kept looking back to make sure Studd and Buxton were still following him. When they reached the house the tribesman stopped outside the door and pointed frantically into the house. 'Mamba! Mamba!'

It was a word the two Englishmen had not encountered before so they did not know what to expect, but the African's manner made it clear extreme caution was necessary. They entered the house. Light streamed through the window and the open doorway, but they could see nothing unusual.

'There, Bwana!' Shamba stood by the door, pointing to Studd's bed.

Studd looked around the room and saw a stout stick that he frequently used on his treks in the bush. He grabbed it and slowly approached his bed. When he was close enough he gently lifted the blanket with the stick. Out slithered a green snake. The sun, beaming through the window, highlighted the brilliance of its colour.

'Mamba! Mamba!' Shamba repeated, from a safe position behind Studd.

The three men all trained their eyes on the deadly reptile. 'Move away from the door, Alfred, and take Shamba with you,' Studd instructed.

Buxton did so but said nothing. The snake, meanwhile, moved away from the bed and began to slither in the direction of the door, its tongue flicking out menacingly. Studd manoeuvred to give the creature a clear path to the exit. When it was close he quickly moved towards it and, with a deft flick with the stick, propelled it through the open door. He followed it into the bright sunlight. To his surprise there were now dozens of Africans around the house, having been attracted by the noise. They, almost as one, stepped back with a gasp of astonishment as the reptile slid on its way before them.

Before Studd could act one of the warriors strode forward and with one thrust of his spear killed the venomous creature. A shout went up from the watchers. Studd sighed with relief but found breathing difficult after all the excitement.

Shamba started talking at a great rate of knots, advising the other Africans of what had happened. Buxton understood some of what was said but Studd, little. The national spoke too quickly. As Shamba's fellow tribesmen and women listened to him, they began to look at Studd in awe.

Charlie found the look unnerving. 'What's this all about, Alfred? Did you understand any of it?'

'Not much, Charlie, I'm afraid. It was a bit too quick for me. I'll ask Shamba.' He approached the African and asked him to explain.

Once more Shamba began to speak at great pace. Buxton signalled to him to slow down.

The African let out a great sigh and began to speak more slowly. This time Charlie grasped the meaning of a little of it, while Alfred comprehended most of what was said.

'I'm still not clear, Alf. What's all this fuss about?'

'As you probably guessed, that Mamba snake is deadly. If it bites you, you don't last too long.' Buxton paused. 'And, they assume that last night it crept into bed with you. Not surprisingly they can't make out why you're still alive.'

Amidst all the frenzied activity the possibility that he had slept all night with a deadly snake in his bed had not occurred to Studd before. A look of horror came over his bearded face.

Buxton noticed the change in colour in his friend's complexion. 'Are you alright, Charlie?'

For a moment Studd said nothing but then he pulled himself together. 'Yes, old chap, I'm fine. If they're right, I've had a close shave, eh?'

'You have, indeed. A bit like the Apostle Paul, when he was shipwrecked and landed in Melita. That snake actually bit him.'

Studd looked down at his lean body and arms and then smiled grimly. 'No sign of snake bites on me, Alf. Hallelujah! Our God is good, indeed, eh?'

He went down upon his knees. Buxton joined him and they prayed their thanks to God, whilst the Africans gazed on in astonishment.

More post came from England advising of difficulties in finding new recruits for the mission. Although five men were already preparing to join the two pioneers, Studd had been repeatedly writing home for a lot more than that, such was his vision. But Studd's reputation in England had declined and few were prepared to back his judgment. During his final days in England the manner in which he had condemned the English Church had alienated many and, since arriving in Africa, the abrasiveness of some of his letters and his split with AIM had caused even more to regard him as an irritating crank.

Buxton advised him to tone down the severity of his letters but he would not listen. Priscilla urged him to come home for a while to attend to affairs on the home front, believing that his presence would make the difference to those who might be wavering. However, Studd was not yet satisfied that the mission was sufficiently well established to return to England. He felt they needed a firmer base in Africa first.

The two men returned to Nala, marked out their land concession, and successfully improved relations with the tribes in that area. Their bikes were still a great source of attraction to the Africans, who ran beside the white men as they pedalled their way through the jungle. The lean, but powerful, black bodies glistened with sweat as the sun's rays peeked through the foliage. When the vegetation was too dense to cycle there was no shortage of volunteers to carry their bicycles. Studd and Buxton could not help reflect that some of these tribes had the reputation for being cannibals, but for the most part the two Englishmen were treated like honoured guests. They moved further west to Poko and Bambili to sight the land there, and then discussed the various possibilities about returning to Britain.

It was quickly agreed that Charlie had to go back, and soon, but what about Alfred? Thoughts of Edith Studd had never been far from his mind so, from a personal point of view, returning to England and then travelling back to the Congo with her as his wife had considerable attraction. But, what was best for the work of God? That was the key issue to them.

When news arrived that the five new missionaries were already on their way it was agreed that Alfred had to remain. It would be his task to further the contacts made with the African tribes and to help the new men find their feet, establishing them in their respective posts. In Bambili the two men said goodbye. Buxton returned to Niangara to await the reinforcements, while Studd proceeded westward along the River Congo and eventually back to Britain.

It was not plain sailing for any of them. On the way to Central Africa one of the new missionaries died; a frequent occurrence for Europeans new to Africa. This set in focus the dangers inherent in their campaign. Alfred was thus left with just four to add to his workforce of one. At first the quartet remained at Niangara to find their feet. By this time Alfred was quite fluent in Bangala and was able to converse readily with the tribesmen as well as preach the Gospel to them. He was even beginning the task of translating the Bible into that language.

It was not long before they had the joy of seeing a handful of the nationals won to Christ, the first being Shamba, and in June 1915 Buxton conducted the first three baptisms. After the new converts had testified to their faith, they went down to the river to be baptised by Alfred, while pistol shots echoed in the jungle air. The shots were not fired by way of celebration. Edgar Coles, a new arrival, was shooting to try to keep the crocodiles at bay. Later, the new missionaries were despatched to other stations. Six months after the first baptisms in Niangara, eighteen converts were baptised at Nala.

Studd, meanwhile, found Britain a different country to the one he had left. She was now at war with Germany. By the time of his arrival, early in 1915, hopes of a quick end to the war were fast disappearing, as the conflict escalated and the casualty toll rose. How could he find men to fight on God's battlefield when so many were volunteering to be annihilated fighting for a lesser king? Alfred Buxton's brother, George, had intended to sign up with HAM, but the advent of the war had seen him enlist in quite a different army. He was killed in 1916.

Though Charlie was delighted once more to be in the arms of his wife, mission responsibilities frequently took him away from her. To him it was all part of God's service. Priscilla was just glad to be able have him close at hand for at least some of the time. She had, though, in spite of her poor health, already established an effective headquarters at their home in Norwood, and this was an invaluable platform for the task he faced.

But, he also found himself in disagreement with some members of the committee. Studd insisted that HAM was to be a faith mission. Individually or collectively, its members were never to ask anyone other than God for money or provision. They were to live by faith in God's bounty. Not all on the committee agreed, so there were more resignations.

In addition, his health was not good, with recurring bouts of malaria and asthma. But war, resignations, poor health and disputes over finance could do nothing to dent his determination to win, not just Africa, but the world for

Christ. Like a warrior of God he soldiered on. He sought 'lion-hearted' men and women 'who rejoice in hardship.' He wanted people prepared to dare nothing less than all for God.

On 1 July 1916 the Battle of the Somme began in France. On that first terrible day the British Army suffered 60,000 casualties, the most it had ever experienced in one day. Two weeks later an army of just eight left England under the leadership of 'General' CT Studd. Its task was to capture Central Africa for God; just part of an overall campaign to win the world to Christ. In the party was Studd's daughter Edith, a missionary with self-confessed mixed motives.

Once more Studd said goodbye to his wife, with the possibility it would be for the last time.

CHAPTER 29

New Life in the Jungle

Though the sea voyage to the Congo was largely without incident, wartime conditions prevailed, with all the portholes being blacked out. A vessel travelling along the same route a few weeks later was, in fact, sunk by a German torpedo.

In spite of further bouts of malaria, Studd spent a great deal of time on board teaching his little army about the biblical principles of missionary work and the practical details of living in Central Africa. The party of five men and three women arrived in Matadi at the mouth of the Congo River just before the end of September, and then travelled twelve hours by train to Kinshasa. There they caught a steamer and began the slow, slow journey up the Congo. On her first Sunday in Africa, Edith Studd recalled singing a hymn, the chorus of which ran:

Death cometh once; hear now his tread,
Soon shall you and I be lying, each within our narrow bed.

She found herself wondering who would be the first of this little party to experience that death which 'cometh once.' It was a solemn start to her missionary career.

The thousand kilometre journey along the river took several months. They found the stifling hot days trying, but the cool evenings brought welcome relief. At the end of their trip by steamer they knew that Alfred Buxton would be waiting for them to accompany them on the last leg of the trek, nearly five hundred kilometres on foot to Nala. Then they would be able to launch into the work they longed to do.

As they steamed along on the final day of the river stage of the journey, Studd summoned his troops up on deck for a Bible reading. The steamer's crew, and the handful of other passengers, had come to regard such practices with sneering contempt, but it made no difference to the missionaries, least of all their leader. As Studd read through the story of Paul before Ananias in Acts 23, his daughter found her thoughts wandering. It had been nearly four years since she had seen her fiancé. She wondered whether she would still love him. Would he still love her? The fact that a few days earlier her engagement ring had fallen irretrievably into the mighty Congo did little to allay her fears. Was it an omen?

Studd concluded the reading, prayed, and the little party rose and went to the side of the steamer, and began looking expectantly for their destination. Very soon they caught sight of a little wooden jetty in the distance. As they drew closer they saw a number of unidentifiable figures, who appeared to be looking in their direction. The Studds gazed keenly at the little group to see if Alfred Buxton was there. Edith was excited and nervous at the same time. She longed to see him, but was afraid he might have changed from the man with whom she had fallen in love.

'Is that him?' one of their colleagues asked. 'There! The one with the beard.'

Edith peered at the group on the pier as the boat drew closer each second. *Surely Alfred wouldn't be wearing whiskers for our first meeting in four years*, she thought. She looked at the man with a beard. He had red hair sure enough but as they drew a little closer it became obvious it was not him. 'No,' she said, 'that's not him.'

She couldn't help but feel a little uneasy because she still could not see her fiancé. 'Can you see him, father?' she asked with concern.

Studd gave a little laugh, amused at his daughter's eagerness. 'Your young eyes are better than mine, my dear. If you can't see him, how can you expect me to?'

'Look! Is that him?' She did a little jump of excitement. 'Yes, it is. It's Alfred.' Her voice increased in pitch at the pleasure of the discovery. 'Oh father, he is there, waiting for us.'

'Well, I told you all along that he would be, didn't I?'

Eventually the vessel reached the jetty. The Studds and their little group went down to the lower deck to prepare to disembark. Before they could do so the slim, scruffy figure of Alfred Buxton had hurried up the gangplank and had joined them on the steamer.

'Hello, old chap,' CT said warmly. 'How have things been going?'

His greeting was met by silence. Young Alfred's attention was wholly on Edith.

'Hm! That's young love, I suppose,' Studd grunted to no-one in particular. He then shepherded the remainder of his flock away, scattering the ship's chickens in the process. 'We'd better leave them for a while, I think. They need to get reacquainted.'

Edith and Alfred both found themselves possessed by an uncertain joy. As they gazed at each other, they soaked in the pleasure of seeing one another once more, yet, somehow, it all seemed so unreal. They had become so used to being apart, they were not quite sure that they knew how to be together. Many times during the past few years they had imagined this moment, but they had never expected it to feel quite so uncomfortable. They were largely oblivious of their surroundings, painfully aware of each other, yet uncertain how to respond.

After what seemed an eternity, Alfred stepped forward and clasped his fiancée's hands. 'It's wonderful to see you, Edith.' The words sounded totally inadequate to him but to Edith it was like music.

If on the trip along the Congo she had harboured doubts about her love, now they had all been dispelled. This quiet, unassuming man, much more mature since she last saw him yet of no apparent difference in character, was the same one who had won her heart four years before.

'You, too, Alfred,' she said. Her voice sounded distant, almost as though someone else was speaking.

He drew her close to him and held her tightly in his arms. As they embraced he felt her tears wetting his shirt, as she cried tears of pure joy. For both of them, now, the uncertainty had gone. They knew their love had survived the stresses of separation. For a few quiet moments they walked the decks together, hand in hand.

Almost as if by set time CT appeared back on deck. He was carrying a new coat. 'This is for you, Alfred,' he said, holding it out towards his friend. 'I thought you would need a new one by now.'

Suddenly, Alfred found himself back in the real world. He let go of Edith's hand and for the first time looked at his future father-in-law. 'Why, that is kind of you, CT. I really appreciate it.' He took the jacket and tried it on. 'How does it look, Edith?'

'Very smart! You'll have to wear that for the wedding.'

'I will, indeed,' he said with a whimsical smile. 'I've certainly nothing else suitable.'

Studd then introduced the new missionaries, who had now reappeared, and they all disembarked together. After a couple of days wait they boarded a smaller steamer and completed the river stage of their journey. They then commenced the last phase of the trek, by foot to Nala.

On the final day they arose early, broke camp and began their tramp over the rugged terrain. Even though it was early in the morning it was already quite hot, and their clothes stuck to them as they fought their way along through the dense growth. After they had been travelling for about an hour they heard a strange noise. Up ahead came the heavy sound of a native drum – not in itself unusual in the African jungle – but accompanied by a strangely, unexpected style of singing. The music sounded familiar to Studd, yet somehow different.

Then, suddenly, bursting through the trees came dozens of Africans. They were an excited reception party from Nala, containing Christians and non-Christians alike, all intent on welcoming back Bwana Mukubwa (Great White Chief). Four of the larger nationals carried one enormous drum, and atop that was a little boy, beating it for all his worth. The remainder were singing at the tops of their voices, in beautiful harmony, something that sounded vaguely like a 'Sankey', though Studd could not quite place it.

The little 'tribe' quickly surrounded the trekkers, a rather unnerving experience for some of the newcomers, and excitedly jostled each other to take their turn in shaking Studd's hand. They then formed a noisy escort for the remainder of the journey, eventually arriving in Nala at about midday, where the missionaries were given a further warm greeting. Amongst the welcoming committee was Chief Baragweni, who had originally opposed Studd and Buxton in Niangara. He was now a Christian.

Studd was weary when they arrived. He was still suffering the after effects of fever. But his delight with what confronted him overcame his physical disabilities. This reception was beyond his wildest dreams. He did not see it as a personal accolade; rather as an affirmation of the triumph of the Gospel.

They stayed three weeks in Nala, while Studd regained his strength and he and Buxton helped the new missionaries settle in. Alfred and Edith made their wedding plans and, like her parents before them, knew they would have to have their marriage solemnised by European officials to make it legal in Britain. They decided to travel to Niangara to be married there by her father, and then have that ceremony followed by another conducted by Belgian officials to meet the legal requirements.

So the three of them set off once more on a trek, accompanied by another noisy group of national Christians, intent on being witnesses to the first white wedding in that part of Africa. After the wedding Edith and Alfred went up river on a brief honeymoon. Studd returned to Nala, which he now regarded as his headquarters, to organise the distribution of his troops to the districts where the mission had already gained a foothold.

The awareness of the missionary presence had spread over a vast area, and some chiefs sent representatives to visit Nala, with the intention of inviting the missionaries to come to their tribe. One such chief was Jabori.

The thought of Jabori and his men approaching a village was enough to send its inhabitants scurrying desperately for cover. For some years he had been a man of frightening reputation and, in recent times, had been used successfully by the Belgians to subdue other tribes. When it was learned that he was on his way with a group of warriors, fear gripped the people.

Studd was a little uneasy, but so much of his life had been spent dealing with danger, from fast bowling on the cricket field to mobs in China and cannibals in Africa, that one more danger did not unsettle him greatly. He called his people together for prayer and waited.

The expected attack came, if attack it could be called. Laden with spears, Jabori and his warriors marched into Nala and demanded to see the missionaries.

Studd came out and greeted him a little cautiously. Jabori stated his purpose and the missionary sat down with the visitors to listen to his story. The chief told Studd about his life as a warrior. He need not have done, for the Englishman was already aware of it, but he listened quietly. Then the African went on to tell the primary reason for his visit.

'You see, Bwana, a few years ago I became very ill. For days my people treated me with our traditional medicines, and the witchdoctor used his charms, but I only became worse. Eventually...' and here he hesitated. 'Eventually, Bwana, I died.'

Studd showed no sense of surprise at the statement. He had seen enough in Africa and China not to be surprised by anything.

Jabori continued, 'Then my friends', the African indicated his travelling companions, 'mourning me, dug a grave and placed me in it, when suddenly, much to their astonishment, I came back to life.' The other Africans began to talk excitedly together, recalling the vivid memories of that remarkable occurrence.

Jabori held up his hand for silence and continued. 'You see, Bwana, not only did I come back to life, but while I was dead I had a dream. In the dream I saw a godlike figure and he spoke to me. His voice was very clear and I know that I truly understood what he said. He told me that I must look for "the English, who would tell me about the true God." We have heard from other tribes that you,' Jabori pointed straight at Charlie, 'are the English, and that you can tell us about this God. Will you tell us? We want to know about this God who can speak to me, even when I am dead, and then bring me back to life.'

Studd was overwhelmed by the story. It seemed to him that 'the English', bearers of the truth though they so often had been, were frequently too spiritually insensitive to have the kind of experience that this African had just related.

Thank God, he thought, *that you Lord have seen fit to speak to this native in this amazing way just like in Bible times.*

The missionary, so overcome with the earnestness of the enquirer, found it difficult to speak. At first his words stuttered out, and the warrior had difficulty understanding his halting Bangala. But, gradually, Studd pulled himself together and with frequent stops and starts began to tell his visitors about Jesus Christ. The Africans sat entranced. The idea of a God who had created them and loved them enough to send His Son to die for them was beyond their experience, but they listened carefully to every word 'the English' spoke.

Such was their thirst for more knowledge about this new God, Jabori and his fellow tribesmen decided to stay at Nala to speak further with this white man. They determined to find out all they could, and then take the news back to their tribe.

Within a few days Jabori had become a Christian. Many of his companions followed soon after. For Studd, such conversions as these made all his sacrifices seem of no consequence. The luxuries and pleasures he had given up all appeared like dross compared with the gold of Africans won into the Kingdom. Immediately Studd began to prepare for a mass baptism. There were already numerous local Christians waiting to be baptised, so he and his associates began to conduct baptismal classes for all of them.

On the baptismal day it seemed that the whole of Nala walked down to the river to witness the event. On one bank Studd and several of his fellow missionaries stood with the candidates, listening to each one's confession of faith. Beyond the river, on the opposite bank, hundreds stood watching in excited anticipation, and dozens more lined the bridge which straddled the river. Drums beat, horns played, voices sang and glistening, black bodies swayed, all in enthusiastic celebration of the occasion.

The first group of a dozen Africans went down into the water and were baptised. The occurrence was greeted by cheers and more singing from the crowd. Then the next dozen followed them; more shouts and songs of praise. Then, as each succeeding group took its place in the water and the candidates were baptised, the cheering and singing resounded throughout the area. In all over eighty pledged their faith in Christ through baptism that day. The Belgian Congo had never seen the like of it before. Jesus Christ had come to Central Africa.

Yet it did not end there. A few months later some of the newly converted expressed a strong desire to evangelise their own people. To Studd this was the most exciting part of all. He recognised, though, that if they were to do this some appropriate training would be necessary, so he made sure that each prospective evangelist was properly prepared. In Nala alone there were several dozen of these would be preachers, so Studd and his associates divided them into small groups and taught them simple Gospel preaching.

When the first band was ready to depart Studd took them aside, had them all sit down in the shade of a mango tree and gave his final instructions. While they sat he walked amongst them, delivering his message. His manner was earnest. As he spoke he frequently punched his right hand into the palm of his left.

'There are four things I particularly want you to observe', he began. 'The first is this. If you don't want to meet the Devil during the day, meet Jesus before dawn. Prayer is absolutely essential to the work you are about to begin. Secondly, if you don't want the Devil to hit you, hit him first, and hit him with all your might. Preaching the Word is the rod the Devil fears and hates.

'Thirdly, if you don't want to fall, then walk, and walk straight and walk fast.' He quickened his step as he acted out his message. 'And, lastly, beware of the Devil's dogs which he uses to hunt us. Beware of them, for they bite and tear. Beware of the dog of a swelled head. Many have fallen because they became too big-headed. Beware of laziness. You know better than I how many thousands of your people need the Gospel. The need is urgent. Tackle your task with energy and vigour.'

He paused for a moment to organise his thoughts. 'And, then, beware of greed. When the Lord was sending out His disciples, rather like I am sending you out today, he said to them, "Freely you have received, freely give." (Matthew 10:8) Give to people out of your love for them. Expect nothing back in return. And always remember that God is with you.

'Before you depart let's join together in prayer.' Studd went down on his knees, and the beaming Africans surrounded him, likewise kneeling. Studd committed them to God and then slowly, with an effort, rose from the kneeling position. The Africans milled around him, excitedly asking last minute questions.

'Bwana Mukubwa,' one said, 'you haven't told us how long we are to stay away.'

Studd laughed. 'Well, if after one month you are tired out, then come home. If you are not tired, do two months, or even three.'

'Why not a year? We can go so much further in a year.'

Charlie laughed again. 'Well, if you want to do a year, then do a year. I won't stop you.'

By this time a large crowd had gathered to send off the mission's first team of national evangelists. Tears were shed as relatives said farewell to their departing loved ones. Studd felt a lump in his throat as he surveyed the scene. What a change there had been in a few short years; a triumph of the grace of God.

A few weeks after the departure of the evangelistic team another baptismal service was held, with dozens more going through the waters. The work was progressing remarkably. God was truly blessing. Yet not all was plain sailing. Satan has never liked successful sorties into his territory, so he fought back. Some of the earlier converts reverted to their former ways of adultery and violence, whilst others attempted to incorporate the old animistic beliefs into the new faith. Studd was distressed, but not surprised. He had seen it happen on occasions in China and knew well enough that many such things happened all too often in Christian England, also. His method of dealing with the situation, though, was uncompromising. Those believed to be guilty of serious sin were brought before the church and, if unrepentant, were dismissed from it. To CT Studd there was to be no compromise.

CHAPTER 30

Deti

Up until this time HAM had worked only in the Welle Province. However, on one of Studd's treks he journeyed further south into Ituri Province. News of mission activities had even reached the tribes in that region and, as Charlie passed through, he was met by a chief who invited him to visit his tribe. So the missionary accompanied the African and his entourage back to his village. Charlie had trekked often enough through the jungle but, by this time, age and ill-health were beginning to impair his mobility. He had difficulty keeping up with the fleet-footed Africans.

They eventually reached their destination and talks ensued between the two men. The conversation between them was aided by one of Studd's porters, who spoke the local language. The chief's name was Abiengama, and he was the Great Chief of that region. He was a cannibal and a man greatly feared. Though Studd did not know it at the time, a war party led by Abiengama had recently captured and eaten fourteen national porters belonging to an expedition.

Resulting from the discussion it was decided that if Studd agreed to establish a mission station in their territory, Abiengama would donate a hill called Deti for its base. The chief showed his visitor the site and Studd was delighted with it. Set high and already partly cleared of vegetation, it had glorious views of the surrounding forests. Before he left the next day CT promised to send a missionary to Deti as soon as possible.

In the event he sent two: Mr and Mrs John Ellis. The work at Deti proved to be remarkable. The Holy Spirit moved in power almost from the beginning, and the people responded keenly to the Gospel call. Among the first converted was Ndubani. Some years earlier Ndubani had aspired to become chief. To remove such ambitions from him a rival had some of his henchmen blind Ndubani by rubbing pepper in his eyes. Thus crippled, the African had to content himself with a much lower profile in the village.

One night he had a dream. He dreamed that he was walking along a dirt road, when suddenly up ahead the forest burst into flames. He stopped in his tracks, uncertain which way to go. Before he could decide he heard a voice, a strange unearthly sound. It said, 'Wait for the white man with the book and he will tell you how to escape the flames.' The scene vanished and Ndubani found himself awake, lying on his mat, his body bathed in sweat.

When the Ellises settled in Deti the blind man had his son escort him to the home of the newcomers, so that he might learn about the message of 'the white man with the book'. The missionaries were only too pleased to explain the Gospel to him, and it was not long before he found salvation in Christ. From then on Ndubani, led about by his son, could frequently be found walking around the village talking about his new Lord to all who would listen. When that task was completed he went further afield and toured the neighbouring villages with the news of Christ.

Chief Abiengama and his favourite wife also became Christians. Thus the Ellises were then faced with the problem, oft repeated in that part of Africa, of what to do with regard to the chief's other wives. Studd had formulated a policy that if any convert was polygamous, he should be allowed to retain all his wives, but not be allowed to marry any more. This was because the only alternative was to cast aside the unwanted wives, which usually condemned them to poverty and often to prostitution. Ellis explained this policy to the new convert, who accepted it with surprising readiness.

After the conversion of Abiengama, John Ellis supervised the building of a grass-walled church. However, it was not long before that building was too small and had to be enlarged.

One week in June 1918 Studd visited them. His arrival was heralded by a fierce storm. The clouds had been building up as his party ascended the hill and, just as they reached the summit and entered the mission complex, there was a frightening flash of lightning, followed almost immediately by a deafening crash of thunder. Studd jumped at the ferocity of it, and before he had time to recover the rain came down in sheets. The party hurried indoors.

Studd peered out as the world around them was repeatedly lit up by the dazzling flashes. The resounding thunder shook the ground beneath them. Rain seeped through the grass roof and walls.

When the storm had subsided Studd was treated to warm hospitality by the Ellises and their African neighbours. Though few of the nationals knew Studd, all of them had heard of Bwana Mukubwa and held him in awe, a fact which made Charlie feel most uncomfortable.

The next day was Sunday and Charlie was due to preach at the Deti morning service. He arose in the early hours for prayer, as was his regular practice. Soon after dawn he dressed himself as immaculately as his old clothes would allow, and breakfasted with Mr and Mrs Ellis. As their meal concluded the sound of drums could be heard coming from the valley below. Studd shot a questioning glance at his hosts. John Ellis smiled.

'A call to worship, Charlie. If you look out through the door, I'm sure you will already see the natives climbing the hill to go to church. Some of them like to arrive early to make sure they get a good seat.'

'Like a crowd at the cricket, eh?' Studd said, with a laugh.

'Yes, something like that.'

Charlie went over to the door and peeped out. Dozens of figures – men, women and children – could be seen ascending the hill. He turned back to the Ellises. 'Let's have some prayer together before we join them.' The three missionaries went down on their knees and, each in turn, prayed for blessing upon the service.

When they concluded prayer Studd picked up his Bible and a few sheets of paper, and the three of them walked over to the grass-walled church. Charlie could see a large crowd outside the building. He recalled the days when he had attended Moody and Sankey meetings in England and had seen the people milling around outside the meeting place. However, when they reached the church he came to realise why these people remained outside the building. There simply was no room for them inside; it was completely packed.

John Ellis led the way to the front of the church, the three of them clambering over the densely packed bodies. The congregation's collective eye seemed to be fixed on the thin, grey-bearded visitor, with the beaklike nose. When the missionaries reached the front of the church they were still hardly better off for space, as the crush of bodies extended from one end of the building to the other. Abiengama and the other chiefs sat in the front row.

The service was conducted in Kingwana, a language Studd did not know, but when they joined in praise the hymns needed no translation. Studd knew most of them well enough, and he sang along in Bangala, while with the other songs he just seemed to sense the meaning. During the singing of some hymns, the nationals were so carried away that they swayed and danced to the pulsating, drum-accompanied rhythm. The noise in the crowded building was deafening.

There were Scripture readings, prayers, and eventually it was time for Studd to preach. Munganga, a local Christian, fluent in both Kingwana and Bangala, was the interpreter.

Charlie did not like preaching through interpreters. It was awkward and he never knew for sure whether his message was being presented accurately. He began slowly, even hesitantly. He was uneasy about this means of communication. He looked at the eager faces in front of him and knew that many of these people were lost without Christ. How could he reach them? Suddenly a quotation from Richard Baxter came to his mind. 'I'll preach as though I ne'er shall preach again, and as a dying man to dying men!'

This thought so challenged him that he picked up his pace and began to preach with greater fervour. For a while Munganga had difficulty adjusting to the change of speed. Occasionally he left out a phrase, only to be corrected by some of the other Bangala speakers in the congregation. For a while it seemed as though the sermon might dissolve into a farce. However, Munganga recovered himself and managed to keep pace with Studd. The looks on the hundreds of attentive faces made it clear that at least some of the message was getting through.

When Studd finished preaching Ellis announced another hymn and, after it had been sung, closed with a few further words of challenge. Slowly the bulk of the great crowd dispersed, though some of the Africans stopped behind to talk with the missionaries.

Later when the Britons had returned to their hut John Ellis approached Charlie. 'I hope the dancing wasn't a problem, Mr Studd. It just seems to be a natural expression of worship to these dear people.'

'Indeed, no. I've known such happen on numerous occasions before.

What may not seem appropriate in an English setting can be so here. After all, does not the Psalmist say, "Praise Him with the timbrel and dance"? (Psalm 150:4) Africans don't always conduct themselves in worship in quite the same way as we Europeans do. I remember Alfred and Edith telling me of one character they had in their church who used to roam up and down the aisle during the service. If he noticed anyone's attention wandering, he clapped them around the head and whispered to them, "Pay attention! Don't forget I've eaten better men than you."' The Ellises laughed. 'Mind you,' Studd continued, 'they had to put a stop to that one.'

The rest of that day saw them host many visits from the Africans. The missionaries befriended, they taught and they counselled. Studd stayed in Deti for most of that week and then began the return journey to Nala.

In 1919 Charlie and Alfred discussed the pros and cons of one of them returning to England for a while. It was eventually decided that Alfred, who had now been in Africa for six unbroken years, would return with Edith and their daughter Susan, who had been born just nine months before. With them, too, would go four of the other longer serving missionaries. This would leave Studd with few troops to run the booming stations, for there had been no new arrivals during the past year because of the European war. Indeed, part of the Buxtons' purpose for going to England was to help Priscilla enlist more volunteers.

The little party of missionaries travelled north on foot and later by car, to reach the Nile. They made the next stage of the journey to Khartoum by steamer. During the arduous trip little Susan nearly died. She was able to keep down only one particular type of milk, and as this proved unobtainable for much of the trip she took in little nourishment. Concern about her health grew daily. When they arrived in Khartoum, they obtained fresh stocks only just in time to save the child's life.

Studd, meanwhile, soldiered on with his depleted forces. The stresses he endured were considerable; for a lesser man they would have been intolerable. The departure of half his staff (only three men and two women remained with him) and the absence of new recruits placed a much greater burden on him. Even worse was the backsliding of many national converts, including some of the more prominent ones. The old ways seemed to exercise a strong hold on so many. Even some who appeared to have developed well in the Christian faith returned to pagan ways. Studd found it all so terribly sad, but he did not despair. He knew well enough that even the Lord Jesus in His earthly ministry had suffered the same experience, for 'many of his disciples went back, and walked no more with him'. (John 6:66)

Yet others remained true to their faith in Christ and new converts were still being made. Through all the difficulties this aging warrior experienced, he could see that God still blessed the work.

CHAPTER 31
Reinforcements

The First World War had been a disaster from many perspectives. Virtually a whole generation of young men in Europe had been killed or badly wounded, as had many in such countries as America and Australia. Apart from anything else, this meant that the cause of world mission had been set back, perhaps by as much as two decades. When the Buxtons returned to England less than a year after the war had concluded, they found a society which had changed dramatically from the one they knew. It was less obviously Christian. Many of the young men who had survived the horrors of trench warfare no longer attended church. Their Christian faith seemed to have departed with the loss of so many brave companions. The world seemed less proud, even ashamed, of the wasteful terrors of the preceding four years, yet now, at last, there was less hindrance to the cause of mission work.

When CT Studd had left England in the middle of 1916 he left behind his wife, little more than an invalid. Strangely, even miraculously, after his departure she arose from her bed of illness and, in her husband's phrase, she became a cyclone: a human whirlwind of activity. She attended to mission business with an energy which astonished those who knew her condition.

With other prospective mission workers involved in the war effort, Priscilla had to organise the home affairs of HAM almost single-handedly during the closing days of the conflict. In spite of her efforts she saw the supply of missionary candidates completely dry up. Even the circulation of the mission magazine had shrunk dramatically. But, with the end of the war and the return of her daughter and son-in-law, a new impetus fired the mission.

Dorothy's husband, Reverend Gilbert Barclay, became Chairman of the Home Committee, and brought to the work a vision which paralleled Charlie Studd's. With the enlarging vision, in 1912 the mission became the Worldwide Evangelization Crusade (WEC), with the name, Heart of Africa Mission, being retained for the work in Central Africa.

In the summer of 1919 Priscilla took a daring step of faith. She sent a cable to her husband which read, 'Reinforcements leaving this year.' At the time the telegram was despatched there were no reinforcements, but she and her companions in prayer so firmly believed that a breakthrough was just around the corner they felt compelled to be bold. A week before the year ended, a small party left England bound for the Congo. In it was the Studd's fourth daughter, Pauline, and her husband, Norman Grubb. Early in the new year, two more groups left and by 1922 WEC staff in Africa had increased to forty.

The Buxtons, too, planned to return to Africa, but they were faced with a problem. A son, Lionel, had been added to their family, and they had grave doubts as to the advisability of taking two young children into the malaria ridden jungles of Central Africa. If they chose not to take the children, should Alfred and Edith separate, like the Studds, and live apart for years on end, with Alfred attending to mission affairs in Africa and Edith caring for the children in England? Alfred felt compelled to return to Africa. He never had any doubts about it. Edith was less convinced about her calling. She viewed herself as a 'reluctant missionary'. But the idea of being separated again from the man she loved filled her with horror. On the other hand the thought of being parted from her beloved children was hardly less terrible.

She agonised over the decision during the closing months of 1920 and finally decided to accompany her husband back to the Congo, leaving their children in the care of Alfred's parents. In the winter months of the following year, Alfred and Edith Buxton set sail once more for the hot, humid forests of Central Africa.

****

In 1922 Studd moved his battlefront headquarters to Ibambi in the Ituri province, nearer Deti. His health was still poor and, during one extended bout of fever, Alfred and Edith travelled down from Nala to nurse him. They continued the work there while he was incapacitated. One night Edith was asleep in bed when her husband returned at midnight from nursing his father-in-law. She awoke as he slumped, totally exhausted, into a chair beside her bed.

'Are you alright?' she asked in concern, sitting up. He did not answer.

'Here, let me help you,' she said, rising from her bed. She half helped, half carried the listless form of her husband, and found herself reflecting how much sturdier he had seemed when they had first married. She placed him on the bed, and pulled the mosquito net over him, then returned to lie down again.

The exertions of her day overcame the worries she felt, and very soon she was asleep once more. Her sleep was broken by a terrifying sound. At first she thought it was a dream, a nightmare. But the piercing shriek sounded all too real, indeed too close for comfort. She did not know how long she had been asleep, but was horrifyingly aware that now she was awake, and the scream was coming from her husband. She rushed over to him, and in the dim lamplight saw his body writhing around on the bed.

Then, suddenly, the convulsing ceased and the screams ended. His body lay motionless on the bed. For a moment she thought he was dead, but noticed that his breathing, which moments before had been tortured, was now near normal. Edith called his name, but there was no response. She checked his breathing once more and then ran the two hundred metres to her father's house.

She burst through the door calling urgently, 'Father, father, come quickly. Alfred is very ill.'

Studd quickly recognised the urgency of the situation and ran with his daughter back to where Alfred was. The sick man was still motionless, just breathing lightly. As Studd examined his son-in-law, Edith gave her account of the attack. Studd took his pulse, listened to his breathing, and thoroughly looked him over.

Turning to his daughter, he said, 'It must be some kind of fit, Edith, though I confess I don't know what's caused it. I think the best thing we can do is let him rest and see how he is in the morning. I'll just pop back to my house to get some medicines and come straight back. I'll spend the rest of the night here.'

He rushed off into the night and within in a few minutes he returned with some of his potent remedies. For the remainder of the night the two took it in turns to sit by Alfred's bed, praying for his recovery. Alfred slept soundly for the rest of the night and well into the day. During the few moments he was awake they dosed him with medicine, but he seemed largely oblivious to what was going on.

The next night Studd, who was still far from well himself, returned to his own quarters, and Nzanga, one of the African Christians, sat with Edith on her all-night vigil. Still Alfred did not stir. Edith was confused. Her mind boiled in turmoil.

'Why? Why? Why?' she asked God. 'Why does this good man have to be so afflicted? He's doing your will, Lord, isn't he? Why does he have to be struck down in this way?' But the more questions she asked, the louder was the silence. God seemed so far away.

Shortly after midnight she fell upon her knees and called out in desperation, 'Where are you, Lord? This is hell.' But, still no answer came.

Later she rose from her knees and sat once more in the chair next to her husband's bed. For an age she just sat and looked blankly ahead. Nzanga remained silent. Then Edith picked up her Bible, flicked through its pages, and her gaze fell upon Psalm 139. From verse eight she read:

If I make my bed in hell, behold thou art there.
If I take the wings of the morning, and dwell in the uttermost parts of the sea;
Even there shall thy hand lead me, and thy right hand shall hold me.
If I say, Surely the darkness shall cover me; even the night shall be light about me.
Yea, the darkness hideth not from thee; but the night shineth as the day: the darkness and
the light are both alike to thee.

At first it all seemed to have no meaning. Yet, when she read the passage through again she could see in it God's answer to her. He had used the word hell back to her in much the same way as she had used it. She focused on the words, 'If I make my bed in hell, behold thou art there.' Gradually she became aware that God was with her even in this, the darkest of dark situations.

The sun rose the next morning and Alfred was considerably better. He still slept most of that day and the next, but in his waking moments he was lucid and able to take nourishment. From then on his condition improved, though in later years those violent attacks were still to afflict him.

Charlie was to have attacks, too, but of quite a different kind. Priscilla had begun to bombard him with letters, beseeching him to let her join him in Africa. Charlie would have none of it. He feared for her health in that savage climate and, anyway, he regarded her role in England as too valuable. Every time she pleaded with him to let her come, he refused to agree. On one occasion she even holidayed in Cairo in the hope that her husband would join her there, but once more he refused.

For years a gap of many miles had existed between them, but now a gap of a very different kind began to manifest itself. She felt in a strange, disappointing way a sense of alienation from her husband. Even Alfred was saddened by Studd's behaviour on this matter and challenged him on it. But, Studd did not like being so rebuked.

Back in England the Worldwide Evangelization Crusade was living up to its name. In spite of acute financial problems the committee decided to launch out in faith into other lands. In 1923 three missionaries were sent to South America to work amongst the Indians in the Amazon jungle. When one was soon killed, he was replaced by three more. Two men were sent to Northern India and Tibet, and, later, more to Arabia and West Africa.

Meanwhile Priscilla toured some traditionally Christian countries to stir up interest. She visited America, Canada, Australia, New Zealand and South Africa, establishing WEC councils in each. On her tour of Australasia she participated in over 270 meetings. Priscilla Studd was tougher than her husband and doctors thought.

CHAPTER 32

STRIFE AND BLESSING

Charles Studd believed in giving his whole being to God in service. He held nothing back. His dedication was outstanding, but this not infrequently led to disagreements with others who did not have his high level of commitment.

Studd was now well into his sixties, but his workload was far greater than many half his age. He frequently rose at 2 am to pray and read the Bible, and usually followed this with a session in which he taught some of his church leaders. He would next have breakfast, which was often followed by a brief nap. Then, apart from hurried meals and a brief rest early in the evening, he laboured throughout the day. If his heavy workload permitted, he would go to bed at 9 pm. If not, he would stay up until his tasks were completed. He refused to take holidays, to participate in relaxations of any kind and only ate the plainest of foods.

That he set himself this inhumane schedule was one thing; that he expected it of others was another matter. It was always bound to lead to disagreement. After the war, new missionaries arrived at regular intervals. Many of them found Studd's demanding ways difficult to take. Buxton, who was no less dedicated than his long-time companion, pleaded for a more tolerant approach. Studd thought tolerance was weakness.

In any interdenominational mission the issue of the differing beliefs of its members is always bound to lift its head at some stage, though most often without great drama. But when that 'head' lifted in the Heart of Africa Mission, Studd endeavoured to cut it off. Disagreements occurred over ordination, baptism, the nature of holiness, spiritual gifts and social issues such as the use of alcohol. To Studd there was just one way: the Bible's way. His opponents agreed with that, but disagreed what precisely was the Bible's way.

Studd would have none of what he called 'denominational truth', but failed to see that whatever practice one adopted with such issues as baptism, one followed the tenets of some denominations whilst rejecting the beliefs of others. Both sides in such disputes pointed to the Scriptures to justify their positions. Alfred urged a less dogmatic approach, but Charlie knew no other way. This strife resulted in some of the new arrivals quickly leaving HAM and joining other missions.

In 1924 a party of seven missionaries arrived from America. Their arrival coincided with a difficult time in the infant Ibambi Church. A number of converts had fallen back into sin, with some committing adultery and others practising witchcraft. Studd had a great hatred of sin in the professing Christian. He stated passionately, 'God will never wink at sin and call that exercising grace.' He also believed that such as these could no longer be Christians and should therefore be excommunicated.

The new American arrivals believed that once someone was saved, they remained saved. They thought this was a case of trying to restore brothers and sisters in Christ to a position of consistent Christian living. The argument raged. Alfred Buxton hurried from Nala to mediate, but to no avail. The Americans resigned.

When the news reached England there was much concern. A great deal of effort had been expended in establishing WEC in the USA, and these men were the first group of missionaries from that country. That their tenure with the mission should last only a matter of weeks could mean that they might be the last. Priscilla, who was secretary of the WEC committee, had the unenviable task of relaying to her husband the committee's displeasure. She suggested that stress and tiredness was affecting his judgment, and that he needed a rest. Studd was not pleased with the letter and responded angrily.

Through all this Alfred and Edith Buxton did their best to mediate but their efforts were not well received. One day the Buxtons received a letter from Ibambi. Alfred opened it and scanned the contents. As he did so his face went crimson, and he shot embarrassed glances at his puzzled wife.

'I assume it's from Father,' Edith said.

Her husband nodded.

'I think you'd better read it out loud, Alfred.'

Alfred did so. Studd's letter accused the Buxtons of being disloyal, of not playing the game, and generally not supporting him. Long before Alfred had finished reading it Edith had collapsed into a chair, and sat there listening, but hardly understanding, her head in her hands. Neither looked up until the letter had been read, then they fixed their gaze on each other. Edith's hands were clasped tightly in her lap. Her face wore a blank look of astonishment.

'Are you alright, Edith?' Alfred asked. 'You look shocking.'

Her hand lifted and touched her head, as if to steady it. 'I feel rather faint,' she mumbled.

Her husband rushed to fill a tumbler full of water and took it to her. She grasped the glass and sipped the water. There was silence. Neither seemed to know what to say or do.

Finally, Edith blurted out, 'But it's so unfair, Alfred. It's just not true. No one has been more loyal to Father than you. How could he say those things?' She paused. 'What do we do, Alfred? What do we do?'

Alfred said nothing. For some time he had seen this problem coming, yet now that it had he was no nearer knowing how to handle it. His life was inextricably tied up with the Mission and thus with his father-in-law, and resigning seemed out of the question. Yet remaining with a long-time colleague who no longer appeared to trust him was fraught with difficulties.

That night sleep would not come. Both Alfred and Edith were too disturbed by the contents of the letter. The next day they set about their tasks in the church at Nala with an unusual lack of enthusiasm. Their minds were in a daze and their hearts downcast.

A few weeks later Alfred was taken ill. His improvement was slow and, after discussions with Studd, it was eventually decided that the Buxtons ought to return to England.

On their way home up the Nile Alfred's health, mercifully, showed signs of improvement. But, as they travelled north Edith dropped a bombshell which set him back, emotionally at least.

'I've had enough of this missionary life, Alfred,' she blurted out. 'I don't think I can go back again.'

The events of the last few months had all been too much for her. The comment saddened her husband, but he knew that his own missionary life was far from over. He strongly suspected that when he next returned to Africa his wife would once more be by his side.

They arrived in England to be confronted by the committee, which was still in turmoil over the defection of the American missionaries. After a couple of months rest the Buxtons were despatched to America to try to pacify the committee there, a task which Alfred, ever the conciliator, endeavoured to do.

But, a further letter from Studd, again accusing the Buxtons of disloyalty, made it necessary for them to resign from WEC. Soon after that they joined the Sudan Interior Mission and went to Ethiopia with that organisation.

****

Studd, meanwhile, continued his work in the Congo alongside those missionaries who had remained loyal to him. Although, as has been seen, he could be uncharitable to those who opposed him or appeared to be giving less than their best, he could also be extraordinarily kind to those in need. He frequently provided goods from his own meagre supplies and offered words of encouragement. He would rather go without himself than see others do so. Many missionaries and national Christians alike benefited from his generosity.

At times, though, he felt agonisingly alone, even though he was rarely short of company. The Africans still held Bwana Mukubwa in great esteem, and would flock to his house. The other HAM personnel frequently approached him for help and advice. Yet, somehow, there seemed a kind of barrier between him and other people. Not surprisingly, too, the spiritual temperature of the Mission was at an all-time low. Studd felt they were going backwards, rather than forwards.

Asthma and malaria still plagued him. At times he felt as though his cross was heavy beyond endurance and, like Paul centuries before him, he longed to be with Christ. Yet he was prepared still to labour on in God's service on earth, if that was what the Lord required of him. It seemed that the Lord did.

It became the regular practice for all the missionaries based at Ibambi to gather together at 8 pm in Studd's house for Bible study and prayer. One night they read through Hebrews chapter eleven, and were challenged by the faithfulness of that mighty catalogue of saints, 'Of whom the world was not worthy'. When the reading finished there was a silence that could almost be felt. The atmosphere was charged.

Studd sensed it as, indeed, did the others. He began to speak quietly. The noises from the surrounding jungle gave an eerie accompaniment to his words.

'Could it be possible that such as we shall march up the Golden Street with such as these?' The tone in his voice drew the contrast, and he paused for the question to sink in. 'It shall be for such as are found worthy,' he continued, his voice rising in volume. 'Then there is a chance for us yet. Glory! Hallelujah! Hearts begin to burn! The glory of the deeds of these heroes of old seems to scorch hearts and souls, doesn't it?'

Sounds of agreement echoed round the room.

'How God honoured and blessed them, and made them a blessing to others, in their life time, yes, and right here tonight, if I'm not much mistaken. What was the spirit which caused these mortals so to triumph and to die? The Holy Spirit of God, of course! One of whose chief characteristics is a pluck, a bravery, a lust for sacrifice for God, and a joy in it which crucifies all human weakness and the natural desires of the flesh. This is our need tonight. Will God give to us as He gave to them?'

He paused again. 'Yes! Yes! Of course He will. What are the conditions? They are ever the same. Sell out! God's price is one. There is no discount. He gives all to such as give all. All! All!' His voice rose in intensity as he emphasised the words. 'Death to all the world, to all the flesh, to the devil, and to perhaps the worst enemy of all, yourself.'

As he stopped a compelling silence once more filled the room. For a while Studd refrained from continuing. Then he said, 'I don't know, how does one describe this experience in modern terms? This selfless dedication?'

Once more there was silence. Then one young man spoke up. 'Well, Mr Studd, it seems to me that it's a bit like being in the war. When I was fighting in France, our Sergeant Major used to describe it like this, "The British Tommy doesn't care what happens to him so long as he does his duty by his King, his country, his regiment and himself."'

'Yes that's it!' an excited Studd agreed, rising from his seat and holding his right arm aloft. 'That's what we need, and that's what I want.' He raised his eyes heavenward. 'Oh, Lord, henceforth I won't care what happens to me, life or death, aye, or hell, so long as my Lord Jesus Christ is glorified.'

Immediately the ex-soldier rose to his feet and promised, 'I don't care what happens to me, either, Lord, joy or sorrow, health or pain, life or death, so long as Jesus is glorified.'

One by one each of the remaining missionaries stood up and made a similar commitment. A new feeling of peace and spiritual oneness swept through the group. They fell to their knees and continued to pour out their hearts to God. The Spirit ministered to them dynamically. Time seemed to have no meaning. When they eventually brought the meeting to a conclusion, the nine missionaries had a new dynamic. The Holy Spirit had revitalised a key group of WEC's frontline soldiers.

In the days and weeks ahead the blessings spread to the whole Church at Ibambi and the other mission stations. Missionaries were equipped with new spiritual vigour. New converts were made; backsliders brought back into the church. Where, before, there had been a spirit of frustration and defeat, now there was a sense of purpose and victory.

One of the greatest triumphs at this time was in the life of Adzangwe. He had been a cannibal chief but had forsaken this practice soon after the arrival of the Christian missionaries. He had shown a lukewarm acceptance of the Christian faith but his life had not evidenced a genuine conversion experience, nor had he been baptised. Suddenly there was change in his life.

Adzangwe positively radiated the Spirit of Jesus Christ. The change was dramatic. He became a leader in the church at Ibambi and soon began to visit neighbouring tribes preaching the Gospel. At one stage he was held captive and was only able to escape after some of his captors had become Christians through his witness.

The Spirit of God was moving and the problems and disputes which had so bedevilled the mission in recent times were now pushed into the background.

CHAPTER 33
THE END IS NIGH

CT Studd had never been one to pay too much attention to personal comforts. Because of this his health suffered in a variety of ways. One great problem he had was with his teeth. Practically all of them had fallen out and those that remained gave him considerable trouble. There had been a persistent push from a number of directions for him to return to England for a period of rest and the troublesome state of his teeth just added impetus to that campaign.

'You really ought to go home and have your teeth seen to, Mr Studd,' a colleague advised one day.

'I can't afford to leave the work here just to have my teeth attended to,' was the predictable response. 'If God wants me to have some new teeth, He can just as easily send me some here,' he said with a little laugh.

The colleague shrugged his shoulders resignedly and joined in the laughter. 'Why is it I thought you would say something like that?'

Studd laughed again.

****

Back in England a gentleman named Buck applied to WEC for missionary service. Ben Buck was a dentist. However, the Committee rejected his application on the grounds that he was too old for the rigours of Central Africa.

But, Buck was a determined man. He really wanted to be a missionary and, having heard about Studd's dental problems, he was also intent on solving them. He sold his practice in England and set out for Africa. He travelled by steamer along the River Congo and then by canoe along the Aruwimi River.

Early one morning, as the sun was just beginning to rise in the sky, Buck and his guides noticed another canoe travelling in the opposite direction. When it came close they realised that those on board included a white man and woman. A shout of 'Pull over to the bank!' from the other canoe made it clear that at least one of the whites spoke English. The two vessels pulled over together on to one of the banks and the two parties introduced themselves. The strangers were Studd's youngest daughter, Pauline, and her husband Norman Grubb. They were returning home on furlough.

The two groups spent some time together over breakfast. When they were about to part Buck took Pauline aside and explained one of the purposes of his visit was to make her father a set of dentures. She laughed with delight. She remembered her father's words of some weeks before and reflected on the goodness of God.

Buck continued on his way and eventually arrived in Ibambi. When he met Studd, he introduced himself and told him, 'Mr Studd, God has sent me here first of all to fix your teeth.'

Studd took a step back in astonishment. His hand went to his mouth and he then proceeded to laugh.

'My dear, Buck,' he said, after he had regained his composure, 'many weeks ago I said that if God wanted to give me a new set of teeth, He could send them to me, and here He has done just that. Hallelujah! How great our God is!'

The next day Buck removed the remaining teeth in an extended and painful operation. Later, he prepared dental plates for his patient, which Studd christened 'the upper and nether millstones.' Studd described them as being excellent for singing (though they had a bit of an echo) but not much good for eating. They never quite felt comfortable and he often had to remove them. At times, when he was writing, he used them as a pen holder, a practice that often liberally sprinkled the dentures with ink.

During one service he took them out while a colleague was praying, tied them up in his handkerchief and put them in his pocket. When Studd opened his eyes after the prayer he was greeted by rows and rows of black faces staring at him in wonder. Every look seemed to say, 'Where have his teeth gone?'

Later in the service he made the mistake of pulling his handkerchief out to blow his nose, sending the two plates flying across the little platform.

Every eye became fixed in astonishment on the dentures and then back to Studd's mouth. Studd and Buck took an extended look at what proved to be the shattered remains of the two dental plates. Ben Buck's work in Ibambi was certainly not completed, yet. Later that week, he began making a new set of teeth that, to the relief of everybody, fitted much better.

Studd's temperament mellowed somewhat in his final years and his relationships with his colleagues consequently improved. He frequently showed great concern for the suffering of his fellow missionaries but still showed little interest in his own. His health continued to worsen. He still suffered from bad bouts of fever and asthma. He also developed a heart condition and probably suffered from gall stones. Yet his workload hardly declined. Indeed, he took on another major task.

Alfred Buxton had previously translated the New Testament into Bangala but there was still no translation of any of the Scriptures in the local language, Kingwana. In his late sixties Studd began the daunting task of translating the New Testament into that language. For a man who once had struggled so hard to learn Chinese and was a man of action, rather than a scholar, it was a difficult, demanding job. Day after day he laboured over the books, usually committing the early hours of the morning to the project. After each day's translation work was completed, another missionary typed up the manuscript. When the New Testament was completed he proceeded to translate the Psalms.

****

In 1928 Priscilla decided to visit the Congo. She suspected that her husband had not long to live. She was determined to see him before he died and, perhaps, even persuade him to come home to spend his final days. Charlie protested and advised her against the trip but this time she would not be denied.

Norman and Pauline Grubb were due to return to the mission-field, so Priscilla decided to accompany them. Roads had now been built through the dense jungle of the eastern Congo, so the last part of their trek was by car, in relative comfort. The arrival of the vehicle was greeted by a large enthusiastic crowd of Africans, eager to see Mama Bwana.

Priscilla stepped from the car and looked around her. All she could see was a mass of smiling black faces but no sign of her husband. Then through the throng came a slightly stooped, thin figure, his head balding and his beard grey and bushy. Priscilla was shocked. This was her husband sure enough, but he appeared to be a mere ghost of the man she had last seen twelve years before.

Amidst the crowd they stared at each other like strangers. Neither knew what to say, nor how to respond to the situation. It all seemed so unnatural. Priscilla found herself wishing she had not come. After they had stood staring at each other for what seemed an age Charlie muttered, 'It's good to see you, Scill.'

Suddenly Priscilla's doubts rolled away. She was glad she had come, though she knew that her time in Africa, however short or long it might be, would not be easy. She stepped forward, their hands touched, and Charlie led her to his home.

Her stay, though, was to be brief: a mere two weeks. In that time she addressed the church on several occasions through an interpreter and also endeavoured to persuade her husband to return with her to England. Yet Charlie would not be persuaded. He was determined to spend his final days in the Congo and it did not matter how much anyone pleaded with him, not even Scilla.

Once more it appeared to her that this trip was a mistake, for she had failed in her main intention. Yet she was pleased that she had seen the man her husband had become, and was proud of him for, within the physical wreck that was his body, she saw a spiritual giant.

The parting was as hard as either of them had ever endured. They both knew this would be the last time that they would see each other in this life. They said their goodbyes in the house. Then they walked slowly down the path to the waiting car, neither daring to look at the other. Priscilla climbed into the vehicle, sat down and looked straight ahead of her. As the car turned round to leave, the last sight Charlie saw of his wife was her sitting bolt upright with her eyes glued to the road ahead. The car disappeared in the distance and Charlie Studd felt a strange, overpowering sadness in his heart.

That same year he had several heart attacks and, after a severe one, a Belgian doctor was called in to treat him. The medic administered morphine to ease the pain. Studd never completely recovered from this bout and was a frequent user of morphine from that time. It seemed to be the only way he could continue his work.

CHAPTER 34
To Glory

Studd was old, sick and tired, yet his humour had not deserted him. He wrote home: 'My head will not work as it did. I flog it, but the poor dumb brute turns and says like Balaam's ass, "What harm have I ever done you?" My old heart won't work. My stomach has perpetual nausea.'

Yet through all his physical discomforts there was no shortage of spiritual encouragements. One such was Zamu. He belonged to Chief Adzangwe's tribe and had a terrible ulcer on his foot, which made walking very difficult. The condition proved no impediment to this brave African volunteering to evangelise distant tribes to the south. These tribes had traditionally been his bitter enemies but now he wanted to bring the news of God's love to them. One day he approached one of the lady missionaries, Esme Roupell, and explained his vision to her. She was touched by his dedication but was concerned about the enormous difficulty he would encounter travelling great distances in his condition.

'What about your foot, Zamu?' she asked, pointing to the ulcer.

The African smiled. 'God is, white lady!' was his astonishing reply.

His words halted the questioner for a moment. Then she said, 'The food is quite different in the districts you will be going to. No palm oil, no salt down there.'

'But God is, white lady,' he replied once more.

She hesitated, taking in the significance of the reply again. 'You might starve, or ... be killed. You know better than I that those tribes are your enemies.'

'God is, white lady.'

Roupell was impressed by his simple determination but felt she ought to continue the questioning to make sure that he had considered every angle. 'What about your wife, then, Zamu?'

'She will come with me. God is, white lady.'

The missionary smiled. 'You certainly are determined, aren't you? Go, and may the Lord go with you. I think you had better see Mr Studd, though. With all his experience he is sure to be able to give you some advice.'

Zamu went to see the old soldier. He told Studd his intention and of the conversation he had had with Esme Roupell. The Englishman was delighted. Here he was, coming to the end of his innings, but there were men and women such as this brave African ready to replace him. It was truly a dream come true.

As they sat and talked together Studd rolled up his sleeve and said, 'You see this arm of mine, Zamu?' The African looked at the thin, shrunken limb. 'Once it was very strong but now it is so weak,' Studd continued. 'My time is nearly finished on this earth. I only go on from day to day as God gives me strength. So don't depend on me, depend on God. He is with you. He will keep you. Go in His Name! Don't go with shame. Don't be afraid. Be bold and preach the Gospel!'

'Yes, Bwana Mukubwa, I will,' Zamu said.

'Is anyone going with you?'

'Just my wife, Bwana.'

'Well, if you are true, God will turn the two of you into a great company one day.'

So Zamu and his wife went to the tribes in the south. They experienced much opposition and great hardships but, gradually, their preaching bore fruit. In succeeding years they were followed by ten more national evangelists with the same vision.

CT Studd now knew that Christianity in Central Africa was no longer entirely dependent upon foreign missionaries, and for that he was thankful.

****

'Bwana Mukubwa! Bwana Mukubwa! The post has come.' One of the Africans stood at Studd's door shouting his urgent message, his hands full of envelopes.

'Just put them on the table, would you? I will look at them in a moment.'

The national Christian put the letters down in a pile on the desk and

Studd continued on with the translation work in front of him. It was another hot day in January 1929. Studd was weary. He knew well enough that his life would soon end, so he maintained his seemingly impossible schedule, endeavouring to pack as much as possible into his final days.

It was some time before he ceased working and began to look through the envelopes beside him. When he did he looked quickly at each one to see where it was from. He noticed one from his daughter, Dorothy, and opened it. It contained some terrible news: Priscilla was dead.

Did the letter really say that? Could it be true? He read the fearful tidings once more and was left in no doubt as to its truth. It was like a knife being thrust through his heart. His wife, his support, the lynch-pin of the work in England had gone. The one with whom he had shared so much happiness, sadness, strife and triumph was dead.

He tried to read the remainder of the letter but his eyes were glazed, his mind a mass of confused thoughts. Unable to focus he placed it on the table in front of him, put his head in his hands, and wept.

When he recovered sufficiently he continued to read the letter. Priscilla had been on holiday in Spain and had been taken ill with terrible pains in the chest. She lapsed into unconsciousness and died the next day. The end had been as quick as that.

Studd continued to sit in the quietness of his primitive home, alone in his sadness. His heart became a strange mixture of emotions. Certainly he experienced grief, but the sting had been taken out of it, as it were, by the frequent partings he had had from his wife over the years and the recent long separation. On each one of those occasions, when goodbyes had been said, he had grieved, though he often did not show it. Therefore, the great grief one might have expected to be brought about by her death was lessened. Mixed in with the inevitable sadness, though, was a great peace, even a strange, unearthly sense of joy, such was his firm conviction in the heavenly reward. To him, Priscilla Livingstone Stewart Studd had not died but had gone to be with Christ, and that was far better. He praised God for His goodness.

It was not until another African came to visit him an hour or so later that the news of the loss was relayed to the remainder of the mission. The news of the totally unexpected death shocked everybody.

In the two years after his wife's decease CT Studd frequently came close to death himself or, as he put it, 'went down to the river'. On one occasion he had a seizure during a service, which caused him to fall off his chair, and thus brought the meeting to a slightly premature end. At times his pulse slowed down to about 45, while at other times it raced as high as 160. Often he had high fevers. His legs and arms became swollen. Asthma attacks continued. When health permitted he continued to work all hours but his physical condition allowed that less and less.

In 1931 he wrote to his grandchildren:

My loving advice to you is summed up in a few lines which I want you to learn by heart: 'Only one life, 'twill soon be past; only what's done for Jesus will last.'

Sometimes it seems like yesterday that I was at Lord's playing cricket and my life in front of me. I have seemed to be young for many years; and then quite suddenly old age has come. These last years have been sorrowful and yet the most happy and fruitful of my life. I have come to understand better than before what the religion of our Lord Jesus really is and the awful caricature we have made of it. It is the one really noble thing on earth, and in essence, it is not getting but giving. Our lives must be of this pattern of Jesus. He gave up heaven to come to earth to shame, torture and death on the cross to save us; we must give up earth in order to follow Christ and save our fellow men. Unless we get Jesus to change our hearts we should all go to the place where sin reigns supreme and where there is sorrow for ever. But God sent Jesus to change our hearts, and as we gaze on the marvellous love of God for us, our hearts must love Him and desire to become like Him. The greatest joy anyone can have on earth is to walk with Jesus: and this is what it means to be a Christian.

Now I must finish this letter. I say, love Jesus supremely, more than anybody on earth and do as He asks, then you will live the happiest possible life that anyone can live. Oh is it not wonderful to placard this world with 'Jesus, crucified for us'?

Your loving old grandfather.

On Sunday July 12 Studd was in surprisingly good health, so he despatched his helpers to various preaching places and led the service at the mission base himself. The meeting lasted five hours! He was tired after it but still reasonably well.

The next afternoon he complained of feeling cold and one of his associate missionaries gave him an injection of quinine. That night he complained of severe pains in the right side. For the next two days his condition deteriorated. On Thursday the pain eased, but his general condition showed further decline rather than improvement. Speaking proved an effort and each word he managed was barely audible to those, black and white, who crowded around his bed.

Frequently, though, he was heard to gasp, 'Hallelujah!' And, as he drew closer to 'the river', that oft repeated word of praise was the only one that could be understood. Around 7pm he slipped into unconsciousness and passed into Glory just before 10.30 that Thursday, 16 July 1931.

The next day the news of the death of Bwana Mukubwa travelled like lightning throughout the region. Many hundreds of Africans poured into the mission complex and, as he lay in state in a room in his house, they filed past to pay their tribute. At his funeral some of his national workers carried his coffin in teeming rain, before a crowd of over 1,500. He had left instructions that there was to be no mourning for CT Studd had not really died, he had gone to rejoice with his Maker.

At seventy years of age, CT Studd's greatest innings had finished but the match had not ended. He, in the power of God, had pioneered a new work in Africa, indeed the world, which would go from strength to strength. Thus others would bat on after him, building on the foundation he had established, playing their part in bringing in the Kingdom of God.

Five years after his death the region which had seen his final labours experienced a revival which, through the power of the Holy Spirit, confirmed the work Studd had begun.

EPILOGUE

Many characters have appeared in the pages of *From Ashes to Glory* and then vanished. What happened to them?
- Kynaston (JEK) Studd twice served as Lord Mayor of London and was also knighted.
- George (GB) Studd continued his work in the slums of Los Angeles and died in 1945.
- Moody and Sankey continued their evangelistic work in America and Britain, Moody died in 1899 and Sankey in 1908.
- With regard to the other members of the Cambridge Seven:
- After lengthy service in China, Monty Beauchamp returned to England and served as a Chaplain in World War 1. He inherited the baronetcy and later went back to China where he died in 1939.
- William Cassels continued to work in China, became a Bishop and died in 1925.
- Dixon Hoste became the General Director of the China Inland Mission (now known as Overseas Missionary Fellowship) and died in 1946.
- Arthur Polhill-Turner was ordained in China in 1888, where he continued to work until 1928. He died in England in 1935.
- His brother, Cecil, remained in China (except for a short period in India) until he was invalided home in 1900. He later made seven return visits to China and died in England in 1938.
- Stanley Smith spent most of the remainder of his life in China, though he did leave CIM. He died in 1931.
- Hudson Taylor who, perhaps, did more than any other to assure the spread of the Christian Gospel in China, eventually died there. When Taylor first arrived in that heavily populated land Christians at best could be numbered in hundreds. It is now estimated that there are 60

million Protestant Christians in China. The foundation laid by Taylor, and such as the Cambridge Seven and national workers like Pastor Hsi, proved a firm base for a mighty work of the Spirit of God, in spite of major setbacks.

- Alfred and Edith Buxton continued to serve in Ethiopia but were forced to leave in 1935, when Italy annexed that country. Alfred was wounded in the leg during their escape. He died in 1940. His wife outlived him by more than twenty years.
- Norman and Pauline Grubb remained with WEC. Indeed, after Studd's death, they became its leaders. After a difficult settling in period, they supervised the expansion of the mission into many more countries in Africa, Asia and South America. Today WEC International is active in about 50 countries, with a staff exceeding 1,800, and ministers to nearly 100 groups of previously unreached people.

As CT Studd would say: Hallelujah!

BIBLIOGRAPHY

Many books and other sources were consulted during the writing of this story. The major ones are below.

Broomhall, A. J. (London: 1981-88) *Hudson Taylor & China's Open Century* (Seven volumes), Hodder.

Buxton, Edith, (Cambridge: 1968) *Reluctant Missionary*, Lutterworth Press.

Grubb, Norman, (Cambridge: 1982) *C.T. Studd: Cricketer & Pioneer*, Lutterworth Press.

Studd, C.T. (Gerrards Cross: no date) *The Chocolate Soldier*, WEC.

Studd, C.T. (no date) *Fool & Fanatic* (letters written by Studd), WEC.

Taylor, Mrs H. (London: no date) *Pastor Hsi*, CIM.

Vincent, Eileen. (Eastbourne: 1988) *C.T. Studd and Priscilla*, WEC and Kingsway.

And for details on the Ashes Test and subsequent games the most useful books were:

Illingworth, R. and K. Gregory, (London: 1982) *The Ashes: A Centenary*, Collins.

Berry, Scyld & Rupert Peploe, (London: 2006) *Cricket's Burning Passion*, Methuen.

www.ingramcontent.com/pod-product-compliance
Lightning Source LLC
Chambersburg PA
CBHW062200080426
42734CB00010B/1751